UP-CLOSE & PERSONAL

UP-CLOSE & PERSONAL

IN-COUNTRY, CHIEU HOI, VIETNAM
1969-1970

A Memoir, by

Robert C. Bogison

B Company

"Bushwhackers"

720th Military Police Battalion

United States Army

"The past is never dead. It's not even past."
William Faulkner, *The Sound and the Fury*

ISBN: 9781097969142
Imprint: Independently published

Cover photos: SP/4 Edward "Easy" Aldrich

Frontispiece (over-leaf): the author, having just returned from an emotionally and physically demanding body-recovery mission, April 17/18. 1970.

INTRODUCTION

There were two Vietnam assignments in my life, starting with the Military Advisory Assistance Command (MACV) in 1964 and oversight of the four major training sites, one in each of the Corps areas.

The second tour in 1968 was of a different magnitude and came nearer the time covered in Robert Bogison's fascinating narrative, assigned to an infantry unit the author will recognize at once: Command of the 2nd Battalion, 39th Infantry, 9th Infantry Division. "Bushwhackers" of the 720th MP Battalion were intimately familiar with the 9th, "The Old Reliables."

But Robert Bogison was not infantry. Not his MOS at all. Remarkably, he was a Military Policeman who got the roughest kind of infantry-appropriate, ground-pounding assignments imaginable. An anomaly in U. S. Army chronicles and very probably unique in the history of the Military Police Corps.

What's more, Robert and his band of brothers did the job with consummate military skill, with fortitude, application of loads of common sense, technical savvy, with humor and with no small dash of élan.

Whatever their background, from California surfer to urban street hangers-on, they fought as a team of "heroic hearts," strong in will and never to yield. They represent America's best, young men to whom the nation owes a debt of boundless gratitude.

The 9th Division that Robert and I share affection for — and to whose energetic support we likely owe our survival — is the same outfit in which Sergeant Smith served as a Military Policeman and told about back at Fort Riley, before Robert's in-country perils began. About the ambushes and fire fights Smith survived escorting convoys on the highways of the Mekong Delta.

The 9th was the first infantry division Robert spotted in the octofoil shoulder patch worn by "old-timers clad in worn and faded fatigues" cited in the lively account of his arrival in Vietnam, when the well-worn saddle of a senior sergeant -and Robert's trans-oceanic airline passenger companion -parted with a kindly, "Good luck, kid. Do what they tell you."

Doing what they "tell you" is the easy part. Doing it right when there's no one around to tell you anything is the hard bit. For Robert and for most of us, presence of mind for independent action came later, with experience.

And it was the 9th Division Robert and his squad impatiently awaited for a "special delivery" from the "artillery guys miles away at a place called Bearcat" only to be told that the 9th had a melee of their own to sort out and there was no artillery to spare. I know Bearcat. We share the experience in more ways than just geography.

The Vietnam War was a defining event for me, as it was in Robert Bogison's life. In-your-face combat participation is a crucible that changes people forever. Robert was in Long Bihn ward, Biên Hòa, Đồng Nai Province. My bunk was not all that far away in the Delta at Firebase Dirk, later designated Firebase Schroeder in honor of Lt Colonel Donald B. Schroeder who was killed in action.

We got the same mosquitoes, bugs the size of Philadelphia, venomous reptiles in unbelievable numbers, sizes, and colors, same wet, same mud and the same people who wanted to kill us.

I still have a note written by our chaplain who remembered

vividly how we ran into each other one action-packed night in 1969.

> *It was about 3am and we were experiencing a rather heavy mortar attack which gave evidence of being a prep for a ground attack. We were heading for the perimeter, but in opposite directions. The night was totally without light, except that from exploding mortars, one of which heavily damaged my quarters, and another, but a few minutes later, exploding on top of the sandbags protecting the aid station. 13 of us were in the treatment room when it hit. It was an interesting night.*

The enemy at that time, for Robert Bogison and for me, came mostly from the Viet Cong, but it rapidly was joined by well-trained North Vietnamese Army forces moving down the Ho Chi Minh Trail from North Vietnam. We were involved in several major battles with both elements.

Like the "Bushwhackers" in this book, we conducted routine day and night operations. It was a pitiless schedule made worse by geography and climate. I thank God for allowing me to come through the war unscathed. There is no doubt Robert Bogison would not hesitate to join me with an Amen to that!

A word on recognition of extraordinary service rendered. It is a truism throughout the US military that when individuals get an award it is generally one step junior to the one they actually deserve. But there is little debate that administrative practice in the Vietnam War tilted odds in favor of commissioned officers.

As battalion commander, I had a LOACH observation helicopter at my disposal and took to the air frequently to help guide the battalion's ground movements. Unlike "God's Own Lunatics" the stalwarts who served as combat air crew and had no choice in selecting their sorties, my observer role qualified for award of the Air Medal. That never sat right with me. In that context, congratulations on your Army Commendation Medal, Robert. In your case the symbolism far outweighs the medal's ranking on the awards chart.

I am proud to have served in the same Army, same war zone with Robert Bogison and the 720th, confident of having done our duty.

Robert A. Sullivan
Major General (Infantry)
United States Army
Norfolk, Virginia, February, 2019

Editor's note: *General Sullivan, a native of Sturgis, South Dakota was commissioned as a 2nd Lieutenant, Infantry, in 1952 through the University of South Dakota's ROTC program. He retired in 1982 as Chief of Public Affairs, Office of the Secretary of the Army. In civilian life he was a banker. He makes his home in Norfolk, Virginia.*

GLOSSARY
of Common Acronyms
and Military Terms

Agent Orange: Herbicide and defoliant chemical widely used by US forces in the Vietnam War, 1961 - 1971

AK-47: Soviet-designed Kalashnikov assault rifle; a Chinese variant was issued in quantity to Vietnamese communist forces in 1965

ARVN: Army of the Republic of [South] Vietnam. Pronounced "Arvin"

AVN: US Army abbreviation for Aviation

battalion: Military unit of 400 to 1,000 men usually organized into three or four companies and a headquarters company

CPT: US Army captain

brigade: Military headquarters controlling up to 5,000 men

chieu hoi: "Welcome return," a common greeting and also the name given to the thousands of Viet Cong and NVA personnel who defected to the Southern side, as in "he's a chieu hoi."

CIA: Central Intelligence Agency

Claymore: M18 directional anti-personnel mine that sprays 700 steel balls at human height through a kill range of several hundred feet across a 60-degree arc, triggered by remote control as an ambush weapon

company: Military unit, a captain's command consisting of 100 to 180 men in three or four platoons

corps: Military headquarters directing two or three divisions, commanded by a lieutenant general

C-4: Plastic explosive known as Composition 4 (multiple ingredients

CP: Command Post. Military focal point where a commanding officer of a unit in the field gives/receives orders and exercises authority

C-rats Individual precooked cans of food issued when fresh food was unavailable. In fact, a World War II product replaced with Meal Combat Individual (1958 - 1980) but continued to be called "C-Rations" by US troops

CS: Understandably abbreviated name for compound 2-chlorobenzalmalononitrile, a cyanocarbon. The key element of tear gas used as a riot control agent

CTF: Correctional Training Facility

CW2: Chief Warrant Officer step 2

division: Military formation comprising eight to fifteen thousand men, organized in two or three brigades, commanded by a US major general

DMZ: Demilitarized Zone established near the 17th parallel by the 1954 Geneva Accords, separating the new North and South Vietnams

dust-off: Slang for a medevac helicopter

EOD: Explosive Ordnance Disposal

FSB: Fire Support Base

FNG: Fucking New Guys. Pejorative applied to all fresh troops reporting for duty Vietnam

grunt: Slang for an infantryman

Handgun(s): .38caliber. .45 caliber

hooch: slang for soldier quarters

Huey: Informal name for the Bell UH-1 Iroquois general purpose military helicopter made famous by the Vietnam War

kabar knife: Popular name for the military combat knife first introduced in 1943 and still in service. Named for its manufacturer

LOACH: OH-6 Cayuse, nicknamed "Loach" after the requirement acronym LOH—Light Observation, a military scout helicopter

LAX: Los Angeles Airport

LBJ: Long Bihn Jail (and Lyndon Baines Johnson, US president for much of the Vietnam War)

M14: US Army 7.62mm semiautomatic infantry rifle, standard until 1966-1968, when withdrawn

M16: US 5.56mm rifle, much lighter automatic weapon than the M14 that it replaced, whose 1968 version was prone to jam in action

M60: NATO cartridge 7.62mm-firing machine gun

M67 Baseball-type fragmentation grenade, a replacement for the M33 "pineapple" fragmentation grenade

M79: Single-shot, shoulder-fired grenade launcher

M105: Light, towable 105 mm howitzer

MACV: US Military Assistance Command Vietnam headquartered in Saigon. Pronounced, "Mac-V"

medevac: Medical Evacuation

MOS: Military Occupation Specialty

MPC: Military Payment Certificate generally called "Script" issued in lieu of greenback which easily found their way into the illicit market. Script was not so easily convertible

NCO: Non-Commissioned officer, starting at the rank of corporal with authority similar to a commissioned officer (lieutenant and above)

NLF: National Liberation Front, ostensibly a political coalition but in reality an entirely communist-run movement established in 1960 to promote and direct Southern resistance to the Saigon government

Nook: Vietnamese term for water, and common usage among US troops

NVA: North Vietnamese Army, an American usage adopted in preference to PAVN, People's Liberation Army

PF: Popular Forces, South Vietnam's militia

Platoon: Military unit consisting of 30 to 40 men commanded by a junior lieutenant or senior NCO

PRC 25: Standard US infantry radio that replaced the PRC 10 weighing 25 pounds including battery

Regiment: military unit ordinarily composed of three battalions, commanded by a full colonel

REMF: Rear Echelon Mother-Fuckers. Soldiers far from any action who had power to dispense material good. Legally and illegally

Road Hogs: 720th MP personnel doing convoy escort duty on the dangerous highway system, especially Highway 1

were ambushes and booby traps were notoriously frequent occurrences

R&R: Rest and recuperation - a week-long-out-of-country leave granted to all US personnel at least once during a Vietnam tour, usually in Hawaii, Hong Kong or Australia

RTO: Radio Telephone Operator

ROE: Rules of Engagement whereby US forces were allowed to attack communist forces and installations

RPG: Rocket propelled grenade launcher, a superbly effective communist shoulder-fired weapon delivering a rocket with a range of 150 yards that could penetrate seven inches of armor

sappers VC and NVA elite spearhead units specially trained in the use of explosives

short: Term used by US soldiers to indicate nearing the end of a Vietnam tour, thus especially careful not to risk injury or death

snuffie: Synonymous with "grunt" - a combat rifleman on the ground

SP/4: Enlisted rank of Specialist equivalent to corporal. US Army enlisted ranks start at E-1 (Private) and go to E-9, Sergeant Major.

spider hole: military slang for a camouflaged one-man foxhole favored by the Viet Cong

squad: eight to ten men commanded by an NCO, subdivided into fire teams. There are usually three or four squads per platoon

TAOR: Tactical Area of Responsibility, meaning the geographic boundaries of a fighting unit's responsibility

TOC: Tactical Operations Center

Top: US Army slang for a unit's most senior NCO, also called First Sergeant

VC or Viet Cong: derives from the term Cong San Viet Nam, meaning Vietnamese communists, adopted from the late 1950s, onward

WO: Warrant Officer

TABLE OF CONTENTS

UP-CLOSE & PERSONAL

1
Goodbye Fort Riley and the Correctional Training Facility

I had my fill with all the violence associated with stockade duty six months into my involuntary assignment to the Fort Riley, Kansas, Correctional Training Facility (CTF).

Describing my experience there would require several chapters. Along with a dozen others, I received orders to report to this insane asylum on graduating from the US Army's Military Police School at Fort Gordon, Georgia in June, 1968. Late in December at Fort Riley I was assigned to Building #1380, the Psychotic Block, where the most dangerous and violent people in Army green were warehoused.

Early one morning an inmate, Private Campbell (not his real name), came up behind me and struck my left shoulder with a metal bunk adaptor.

A bunk adaptor is one of four hollow metal tubes, approximately 14 inches long, utilized to stack an upper Army cot to a lower Army cot to assemble a pair of bunk beds.

Instinctively, I turned and punched him with my right fist, striking him directly in the face. He fell backwards striking his head against a wall and then again on the floor. A medical team determined that the man had sustained a concussion and should be transported to the Irwin Army Hospital a few miles away, where he was treated and released several days later.

Subsequently, he was again involved in a minor altercation

with another military policeman while being served a meal. The man died two days later in his cell. Cause of death was "undetermined" and no charges were filed against me or any others who may have interacted with him. In spite of these facts, this incident and the rumors associated with it would follow me.

Early in January, 1969, I completed all the necessary paperwork (Army Form AR-1049) requesting transfer to serve in a Military Police line unit in the Republic of South Vietnam. Repeated visits to the personnel division with the NCO-in-charge proved fruitless. With no response by mid-April, I requested to speak with the Officer-in-Charge of the personnel division for some explanation as to why I hadn't received any response.

The captain there was not receptive and chided me severely for bothering him.

Undaunted, I responded with something close to, "Sir, I am respectfully requesting to know the status of the 1049 I submitted regarding my request for transfer to Vietnam. It's been over two months and I haven't heard anything!"

Suffice to say, my insistence in the matter coupled with my demeanor did not go over well. He did, however, remove all doubt of what I had suspected all along when he rose from his chair and roared, "Bogison, get it in that thick head of yours and let it sink in. You ain't going to Vietnam. You have a critical MOS (Military Occupation Specialty) and you *will* remain right here, at the CTF until the Army decides where you go. Not you. You *will not* come into this office again. Now get the fuck out of here!"

That was clear enough. Undeterred, I had already decided to change to a different strategy.

When I enlisted into the Army in February, 1968 I expected to be sent to Vietnam, just as my father and his brother had been dispatched to a combat zone during World War II when they deployed to the Pacific Campaign. As naive as it might appear now, I volunteered three years of my life by enlisting in the US Army because I believed it was the right thing to do. I was not about to pull stateside duty while the country was engaged in a war, regardless of its unpopularity. It just wasn't in my character.

I became more frustrated with the system when later that month I learned that half of the guys who were sent with me to the CTF from Fort Gordon deployed to Vietnam, and they hadn't even volunteered. Among them was my good friend Al Drever.

Like Al, all of them were two-year draftees with less than nine months left to serve. None of this made any sense. Six draftees with the same critical MOS with no particular inclination to serve in the Army deployed to Vietnam, while a fool like me with over a year-and-a-half left in his enlistment, volunteers to go and is rebuked for doing so.

I turned to what worked for me in junior high and high school, whenever I needed information or material for a school project. I would carefully construct a sensibly written letter — usually to a government source — that had the answers I sought.

Ironically, as a junior in high school preparing a term paper for an International Relations class in 1965, I wrote a letter to the State Department requesting any information defining the role of the United States in what was then termed in the newspapers as a "Police Action in Southeast Asia."

Within days I received a series of papers, pamphlets, and photographs associated with the political and social structure of South Vietnam. Propaganda actually, but highly informative about a place I had never heard of, or at the time really cared about.

Thinking about this experience I recognized that every time I corresponded with the US government, I always received a polite response. I reasoned this would now be the solution to my dilemma. I also recognized that in doing so, I would be committing the biggest sin an obscure and lowly enlisted man could possibly commit in this grand "green" (the Army's uniform color at that time) food chain.

Such action demonstrated a total disregard of the fundamental doctrine ingrained in every soldier, from private to general: launch an unauthorized communication outside the authority of a clearly defined "Chain of Command."

The very worst that the Army could do to me was send me to the very place I was volunteering for in the first place. In 1969, any young man asked what he thought was a terrible fate, nine times out of ten he would have replied, "Go to Vietnam."

About the fourth week in April I fashioned a concise letter explaining my desire to volunteer my services in the war. I mailed a copy to the Army Chief of Staff, one to California Governor Ronald Reagan, and one to my US Senator, George Murphy (who, coincidentally, was a member of the Armed Services Committee). Within days, I had the desired results with polite responses to my letter.

> Governor Reagan's office suggested that, since "the armed forces are separate from state government, the Governor is not the appropriate official through whom your request should be made . . . the Governor has, however, asked me to send your letter to Senator Murphy."

> Senator Murphy was more direct: "I have asked the Department of the Army to look into the situation and advise me of the possibility of your assignment to Vietnam."

The Army, however, was already out in front and before I had seen those responses, I had been advised: "I am pleased to inform you that your request has been approved. In the near future, you will received orders assigning you to Vietnam for movement during the month of July 1969. Your desire to serve our country by joining the forces in Vietnam . . . is appreciated, and you have my best wishes for success in your forthcoming assignment."

Victory is a good thing but often comes at a price, and this one was no exception. I quickly learned that shaking a tree hard enough can bring unintended consequences. In this case it came swift and loud. Within a week of the welcoming news I found myself standing tall in the office of my Commanding Officer, Captain Z. Like one of Joseph Heller's characters in the novel "Catch 22" his middle name was a repeat of his first name. Fitting, because he was a strange man. Nobody liked the guy.

A typical Ivy League college graduate raised in some small town on the east coast.

When I first arrived at Fort Riley, I mistakenly believed that because of his education coupled with the fact that he was about eight years senior to my twenty years, he had all the attributes of a good leader.

Within a week that perspective changed. It was disturbing for me to witness his condescending demeanor as he berated his seasoned, combat-hardened non-commissioned officers. All of these guys, senior NCOs, had over 15 years in the Army and most had served at least one tour of duty in Vietnam. Captain Z was raw, untested. Some of the old war horse NCOs reckoned that his lack of leadership qualities could get him killed in Vietnam. I knew what they meant.

With one week left to fulfill my obligation and forever be rid of any and all vestiges related to this square mile of insanity, I found myself standing tall and receiving my exit interview with the captain, soon to be my ex-commanding officer. After a rather lengthy lecture about his interpretation of the US Army's definition of precisely what the chain of command means and my total disregard in following it, I received an equal earful on how I was going to be repaid for my blatant disrespect to my superiors.

The one-sided conversation went something close to the following:

"Well, Bogison if it were in my power I would bust you down to PFC (Private First Class) for pulling off what you did. You may have won a little battle here but I can just about assure you that you will spend your time in Vietnam doing the same thing you did here. You're headed to LBJ (Long Binh Jail), boy. I will be going to Vietnam soon myself. Unlike you, however, I will be going to a military police unit. So it is very doubtful that our paths will cross. You made this bed now you're gonna have to go lie in it. That's all. Check all your equipment with the supply sergeant. And I mean everything. Good luck Specialist. Get out!"

It was a slightly painful experience as I hadn't been berated quite to that degree in a one-way conversation in my life. Particularly galling because I had freely volunteered to serve in a combat zone. When I reported to the supply sergeant, name forgotten but not his idiocy, he made it clear that I would not be receiving a coffee mug or standard plaque-mounted, custom-made CTF certificate of appreciation for meritorious performance of duties for my time assigned to the unit, as was customary for any other troop transferring out.

Not that I really cared about such nonsense. But angered by his condescension and sanctimony, two days later I broke into the building and took a handsome forest-green mug with the ornate gold lettering of the Unit logo (green and gold being the US Army's Military Police Corps colors).

I got the same cold shoulder when I reported to the personnel division to pick up my records and transfer orders. So much for all things CTF.

2

Home on leave: May 29 - July 5, 1969

The Army usually gave a soldier a thirty-day leave before he would ship out to a combat zone, and I was no exception. On May 30, 1969 I left Fort Riley in my 1952 Chevrolet panel truck and drove home to Granada Hills, California. My high school buddy, Karl Nielsen, also a soldier, was already there from Germany on a 30-day leave to marry his high school sweetheart, Debbie. Glenn Carpenter, another high school pal, managed to obtain a two-week leave from his assignment in Washington D.C. with the US Army's legendary Old Guard.

Rick Hart, a close friend since grammar school, had been ordered to Vietnam earlier that year and was serving with the US 4th Infantry Division at Pleiku.

That left Glenn and me to stand up for Karl at his June wedding. Ironically, the ceremony took place at the same Presbyterian Church — across the street from Granada Hills High School — where I used to tell my parents I was going on all those Sundays when I was restricted from any recreational activity.

Bob Hanner, an old friend from Little League days managed to survive his tour of duty with the Marines at Khe Sahn (scene of a 77-day battle — 21 January to 9 July, 1968) and return home in February, 1969. He was engaged to Sandy. During my time home, Lorraine and I doubled-dated with Bob and Sandy. We went to the beach a couple of times, saw a couple of movies together and spent a day at Knott's Berry Farm.

Bob and I didn't talk much about Vietnam but he couldn't understand why I had volunteered when the Army was content with having me spend the remainder of my time at Fort Riley.

He harassed me by repeatedly saying, "I guess you didn't buy into that shit I wrote to you about what it was like when we were under siege at Khe Sahn. I send you to school, then you throw away the books, then eat the teacher. You are out of your fucking mind."

I spent most of those days surfing waves at beaches along the Los Angeles-Ventura County Line. Each day seemed better than the day before. The waves were always glassy, not choppy and they came consistently in sets of six and eight at a time, six to eight feet in height. Mysteriously, I found myself mastering magnificent maneuvers on a surfboard that were previously beyond my natural abilities. Was this some kind of omen? Why am I now able to perform all these feats? Was this a good thing?

The time flew and I savored as much as I possibly could knowing that these days could be among my last.

Lorraine and I spent my last day home on July 4th with Rick and Patti Ford. Rick, a very close friend since the 6th grade and Patti a friend from high school were among the first in my circle to become a married couple. As the evening came to a close, Patti gave me a big hug then ran away crying. Glancing at Rick I asked, "What's that all about?" to which he barked, "What did you expect? She's scared for you and so am I." In a farewell shaking of his hand I thought to myself, "Better me than you." It was a solemn goodbye.

On July 5, 1969 about mid-morning I packed my duffle bag, suited up in my khaki uniform, embraced my mother, my sister and Lorraine and said that I would see them in one year. I stepped into my father's car and as he drove away I waved to them as they stood in the driveway, waving back. No one had shed a tear but the atmosphere was tense. The Army offered a, "five month early-out" by voluntarily extending your combat tour to a date exactly five months before your military service expired.

Do that, and the Army waived the additional five-month obligation with the award of an Honorable Discharge.

Our drive to the airport was a somber affair and almost wordless. I do remember saying to my father, "I don't know where I will end up over there but if things get really hot I will be home one year from today. If things don't get hot, I am going to extend my tour an extra two months so that when I come home I will be out of the Army." All he said was, "Just get your ass home and no hero shit."

At LAX I got out of the car, slung my duffle bag over my shoulder, looked at the old man square in the eye for the first time since we left the house, shook his hand and said, "I'll see you in a year." As I turned to walk away, he repeated what he said earlier, "Just get your ass home. No hero shit."

I didn't look back.

3

Fort Lewis, Washington

From Los Angeles I flew to Seattle where I caught a bus to Fort Lewis, one of several processing centers for Army personnel deploying to South Vietnam. Waiting for the bus outside the terminal, an attractive young girl handed me a Seattle World's Fair plastic pin, gave me a brief hug and simply said, "Good luck, soldier," then turned and walked away. This wonderful experience would be among the very few I encountered while wearing the uniform of the United States Army.

Over the years I found myself reflecting on that encounter, reasoning that she must have had a boyfriend serving in Vietnam, or perhaps it was a brother, maybe even a father. Then of course the darker side of my inner thoughts suggested that maybe she lost a brother, a friend, a boyfriend, or her father over there. I'll never know.

All I do know is that it was one of the most thoughtful gestures I have ever received from someone I never knew. The human condition at its very best.

The Overseas Processing Center at Fort Lewis burst with activity. Hundreds of soldiers filling out forms. Hundreds more were discarding unnecessary uniforms and personal items, and others were being issued new jungle clothing and gear for Vietnam.

Simultaneously, hundreds of other older, exhausted looking soldiers wearing worn, faded and torn jungle fatigues were being issued clean dress-green uniforms.

These guys were gaunt, had dark circles under their eyes and they didn't seem to engage in any conversation, even among themselves.

I found myself studying them only to realize that these guys weren't old, some of them were probably my age, some maybe even a year or so younger. In twenty days I would be twenty-one years old and I asked myself, "Am I going to look like that?" I reasoned that most of these guys were probably infantryman.

I was a Military Policeman and I just knew I wasn't going to have the experience that these guys probably went through. Military Policemen enforce Military Law, escort vehicular convoys, perform traffic control, and provide physical security at military installations. They don't engage in combat infantry tactics, set up ambushes, sleep in jungles or do any reconnaissance duty. MPs aren't trained in those kinds of things.

After an entire evening and the better part of the early morning of the following day I was finally processed and ready to be transported to Southeast Asia. With a few hours of sleep — in a temporary barracks with a hundred other guys I had never seen before — we were rudely awakened and told that our bus was ready to take us to McChord Air Force Base for our flight to Vietnam.

After a ten minute breakfast of greasy bacon, burnt scrambled eggs, some form of potatoes, grits, coffee or milk, we shuffled off to two buses, engines running, with a young-looking corporal standing between them screaming, "Let's go people! Get your gear and get your asses in the bus! This ain't a war of convenience!"

The corporal was not some overzealous toy soldier. He

sported spit-shined "Jump Boots" which defined him as parachute qualified, a 101st Airborne patch on the upper right arm of his uniform sleeve identified him as having served in a combat zone, and on the left chest of his uniform shirt was a Combat Infantry Badge, airborne badge and Vietnam service ribbons including a Bronze Star with "V" for Valor and a Purple Heart.

When he spoke, even the old guys listened.

4
Off we go

On the tarmac, a Continental Airlines Boeing 707 was waiting with passenger and fuselage storage doors open, and all engines running. Everybody was hustled off the bus, directed to load their gear on baggage trailers positioned adjacent to the plane, and ordered to double-time to board the plane.

Every seat from the back of the cabin to the front was occupied by various ranks of men clad in newly issued olive- drab jungle fatigues. I happened on a window seat just behind the left wing of the aircraft and within ten minutes or less, we were in the air.

Less than twenty-four hours earlier I had been home in Granada Hills waving good-bye to my mother, my sister and Lorraine.

As I looked around me it appeared that I was not alone in my thoughts. Every man on board stared straight ahead, deeply engaged in the privacy of his mind. I hardly noticed the guy sitting next to me, on my right. All of us were strangers to one another. Just as the plane leveled off at thirty thousand feet, my memory drifted to the sorrowful look on my father's face before I turned away from him, after shaking his hand.

Crying was completely out of the question. I was in the company of warriors and it would take every fiber of my entire being to prevent tears from happening.

It was during this inner conflict that I received help from an unexpected source.

Suddenly, the air came alive with a strong scent of coffee mixed with some kind of liquor. Just as my senses attempted to identify this unusual aroma, I felt a sharp nudge on my right forearm — atop the armrest of my seat — by the elbow of the guy I had hardly noticed next to me. He was offering this well-worn, flat shaped silver colored liquor flask, loosely held in his right hand, while he stared out of the passenger window.

Instantly, and without studying the man's features, I blurted out, "What the hell is that stuff?" As he turned towards me he replied, "Well son, it's a combination of mess hall coffee, some heavy cream and the Brothers Christian."

As he spoke, I looked at his face, the furrows on his eye brows and the decades of life experiences associated with them. Within milliseconds I realized that he was a salty old World War II era Master Sergeant, old enough to be my father, and what we young soldiers referred to as a "Lifer."

That is, a non-commissioned officer with nothing in his life but the Army.

"What are the Brothers Christian?" I sheepishly asked. "Christian Brothers Brandy. Don't you know anything?" He paused for a moment studying my face, then concluded. "No, you probably wouldn't know that" and then withdrew his offer of the concoction while stealthily placing the flask into his right front pants pocket.

Several minutes of silence passed with only a faint conversation or two mixed with the loud drone of the air flow of the jetliner as it cut through the sky. Time to reflect on what had just occurred. I reasoned that my interaction with the master sergeant was inappropriate and determined that all the man was trying to do was reach out. It was all those years of life experiences and his extensive understanding of what it means to go into harm's way for the first time. He knew what was spinning in my head without me uttering a word.

I quickly appreciated the old timer and engaged him in conversation. The man had served as an infantryman in World War II and again in the Korean War. This trip was to be his second tour with the 9th Infantry Division somewhere in the Mekong Delta area. He told me a lot about the Viet Cong, the North Vietnamese soldiers and the cultural differences between the various sects of the South Vietnamese people. By the time we landed in Honolulu for a two hour layover, all previous designs of feeling sorry for myself were dashed.

We left Hawaii to our next destination for a short layover at Clark Air Force Base in the Philippine Islands. The old-timer filled my head with personal experiences during his first tour in Vietnam. He talked about his experiences in firefights and ambushes and what signs to look for in avoiding booby traps. I had no way of knowing at that time how valuable this information would be for me later. For a "Grunt" (slang for infantryman) confiding so much to a young MP was a rare thing, as just about every GI disliked MPs. Especially Infantrymen.

The difference between our respective MOS, his 11B Infantry, and mine 95B Military Police, did not matter to him.

5

Clark Air Force Base, Philippines

We arrived at Clark AFB in late afternoon. It was now July 7th, a whole day later as we had crossed the International Dateline. The old-timer was quick to advise me that we had already finished the first day of our 12-month tour without setting foot on Vietnam soil. Only 364 days left.

Shortly after stepping off the plane I panned the entire 360-degree horizon. I saw old buildings and hangers for aircraft that had been inhabited by US Army and Air Force guys before the outbreak of World War II. In December, 1941 the Philippine Islands were invaded by Japanese Imperial Armed Forces, and after bitter fighting, the greatly outnumbered, exhausted and undersupplied US armed resistance surrendered.

My father served as a radio operator in a C-47 (twin- engine transport plane) with the Army Air Force during the US liberation of the Philippines early in 1945. His plane had crash landed somewhere on this airfield. It seemed odd to be standing on the very same ground where my father served in a global war almost a generation earlier. And here I was on my way to serve in a conflict the United States deemed necessary a thousand or so miles further west.

Ironic I suppose, that in 1945 the United States had invaded the Philippines to liberate its people from their Japanese invaders, and now twenty years later the United States was in South Vietnam to liberate the South Vietnamese people from the communists of North Vietnam. The same place the US and its allies helped liberate the Vietnamese people from their Japanese invaders in 1945.

   Minutes later we were back on the plane enroute to our next stop-over destination, Yokota, Japan. The old-timer decided to get some sleep and suggested that I do the same. I tried but I couldn't. I was too wired to even think about sleeping. All I could think about was wondering where in Vietnam I was going to do my tour of duty. I heard how nasty it was in the Central Highlands near Pleiku. Rick was already there with the 4th Division and I wondered how he was doing.

   Sergeant Smith back at Fort Riley told me all about 9th Division MPs he served with in 1967, and the ambushes and firefights he experienced escorting convoys on the highways of the Mekong Delta. Bob Hanner told me what the Marines and Army guys had to deal with at Khe Sahn, Hue, places north and near the DMZ (Demilitarized Zone), and places south of the city of Da Nang.

   I was told that duty with the 716th Military Police Company tasked with patrolling the streets of Saigon was no picnic, either. Then there was the dreaded thought of possibly being assigned to the infamous Long Bihn Prison as Captain Z had threatened he would do if he had anything to say about my prospects during my exit interview. He couldn't possibly have that much influence, or could he? The thought of it made me cringe so I convinced myself that this would not happen and blocked the possibility from my head.

6
Japan

It was evening when we descended on our approach to Japan and still light outside. I peered out the window to my left and could see the mainland of Japan just ahead. My thoughts turned to Colonel Jimmy Doolittle's surprise bombing raid on Tokyo in April, 1942, the crash landing of Captain Ted Lawson's Mitchell B-25 "Ruptured Duck" off the coast of China after the raid, and the book he wrote, "Thirty Seconds Over Tokyo" which I read cover to cover twice when I was nine years old. I also thought about what my Uncle Charlie endured as a Marine in savage fighting with the Japanese on Cape Gloucester, and the islands of Pelelu and Okinawa.

Twenty-four years later his nephew was about to land on the soil of Japan, a place in which he would surely have been fighting for his life had the atom bomb not been dropped on the cities of Hiroshima and Nagasaki in August, 1945.

Just as we touched down at Yokota, I woke up the old-timer. After he stretched and yawned, he said, "Well, it's just us and the pilots from here on. No stewardesses with us to our next stop. Take your last look at a round-eyed woman. Where we're going there ain't any."

Just before disembarking from the plane, all the stewardesses who had accompanied us on this journey were standing in the front of the cabin facing us. A 2nd lieutenant speaking over the PA system advised that we had a two-hour layover to let the ground crews prepare the plane for our final destination, and that we were to remain in the terminal. The lieutenant then handed the microphone over to one of the stewardesses.

With her voice slightly breaking, she wished all of us the best of luck and recited a very short prayer on our behalf while two of the stewardesses were tearing up with the remaining two stewardesses about to. You could hear a pin drop.

Seconds later the girls scurried off the plane. It seemed obvious that this was not the first time they had experienced the transfer from plain old airliner protocol conditions, to the cold reality of preparing troops to enter a war environment.

I don't remember much walking around in the terminal at Yokota, and I didn't wander very far. Mainly, because I was in the middle of a huge sea of small Japanese coming and going in every single place I turned. I recall seeing a camera shop in this ocean of people and was curious to find out what a good camera would cost me. I heard that everything was cheaper in the Orient than anywhere else in the world. I never made it to the camera shop as the human wave kept pushing me further and further away from my gate.

The experience was like trying to swim to the shore of a beach while caught in a riptide.

Soon after coming into this forced stroll I decided to turn briskly and stumble my way back to the departure area. I remember being the tallest figure in the crowd, with no Americans or round-eyed people in sight. It was a strange feeling I would soon learn to get used to.

An hour later I was back in the same seat on the plane. As the co-pilot closed the passenger door, the pilot made an announcement on the PA system.

He said something along these lines: "Gentlemen, we will be departing now and we will be landing at a place called Cam Rahn Bay, Vietnam, in several hours. It will be nighttime when we arrive and we will be putting the aircraft down very quickly. When you depart from this aircraft it is important that you do so in a swift and orderly manner as it may become necessary for us to get this aircraft off the runway and back into the air. However, I do not anticipate this. I will keep you advised."

Needless to state, the atmosphere in the plane was solemn. The reality of what I had volunteered for finally sank in. Now, I was concerned about how I would conduct myself as a soldier.

7
Hello, Cam Rahn Bay

We were flying near 30,000 feet on our approach to Cam Ranh Bay when I clearly saw what appeared to be little fires scattered along the pitch-black terrain below. I mentioned this to the old timer and he nonchalantly explained, "Those are probably villagers cooking meals. Could be Vietcong camped out there roasting monkeys for dinner." "Monkeys? You've got to be shitting me," I replied. "No son, I'm not. You are going to see a whole lot of things over here that you would never have believed if you hadn't seen them with your own eyes."

I had more questions about this monkey eating thing when the pilot announced that the air traffic controller on the ground reported having received several sporadic rocket attacks earlier in the evening, and that the base was on alert.

He further advised us to fasten our seatbelts and repeated his instructions to swiftly exit the plane in an orderly manner through the doors on the left side. This time he added, "When you exit the plane the engines will still be running. Do not linger around the plane. You must double time it to the sandbags about 100 yards in front of you. A ground crew will unload your gear in a matter of seconds. As soon as the gear is unloaded we are taking off. Good Luck and God bless all of you."

Now what the hell did I get myself into? The old-timer read my mind or face or both and said, "Stick close to me out the door. I know where the bunkers are. The VC (Viet Cong) throw incoming rockets on every base in Vietnam just to let us know they are out there. Don't sweat it."

The plane now plunged into such a steep dive that the safety belt dug deeply into my gut while both of my feet braced the framework of the seat in front of me. It felt as though I was standing up because my ass didn't feel like it was touching my seat. I had no idea that commercial airplanes could dive at such a steep angle, and so fast.

Now I found myself more concerned about this steep dive than what surprises might be waiting for us on the ground. Within seconds we were on the tarmac rolling at a very high rate of speed. But before I could even concern myself the pilot braked the plane very sharply, causing my seatbelt to dig deeper.

Seconds later the plane stopped with the engine running. This pilot was good.

The sounds of seatbelts unsnapping and the opening of doors on the left side of the plane signaled everyone to exit. No panic or pandemonium, just an orderly movement of personnel toward the exit doors. As I stood in the aisle I bent over and peered out of a passenger window. Nothing visible. I heard the sounds of men in boots running and people yelling obscenities on the left side of the plane, but as I peered out I couldn't see anything.

Just before reaching the door, the old- timer pushed me aside, moved in front of me and said, "Follow me."

As soon as I reached the door, it felt like I had been hit with a blow torch and thrown into a closet with the door closed. The air was thick, hot, and damp filled with some lifer screaming "Get the fuck off that plane and move, God damn it! Move! Move! Move! Straight ahead. Move!" Of course, visibility was nil. I could barely see the hard ground in front of me which added to the confusion. All that guided me forward were the sounds of running boots in front.

Just up ahead I could see a faint red light. A flashlight with a red filter over the lens waving us forward.

I was relieved when I recognized what it was, because we trained with them in the Vietnam Processing School back at Fort Riley. After I ran past the red light, a familiar voice said, "Kid over here. To your right." It was the old-timer but I could barely see any figure eight to ten feet away.

My eyes started to adjust to the darkness. As I approached him, he said, "We're going this way. It's safer." Seconds later we entered a sand bagged structure occupied by two Army MPs and an AP (Air Force Police.) "Hello boys. Mind if we join you here for a few minutes?" Never know if "Charlie" might want to send us and that plane we came in on a 122mm rocket for a welcoming present," breezed the old-timer. "Come on in sarge. Got some coffee here if you want some," replied one of them. Before we could respond, the plane we came in on was throttling its engines and within seconds, it was airborne.

That plane couldn't have been on the ground any more than three minutes, possibly less.

I remember being pretty impressed by the speed and efficiency displayed by both pilots and ground crew. These guys were damned good at what they did.

Just as the old-timer poured himself a tin of coffee, a whistling noise growing louder and louder approached us. At first I thought why in the hell would anybody shoot off fireworks in the middle of the night to celebrate the 4th of July when it was already the 7th? Before I could make a fool of myself by uttering those thoughts out loud, the old-timer said, "This is gonna be close, God damn it!" One of the MPs yelled at me, "Get your ass away from there! You wanna die?"

Standing in the entry way I quickly moved inside and it was then that I figured this was some kind of artillery round. And it was coming our way.

The whistle blew very loud and ended with one big BOOM! The cement beneath me shook violently, sandbags moved and shards of asphalt and concrete whizzed over our bunker. "Son of a bitch! Why the fuck is it that every time I come to this place I have to be greeted with this shit? This is almost like an R & R (Rest & Recuperation) area for Christ's sake," shouted the old-timer.

"I don't know sarge. Lately we've been catching 122s and some of our perimeter APs and their dogs have sniffed VC just outside the wire. Don't know what to make of it sarge, but something's going on," said the AP. "What's with the FNG (referring to me) sarge? He with you?" asked the MP that yelled at me to get away from the entry way. "Oh, yea, right. First tour. You know. Hey, he's an MP just like you boys." "Shit." is all the other MP replied.

Silence now, just the one rocket.

What the hell is an FNG I asked myself? I didn't dare ask out loud. All I knew for sure is that they meant me. Sometimes keeping your mouth shut is a good thing. The old timer conversed with the guys as I tried to make out what had just happened. I noticed that the MPs were armed with .45 caliber automatic pistols and one M-16 rifle between them. The AP was armed with a .38 revolver and an old M-14.

I wondered why these guys were armed with M-14s and not newer M-16s. I didn't see any grenades, no M-79s (grenade launchers), no M-60 machine guns or ammo in this bunker. I wasn't real comfortable not being armed myself.

What the hell was I supposed to do without a gun in a war zone? I sure hoped they (the Army) knew what it was doing.

It didn't.

The old timer finished his coffee and said, "Later boys. We gotta go." From there, we jogged several hundred yards away and entered a well-lit, large rectangular shaped wood framed, screened-sided structure boasting a large placard with the words, "RECEPTION CENTER" hanging above the double screened door. We joined the rest of our group along with several hundred other men all clad in fresh dark green jungle fatigues. Mingled with us were men of various ranks clad in the same attire, only their fatigues were worn and faded, which suggested to me that these were not new guys like us.

As I studied my surroundings, the old-timer slapped me on the back and said, "Good luck kid. Do what they tell you. Maybe I'll see you around about the same time next year when this tour is over."

I watched him walk into the crowd and greet some other old-timers clad in those worn and faded fatigues sporting 9th Division shoulder patches. This would be the last time I would ever see the man whose name I cannot remember. Over the years I wondered if he ever made it out. Guys like him usually did.

I spent the next two days and nights filling out forms and waiting for my assignment to a military police unit. Cam Ranh Bay was truly a beautiful place with its white sandy beaches and the blue green water of the South China Sea. Further inland and far beyond the barbed wire of this military post lie lush green flora along with dark green rolling hills and mountains beyond that. I noticed all types of naval and commercial ships in the bay.

The air was alive day and night with the sights and the unmistakable "wop-wop-wop" of Huey helicopter gunships flying overhead, interrupted occasionally by the roar of all types of fighter jets, commercial jets, transport planes, and even some World War II era aircraft. In spite of all this assurance in the air and all the Army and Air Force armed personnel in the area I still felt uneasy not being armed myself.

What was I and the hundreds of unarmed guys with me supposed to do if we were attacked? I didn't sleep well there, either. I wanted to be sure I was awake and prepared to run into the nearest bunker for the next rocket attack, which never happened.

8

Biên Hòa Airbase

E arly in the morning on my third day in Vietnam I was directed to board an Air Force C-130 transport plane to Biên Hòa Air Base just outside of the city of Biên Hòa in III Corps. The Army divided Vietnam into four Corps. III Corps was located geographically in and around Saigon, Biên Hòa, and parts of the Mekong Delta. From Biên Hòa I would be transported to the 90th Replacement Center on Long Binh Post. There, I would receive my assignment to a military police unit.

This was my first military transport plane and on entering the cabin I noted that the interior was completely devoid of any and all human comforts. Just an olive drab metal interior with about 25 small seat cushions positioned about a foot apart on both sides of the cargo space. A few windows were at least four or five feet above your head. We sat on the floor with backs resting on the hard metal fuselage. Twenty-five nervous souls on one side of the plane facing twenty-five other nervous souls across the aisle. No seatbelts, no arm rests.

I was among the last of the passengers to board and no sooner did I sit down when the turbo-charged engines cranked over and burst into a deafening roar.

The Crew Chief, a salty old Air Force Master Sergeant screamed, "Remain seated during this flight. Do not stand up unless directed to do so." He had to scream because the noise was that deafening.

I thought that as soon as he closed the passenger door the noise would be less annoying. It was not. The engines grew increasing louder while the entire cabin felt like it was shaking apart as we taxied down the runway. And we hadn't even gotten off the ground yet. Then the roar grew even louder and the increased speed and the forward motion of the plane told my senses that we were taking off.

In seconds we were airborne. No respite from the noise and no idle conversation with the guy seated on either side of you as it was next to impossible to hear or understand him without reading his lips.

At first I could not understand how these Air Force guys dealt with all the noise. Half-way into our ascent I saw the crew chief place earphones on his head. Then I understood.

Sometime during this loud but uneventful journey I saw several small holes through the floorboard, about three feet out from my seat between my boots and the boots of the guy on my left. I pointed them out and we just looked at each other. Without either of us uttering a word I am sure we thought the same thing. They can't be bullet holes, can they? As I looked up I saw the crew chief, seated across from us smiling and nodding his head in an affirmative manner. Simultaneously, he was pointing to a steel helmet he had positioned on the floorboard, directly below what appeared to be a fairly solid-looking metal chair he was sitting on.

No mystery now, they were bullet holes.

It occurred to me to ask myself what are the chances of this noisy beast catching some ground fire, and me getting shot in the ass? How do you explain that? I cringed at the very thought, and so did my ass. We landed without incident. Both my ass and I were relieved to get out of that bucket of bolts.

The instant I exited the aircraft I felt the heavy, wet hot air infused with the stench of jet fuel, burnt rubber, and other unpleasant odors unfamiliar to me. The temperature here was much hotter than it was at Cam Rahn Bay and even more humid, if that was possible. This huge concrete city was chock-full of activity that rivaled the activity of any major airport in the world. Dozens of Air Force guys hurried about performing maintenance on every kind of fighter jet and bomber. Some, I was familiar with and some I had never seen before.

Dozens of men were refueling commercial airliners while others were busy performing Army helicopter maintenance. Numerous large metal half-moon shaped hangers housed all types of helicopters and jets were positioned on the fringes of the runways. Revetments comprised of green sandbags were neatly stacked some twenty feet high and scattered throughout the area. Numerous two-man Army military police jeeps and two-man Air Force police jeeps patrolled both the interior and exterior perimeter of the base.

The air was filled with fighter jets landing and taking off, coupled with the sounds of helicopter gunships constantly circling.

9

FNGs and the 90th Replacement Center, Long Binh Post

We were immediately loaded onto an Army olive drab bus. The engine was running and the driver, a SP/4, barked out seating assignments for each of us as we scrambled aboard, two abreast. I was seated on the driver's side in an aisle seat next to a PFC named John from Nebraska with an infantry MOS. I can't remember his last name in spite of the fact that we later corresponded with each other.

As John and I got acquainted we noticed that the rear window and all of the passenger windows were adorned in a heavy-gauged olive drab chain-linked metal pattern affixed securely to the outside of the glass. My new friend asked the driver, "What's with the windows?" to which an unfamiliar voice several seats behind us, bellowed, "That's so the Zips can't toss a grenade into the bus and blow your dumb ass up. Fucking New Guy!" It was then that the light bulb flashed in both of our heads. John and I had finally figured it out without either of us having to admit it.

After three days of hearing people like us being referred to as FNGs, it all made sense. We are Fucking New Guys. Body language and facial expressions often telegraph so much about what our minds are thinking. That was half of the equation. Now, what did that guy mean by Zips?

The bus was loaded and as the driver smashed the accelerator pedal into the floorboard, he shouted, "Welcome to Vietnam. Now hold on to your seats. We are headed to the 90th Replacement Center on Long Binh Post just a few miles away." It didn't take long to figure out why we needed to hold on to our seats.

The streets were congested with every motorized and human-powered transportation device known to man, all travelling at unsafe speeds. Military jeeps and trucks of every size — including semi-tractors — weaved in and out of the flow of traffic.

Hundreds of bicycles, rickshaws, motorized bicycles, motorcycles, and mopeds usually occupied by two or three passengers, were everywhere.

Dozens of three-wheeled miniature camper-type trucks called Lambrettas. These strange machines retained an arched shaped, tin-roof that draped over a small rear cargo bed equipped with bench seats for no more than four to six passengers, each facing the other. In fact, all were loaded with no less than eight to ten people and well beyond the machine's carrying capacity.

There were early 1940s-era French black four-door vehicles similar to those I had seen in motion pictures depicting German soldiers driving in the streets of Occupied cities during World War II. Mixed in were 1940-1950 vintage American cars and trucks, along with occasional sightings of a late model GM, Chrysler or Ford. In addition to this conglomeration of machines were scores of unidentifiable commercial-type trucks comprised of mixed American and foreign auto body parts of all makes, models, and years of manufacture.

The contraptions had no discernable features that might point to a recognized make or model.

The walkways and sidewalks along the masses of moving metal and smoke exhaust were occupied by hundreds of open air markets where the indigenous population sold wares of just about anything imaginable. Most of the women wore thin, black silk pants with a white long-sleeved blouse that extended to the ankles. An open slit along the length of the outer portion of both legs exposed long black pants underneath.

A woven bamboo cone-shaped hat adorned their heads. Men wore assorted colored pants or shorts, a light colored long or short-sleeved shirt and a bamboo cone-shaped hat or a green US Army-issue baseball cap.

All the men and women wore black rubber sandals (we called "Ho Chi Minh Sandals"), cut from old tires. The entire town bustled with activity. I could only imagine what Saigon might be like.

There were no real rules of the road in Vietnam. The pecking order was simple: the biggest and fastest vehicle always wins and creates the right of way. Literally, trailing only a few feet behind the largest beasts were no less than a dozen motorcycles. Much like the symbiotic relationship that small remora fish share with the great white, using the shark as a protective shield.

As our large bus weaved recklessly through the streets, I felt sorry for these poor people and the conditions in which they lived. Children played in the same mud and dirt with pigs, chickens, and water buffalo. Sheet metal shacks for homes with river water for cleaning pots, pans, and laundry, with tall weathered, leaning wooden poles next to them.

A single electrical wire was routed to other poles from which dozens of electrical wires sprouted in different directions. All provided an unquestionably unsafe but rudimentary workable electrical source.

The air was filled with a mix of engine exhaust, dead fish, garbage, animal and human waste. This place was far removed in time, space and technology from the world I grew to know. And why was it that our driver had no concern about the lives of these people as he careened into several parked bicycles nearly striking several women? The perplexed and concerned facial expressions of most of us were dispelled by the laughter of a few who appeared to understand why this was happening.

No one ever questioned the practice.

It was late morning when we arrived at the main gate to Long Binh Post. The olive drab armor-plated guard shack was surrounded by green sandbags stacked waist high and manned by no less than four Army military police armed with M-16 rifles. An MP waved our driver through the barbed wire gates where I saw hundreds of rectangular, wood- framed, sheet metal-sided buildings with green 55 gallon drums, and waist-high green sandbags stacked all around.

The place was a sprawling 20-square mile military complex surrounded by two defensive barbed wire fences ten feet tall spaced just yards apart. Each horizontal tier of barbed wire had twelve ounce cans of assorted types of empty beer and soft drink containers fixed to them. Later, I would learn that each can contained several rocks for the purpose of making a loud rattle that could alert and detect movement within the perimeter, if disturbed.

On the very top of the fence were circular rolls of concertina wire (razor blade sharp) — about three to four feet in diameter — to serve as a scaling deterrent against an enemy raider penetrating the post. Strategically positioned behind the rear interior perimeter fence were machine gun bunkers and guard towers. Anyone attempting to penetrate the fence line entered the "kill zone."

Headed for the Replacement Center I was surprised to see that all roads were paved in black asphalt, complete with street names and traffic signs. The entire place was a hive of vehicular traffic.

Five-ton tractor trailer trucks, tanks, armored personnel

carriers, heavy duty dump trucks, bulldozers, road graders, jeeps, and V-100 escort vehicles manned by MPs. The V-100 was a highly mobile, fully amphibious armored car used for reconnaissance, convoy escort, riot control, security and as a personnel carrier. The vehicle protected the crew from small arms fire, grenades and anti- personnel mines. All surfaces were angled for maximum deflection and the armor was a 1/4 inch thick.

Power was provided by a Chrysler V8 engine that could reach speeds up to 70 MPH.

This was the workhorse for all the MP units assigned to convoy escort duty on the highways in Vietnam. As the V-100s passed by I envisioned myself being assigned to one of their units. I looked forward to going to a real military police company doing real police work.

At the Replacement Center we stepped off the bus, bags over our shoulders, and entered a huge wood-framed, corrugated metal roofed, cigarette smoke-filled screened-in structure occupied by hundreds of soldiers milling around nervously talking among themselves. After throwing our duffle bags down in front of us, John looked up and said, "What a cluster-fuck this is."

To which I said, "Yea, I wonder where we go from here." Just then a voice yelled, "Attention!" causing all present to face in the direction of the command followed with the sounds of boots locking together, with everyone silent and standing at attention. Thirty yards or so away, we saw a major quickly walking up several steps onto a wooden platform. After a few seconds of surveying the sea of men clad in green he calmly ordered, "At ease gentlemen, and welcome to the 90th Replacement Center, Long Binh."

It was during the major's short and well-rehearsed presentation that we learned the following three days would require some in-country training comprised mainly of familiarization with assorted weaponry, identification and recognition of enemy booby traps, personal hygiene and indoctrination courses associated with the culture of the North and South Vietnamese People.

This would be an advanced course version of what I got when I got my ass kicked back at Fort Riley, attending the five-day Vietnam Indoctrination Course. I figured that this three-day training period would enable the paper-pushers sufficient time to assign all of us to our final destinations. I also reasoned that Captain Z couldn't possibly have any influence here, not in all this mass confusion.

10
Long Binh Jail

T hree days later, the necessary training completed, people all around me received orders directing them to their duty stations. John got his, no surprise, to the 199th Light Infantry Brigade. He gave me the mailing address and I promised to drop a line when I got to my unit. We wished one-another good luck. He climbed up into the back end of an open-bedded "deuce-and-a-half" (2 1/2 ton truck) filled with grunts, destination unknown. He would need luck. Infantry guys get it the worst.

By the end of the day I hadn't received any orders and my patience was growing thin. I was assigned to various work details, mainly involving picking up trash and some mess hall duties. Finally, in the early evening of the fourth day, I received my orders:

SP/4 Robert C. Bogison is to report to the 284th Military Police Company at the US Army Installation Stockade at Long Binh for permanent assignment.

Long Binh Jail — official title, US Army Vietnam Installation Stockade (USARVIS) — was the primary incarceration center in Vietnam. Designed primarily to house Army malcontents and criminals, it also received Navy and Air Force prisoners. I wanted to throw-up. How could this possibly happen to me? Just how much juice could Captain Z possibly have?

Apparently more than I thought.

Early that evening I climbed onto a crowded "deuce-and-a-half" for the short haul to the 284th MP company area, about a mile away. An Army company typically comprises of 80 to 225 soldiers, usually commanded by a 1st lieutenant or captain. After jumping off the truck I watched it drive away, hearing the sound of grinding gears and leaving me in a fog of diesel smoke and dust. I looked around and tried to find the stockade referred to as Long Binh Jail, nicknamed "LBJ" and "Silver City" for its colored metal structures and perimeter fencing.

Established in 1966, the stockade moved from its original location at Tan Son Nhut Air Base, near Saigon to Long Binh Post. As the US military buildup continued, so did growing demand for confinement space for Americans found guilty of violating the grimmer chapters of the Uniform Code of Military Justice.

The men either served their terms at Long Binh Jail or were sent to the US Army Disciplinary Barracks at Fort Leavenworth, Kansas. "LBJ" had a notorious reputation which began during a week-long riot in August, 1968 when approximately 200 black inmates began systematically destroying the camp. During this assembly, white inmates and guards were beaten with any impromptu weaponry the rioters got their hands on, including wooden planks and bars from dismantled beds.

At the end of the ordeal over a hundred MPs and inmates were injured. One military policeman was murdered.

11
284th Military Police Company

The Company area I stood in was a series of sheet metal-roofed wooden framed, screened-in structures all of which had neatly placed OD green and bright yellow painted rocks delineating the borders of a three-foot wide, pea-graveled pathway. Nothing here resembled anything close to a stockade, as I knew it.

I wandered through the graveled pathways searching for the "CQ building (Charge of Quarters or Company Commander's office). The air was filled with loud mixtures of every kind of music. Rock and roll, Motown and Country-Western. A dozen or more MPs clad in standard OD green jungle fatigues, sporting white helmets with large black MP letters embossed on the front, walked towards me.

As they passed one of them said, "Hey FNG, you're gonna love it here at "LBJ." Forty and a wake-up you fuck!" The "forty and a wake-up" meant the guy only had forty days plus one morning left to do in Vietnam. I knew what he meant by, "you're gonna love it here at LBJ." Having spent almost a year at Fort Riley's CTF, this would be nothing new except that the inmates here would be more desperate and — without any doubt in my mind — more violent.

At the CQ I was met by the Company Clerk, a SP/4. His

uniform was impeccably maintained, his demeanor was all military and he was black. He introduced himself and welcomed me to the unit and escorted me into the First Sergeant's office. There, sitting at this paper-cluttered desk was this 300-pound lifer.

I cannot remember the man's name. I do remember he was lazy and very dislikeable. A First Sergeant is generally classified as an E-8 (enlisted rank) with a diamond insignia placed between upper and lower chevrons. Race had absolutely nothing to do with it. Simply put, he was a disgrace. After the company clerk introduced me, the First Sergeant rattled off some of the do's and don'ts and told me I would be assigned as a gate guard, commonly referred to as "turn-key," at the Reception Compound for the night watch. Within the hour.

He assigned me a cot number in the Gate Guard Hooch. Every building or structure was called a "hooch."

The company clerk took me to my new home just a few structures away: a grey, wood framed screen-covered tin roofed building about twenty-four feet wide and at least a hundred feet long. I was surprised that the floor was concrete. From the entry and along both sides to the very end of the structure were rows of bunk beds, four to a section separated by a four foot-wide walkway.

Each section boasted four metal wall lockers, aligned. A pair of wooden footlockers positioned against the wall served as headers and another pair of footlockers served as footers to the bunk beds. The sections were formed into fours: four beds, four wall lockers and four footlockers allowing just about seventy square feet of living space for four residents. About 132 men called this home.

The first three to four sections on both sides were occupied by black soldiers playing Motown music. The remainder of the building had sections occupied by southern boys and mid-west boys who entertained with the likes of Hank Williams. West

Coasters played Beach Boys and some of the Easterners took to Four Seasons and Do Wop music. A mixture of Beatles, Doors, Jimmy Hendricks, Jefferson Airplane and a dozen or more other rock groups added to the nonstop noise.

The place churned with activity. Poker games, dice games, laughter and debates filled the air. Joining in the action and sound was the constant drone of dozens of portable electric fans that could actually transform the clamor into a sort of tolerable background calm.

Silence was nonexistent.

I got a bottom bunk just about midway from both ends of the building. And lucky to be assigned to a section with Jim Connell from Long Beach, California, Tom Bacon from San Diego, California and a guy named Bill (I think) from a small town in Michigan. They were newly in-country as well. No mystery: they wore freshly issued jungle fatigues, like mine. Jim, who arrived a few days before me, suggested that we get something to eat at the mess hall before beginning our watch.

I threw my duffle bag into the metal wall locker and we went off together.

I liked Jim. He was my age, a few inches shorter with a stocky build, and he was a no-nonsense kind of guy. You knew right off that if you ever needed help, Jim would be there. As later he proved to be on more than a few occasions. On our walk I asked Jim where this LBJ was. "We're headed there now. The mess hall is inside the place," he said. "You mean we have to eat in the same place these shitbirds do?" I asked. "Yea. Every day," he replied.

Within a few minutes this large silver installation came in view. A towering 12-foot chain-link fence, interwoven with some form of silvery canvas and topped off with rolls of concertina wire four feet above that.

Armed guard towers thirty feet tall were strategically

positioned along the entire outside perimeter of this complex. It was an imposing and depressing place from all appearances. Far more so than my visits to Leavenworth, back in Kansas. As we entered the sally port the two guards looked at us and asked us to produce meal cards. One of the guards, a white guy said, "FNGs. You FNGs with the 284th, huh. Well you be sure to have a happy time while staying at the LBJ. You're gonna love it here. Careful now. We don't want you to get your young asses kicked before you get into the mess hall. It's better to get your ass kicked on a full stomach."

In the main yard Jim said, "Don't pay any attention to that shit. They've been telling me that shit for the past three days. I guess that's the way it is with some of these people. They just don't give a fuck."

Daylight was fading. All around me was a large expanse of black asphalt, with assorted wood-framed screened-in silver structures divided into compounds. The mess hall — just ahead of us — was within the confines of the Minimum Security Compound. Lots of activity here. Prisoners marched in platoon formations led by MPs. Other inmates were assigned to work details painting signs or pushing brooms around buildings.

The mess hall was operated by prisoners and supervised by a detail of MPs. The food was less than desirable but it was hot and the water was cold. You couldn't help but wonder what these fallen angels might have done to the food they were serving you.

Regardless, the food here was far better than what poor bastards like John ate and drank out in the jungle.

Each compound had a gate manned by an MP armed with a standard issue black wooden night stick. All exits and entries were secured by lock and key. Each compound was like a prison unto itself and all retained a 10 foot tall chain-link perimeter fence. The Medium A and Medium B Security Compounds were designed to house prisoners who had committed minor infractions of the Uniform Code of Military Justice, or were adjudicated in a Special Court Martial in violation of a significant crime.

Minor violations of the UCMJ, or results of a Special Court Martial, brought a sentence up to but not to exceed one year of confinement and demotion to the grade of Private E-2.

The Maximum Security Compound housed prisoners who were adjudicated during a General Court Martial having committed major crimes like murder, rape, robbery, and the like. These men received sentences ranging from incremental years of confinement to Death plus One. "Death plus One" in military terms" (irrationally) meant that you had to die (regardless how), then live one day after your death to complete your sentence.

If you were sentenced to serve six years plus one day, you served six years and one day. No time off for good behavior.

Generally, these prisoners were only held in Long Binh Jail temporarily (up to three weeks, possibly longer) until they could be transported to the Disciplinary Barracks at Fort Leavenworth to complete their sentence.

The "Psychotic Block Compound" housed prisoners who were extremely violent, could not care for themselves, and could not interact safely with staff or other prisoners (regardless of what crime or sentence they received).

The "Intensive Training Area Compound" or ITA housed the most insubordinate prisoners, regardless of their crime or length of sentence. Each day, beginning at noon, this category was forced to run in circles for ten minutes, then perform the US Army Daily Dozen exercise routine, run for another ten minutes and repeat the entire sequence until a dozen Daily Dozen routines were completed.

This form of punishment generally consumed three hours on a black asphalt staging area directly in front of the Reception Compound, within the Maximum Security area with the Psychotic Block on one side and the Intensive Training facility on the other.

Inmates slept in converted Conex shipping containers, where temperatures could easily exceed 115 degrees. Inmates considered this to be a form of torture, and the practice contributed to LBJ's reputation as the worst place to be in Vietnam.

Above: Metal Conex Box housing a Viet Cong POW. These metal boxes were the same type utilized to confine American prisoners in the Psychotic Block and the Intensive Training Area Compound, Long Binh Jail (LBJ).

I spent my first two evenings working the AM Watch (18:00-06:00) as a gate guard for the Reception Center Compound and the Intensive Training Area. Better this than Tower Guard. There was no relief from the stifling heat there as the evening wore on. At least working a gate kept you busy opening and closing access for personnel traveling in and out of these places. Confined to a tower allows too much time to think or, worse, fall asleep.

Between angry rants from prisoners locked inside their metal boxes in the Intensive Training Area and incessant screams from lunatics in the Psychotic Block, it was just about enough to make me want to walk away from my post and never report back.

Breaks were good. Short as they were, you could walk over to the mess hall and drink some strong over-brewed, scratchy Army coffee. After being relieved at my post I went straight to my bunk, removed my sweaty garb then entered a partially open air, gravity fed, cold water shower. There was no such thing as water pressure, hot water, urinals or flushing toilets in the Vietnam I was in. After the sixty second shower I fell on my bunk to the drone of all those electric fans and the loud and varied music.

On the morning of the third day at my new home — and just about one hour into a fairly deep sleep — I was awakened by the PFC assigned to the company commander's office and directed to report immediately to Captain Fortenberry, the Company Commander. What now? This could mean anything. A reprimand, a change in orders, anything. I was reasonably comfortable with the thought that it couldn't be anything bad as I hadn't been there long enough to screw anything up.

The CQ escorted me to Captain Fortenberry, a black officer in his early 30s, seated at his desk. A stocky build inside impeccably maintained jungle fatigues suggested he was career military.

Stepping up to the front of his desk I assumed the position of attention and bellowed out, "Sir! Specialist Bogison reporting as ordered, sir!" and threw a sharp salute. Without standing he quickly returned the salute and ordered me to stand at ease. He was direct and to the point and said, "Bogison. I am assigning you to work in the Reception Compound immediately. You will report to SP/4 Johnson. He will be rotating back to the states next week and you will do everything he tells you because this will be your permanent assignment. Any questions?"

He was giving me a decent assignment because of my experience at Fort Riley. No guard tower duty, no gate guard posts and no dealing with the lunatics in the Psychotic Block or supervising the idiots in Intensive Training. I probably should have been grateful but I just had to respond with, "Sir, with all due respect, when I submitted my 10-49 this was the last place I wanted to be assigned. I didn't come over here to babysit. I did enough of that back at Fort Riley."

Before I could request a transfer to a military police unit, he stormed at me — not without cause — "I don't give a shit why or how you came to Vietnam. Your MOS is 95C40. That is Military Police Security Specialist. That's what you are and that's what you will do. So forget it. You will do your entire tour right here at Long Binh Jail. When your tour is up you can request a transfer to another unit. Now get the fuck out of my office and report to Specialist Johnson. Now!"

Well, that was that. What kind of an idiot leaves the comfort of his own country to travel ten thousand miles to do the same kind of crap working in this depressing shithole. Maybe I should have kept my mouth shut and waited a few weeks before requesting a transfer. Maybe I should have remained at Fort Riley and finished my time in the Army there. Or maybe I should have taken that opportunity to go to Fort Belvoir to prepare for an appointment to West Point. Maybe. A lot of maybes.

I made this bed of shit and now I would have to lie in it. Thank you Captain Z.

Less than enthusiastic, coupled with having virtually no sleep in almost 48 hours, I reported to Specialist Johnson at Reception.

Specialist Johnson, "JJ" as he referred to himself, was a draftee about a year or two older than me. He was about 6' 2" with a large build and hailed from Buffalo, New York. When he spoke it was loud and confident. He spent most of his tour of duty serving with the 557th Military Police Company (just across the way from the 284th) assigned to street patrol in the city of Biên Hòa and the villages of Tân Hiệp and Tân Mai.

He loved to talk about his experiences with a sense of bravado. It got a bit old but he was entertaining and a good instructor. Ultimately, my entire orientation for this job lasted only four days as "JJ" received his orders back to civilian life sooner than expected.

It was monsoon season now and what a different world this was. Rain so heavy, so loud, so thick and so much of it all the time. Often, you couldn't see past three feet in any direction. Stand under a roof, the hard and heavy drops exploded on the asphalt and splashed your face. The volume, coupled with the force of the stuff, was incredible. It could last several minutes or an hour, or longer. And as fast and furious as it arrived, it abruptly stopped. Within minutes all traces disappeared.

Everything became dry, the soil dusty and the mud would return to clay. Within the hour the whole process would begin again. I had never experienced anything like this and I haven't seen anything close to it since. The monsoon season generally ran from July through December and into January.

My job was fairly simple. Reception was a single wooden-framed, aluminum-roofed barn and positioned directly behind Maximum Security, between Intensive Training and the Psychotic block. The place itself was very small. Incoming prisoners were processed and housed here prior to being assigned to a compound. Generally, a prisoner would be evaluated, processed, and delivered to his respective compound within 12-24 hours of arrival.

I would do the evaluation based on a statement of facts from his company commander and in accordance with the infraction or crime he was convicted of.

Predicated on those findings, coupled with the prisoner's demeanor, I would then send him off. My building had a maximum capacity of 25-30 prisoners. However, a population of 7-10 were usually in residence here at any given time. I was the only MP assigned to the building and my only back-up would be Jim, the

MP assigned to the entry/exit gate. My former assignment.

The passage of time does not allow for an accurate count of the prison population, but I estimate that it was well over 300 — and overcrowded. My survival in this environment relied heavily on an ability to immediately judge which of the prisoners was potentially dangerous to me and others. Any display of weakness or uncertainty on my part was not an option.

It was a world in which only the fittest prevailed, both MP and prisoner. Insubordinate and violent prisoners were immediately escorted to either the ITA or Psychotic Block. No exceptions. Consequently, virtually all major disturbances in Long Binh Jail erupted in Maximum Security, the Psychotic Block, or the Intensive Training Area. This had been the case during the August, 1968 riot.

Long Binh Jail reflected American society. Voluntary social segregation was the norm. Blacks with blacks, Hispanics with Hispanics and whites with whites. The atmosphere was dangerous and frustrating for inmates and guards alike.

Maintaining any kind of morale was a continuous challenge for MPs assigned to the facility. Our curriculum at the Military Police School, Fort Gordon, specified enforcement of military law, traffic control, self- defense, firearm training, along with foot and motorized patrol procedures. With the exception of several days of instruction in riot control techniques, MPs assigned to LBJ had no real corrections training but were tasked daily with maintaining order in a very volatile and hostile environment.

LBJ had a notorious reputation which, in turn, bred curiosity among the news media. Information concerning any aspect of the facility was closely guarded by the Army, which only added to the prison's mystique. "Life Magazine," a popular monthly at the time, offered $25,000.00 for the acquisition of just one photograph depicting anything inside the facility. If any were ever obtained (highly unlikely due to tight security), none was ever published.

Real, verifiable information was minimal. Administration of military justice was generally swift, usually severe and more often than not unjust.

My personal view then and now.

As previously indicated, virtually every inmate sent to LBJ had to be processed through Reception. But there were some rare exceptions. A truly combative prisoner bypassed Reception and was escorted directly to Intensive Training. An officer sent to LBJ was housed in a special building within Minimum Security. Special Operations Personnel went to another special building in Minimum Security which had a special guard detail.

Soldiers connected with a series of "incidents" (euphemism for assassinations and big media focus) involving Green Berets engaged in secret CIA-backed counterinsurgency operations in 1968-1969 with North and South Vietnamese double agents, were housed in LBJ during the summer of 1969. Journalists on this story got stonewalled on details. Access to some of these people and any information associated with them was withheld from all of us.

All of us were ordered not to discuss, ask questions or comment in any way about these men. They remained incommunicado for weeks at a time.

None of us were ever told the whys and wherefores of the Phoenix Program, as it was called, and to this day I have no clue what it was all about. Based on my experience, anything that could possibly reflect negatively upon LBJ or the US Army was censored and remained among the government's best kept secrets during and after the Vietnam War.

୬୨୨

12

Justice: Not Necessarily For All

Circumstances that brought soldiers, sailors and airmen to LBJ could be as bizarre as the punishment they received. I learned of one such example very early on.

Exactly one week to the day I departed Cam Ranh Bay we learned that Viet Cong sappers — engineers serving as commando raiders — had penetrated the base perimeter, crossed the air field, and staged a surprise attack on the field hospital killing and maiming scores of guys in their hospital beds. The increased VC activity and rocket attacks MPs were talking about back in that bunker on my first night in Cam Ranh Bay was a precursor to this very incident.

A week later I received two Air Force policemen formerly assigned to physical security duties on Cam Ranh Bay Air Base tarmac. Both had been convicted for assorted violations of the UCMJ, including insubordination and the infamous Article 134, a catch-all for any act reflecting discredit on the prisoner or his respective branch of service.

Both were stripped of their ranks, one a sergeant the other an Airman First Class. Both were sentenced to six months plus one day confinement. In essence, the statement of facts authored by their commanding officer indicated that the men uttered blasphemous profanity over the radio while requesting assistance, adding that both had been insubordinate and disobeyed a direct order from a superior officer.

While seated at my desk reviewing the statement of facts, the two men stood in front of me at the position of attention. After reading the brief, I directed them to stand at ease and asked the former sergeant if this was related to the Viet Cong sapper attack at the hospital at Cam Ranh Bay we had heard about. He confirmed that it was and requested to explain his version of the events, which I allowed.

The ex-sergeant said that he and the airman were patrolling the runway in their jeep during the early evening hours when they observed about a dozen pajama-clad Viet Cong soldiers firing AK-47 rifles and tossing grenades at several aircraft parked in revetments on the tarmac. The sergeant and his partner were each equipped with a six-shot .38 caliber revolver sidearm, and only one 7.62 caliber M-14 automatic rifle locked and loaded with one magazine containing 18 rounds. No extra magazines or additional 7.62 or .38 caliber live rounds had been issued to them.

Engagement with the Viet Cong used up all of their ammunition. In the fire-fight, the sergeant transmitted over the radio something to the effect, "We're out of fucking ammo. We need some fucking people over here, now." The response was, "Report to the OD (Officer of the Day) immediately." The sergeant admitted that he was angry at the time and that his last transmission on the radio was, "Fuck you."

The pair then proceeded to the nearest security bunker and began collecting magazines loaded with live rounds for the M-14 Rifle. They were approached by an Air Force 2nd lieutenant demanding to know what they were doing. The airman said they were returning to the runway to intercept the Viet Cong. The lieutenant ordered them both to report to the OD to which the airman replied, "We don't have time for that, Lieutenant." as the sergeant and the airman ran towards their jeep. The officer shouted, "Stop! That's a direct order."

The sergeant admitted that as he and the airman sped away in their jeep he responded, "No, sir." Within 72 hours following the incident, both men were under arrest, placed before a court martial, convicted, and sentenced. Days later, here they were assigned to me.

I studied both of them carefully. They were articulate and intelligent. Well groomed, sharply clad in their uniforms and both demonstrated a respectful and serious military demeanor. These guys did not belong anywhere in this place.

The sergeant, black, 22-23 years old enlisted in the Air Force several years earlier and had maintained a clean military record. The airman, a white kid, 18-19 years old, was less than a year into his four year enlistment, also with a clean military record. Maybe somebody had an ax to grind. An inflated ego. Perhaps a racial component played out in this equation. That might explain the sergeant's situation, but what about the kid? Who had it in for him?

I could only speculate, and as I came to learn many times, in the military no sense often makes every sense.

I couldn't wallow in the whys. Time didn't permit it. Besides, what the hell could I do? Something didn't ring right, that was for certain and now I had only 48 hours to determine where these guys would have to spend their time in this hellhole. APs were just as unpopular as MPs among all branches and all ranks of the military establishment. The chances of these men surviving in this environment would be minimal. Defining the dilemma as a daunting challenge is an understatement.

Ultimately, I did what I always found successful when an

issue became multifaceted and clearly over my head. I utilized that "chain of command" and presented the problem to an older and wiser higher ranked non-commissioned officer for resolution. In this case it was a master sergeant, name forgotten. My intervention resulted in the sergeant and airman being placed in Minimum Security temporarily.

Both got job assignments outside the facility, with parolees. Parolees were prisoners completing the remaining days of their sentences and housed in one of two barracks outside the LBJ compound, pending orders directing them back to their units. After only a few weeks in Minimum Security the pair were moved into one of the Parolee Barracks where they remained until their sentences were completed.

I do not know what became of them after they were released, but it was very clear that neither should have been sent to us in the first place. The master sergeant to whom I had appealed was a World War II and Korean War veteran. He hailed from Philadelphia. A straight shooter and I respected him. I often turned to him for guidance.

Several weeks later Private Joe Clemintine, assigned to one of the Light Infantry Brigades (199th or 196th), stood before me awaiting direction. Joe had been caught by an NCO smoking a marijuana cigarette while in the company of other members of his squad one evening at his base camp. He was court-martialed, convicted and sentenced to serve six months. Members of the squad who were with him at the time of the incident were left unscathed. Joe had already served six months as a rifleman in the field. There had been no prior issues.

At LBJ, everyone served his sentence, returned to his unit and was sent back into the field for six more months before rotating to the States. Time served in confinement here was the same as it is anywhere else. Dead time.

Eighteen months of service in Vietnam was credited with twelve months.

Joe was singled out by his NCO because of a personality conflict that had escalated during the weeks prior. The scenario was all too common. This particular event stood out because justice was not administered equally and the punishment — in my estimation — did not fit the crime.

Joe, who called himself "Pothead Clem" was a draftee about my age, who grew up in Brooklyn, New York. His service record had been excellent until now. His commanding officer could easily have meted out a reduction in rank and assignment to some crummy work detail in lieu of a court martial. There was no common practice in the enforcement and administration of the Uniformed Code of Military Justice.

A man like Joe could be sentenced to LBJ for six months of dead time, while another man who committed the identical offense could be slapped on the wrist with a warning. I saw a lot of Joes come and go. He was a likeable guy and didn't belong here. As it turned out I wasn't the only one who thought so. When the master sergeant made his daily rounds he took a particular interest in Joe's situation and arranged for him to be assigned to Reception as my Trustee Assistant.

That is to say, Joe was trusted with responsibilities denied to most prisoners. For several months, he helped me in virtually all of my duties, including typewritten logs and reports. In return, I received a thorough education on just what grunts out in that jungle were confronted with every day and night. These lessons were invaluable, as I would later learn.

At about this time that I received my first and only letter from John. He wrote about the hardships of duty in heavy rain -made evident by the letter's blurred, water stained ink. He described canned food, referred to as 'C Rations' or 'C Rats' as all but indigestible. The mud physically exhausting to move in, the leeches plentiful, the mosquitoes numerous, the fear factor immense.

I remember thinking how fortunate I was not having to live in such conditions. How could I possibly complain about anything? I had a dry bed, hot meals, a shower every day and a roof over my head almost all of the time. No more complaining about creature comforts. I was living well. There was never another letter from him nor a response to the two letters I sent in reply. Either he got wounded and sent home, or worse.

13
The Riot

About the middle of October, 1969 in the early evening hours LBJ experienced its second riot. Numerous disturbances from Intensive Training and Maximum Security got both compounds into "Lock Down Mode." The atmosphere reeked hostility. In the preceding week tensions had developed along racial lines throughout LBJ. Physical altercations occurred and several military policemen were assaulted. Convergence of these events interrupted work details. Scheduled activities were curtailed. Productivity all but ceased.

As the week ticked by our population of newly arrived prisoners in Reception mushroomed dangerously, from ten to over thirty.

Prisoners in Maximum Security started destroying property. Military policemen assigned there abandoned the area. Chaos rapidly spread to Intensive Training and the Psychotic Block. Within the hour, elements of the 720th, 716th and the 557th Military Police Companies in riot gear staged near the mess hall. Personnel assigned to Intensive Training and the Psychotic Block evacuated their posts under orders. Large numbers of prisoners began breaking out of their cells.

It was Jim who yelled to me from his post, "We have been ordered out. The gate is open. Let's get the hell out of here, now!" At this moment the riot-geared military police entered the Maximum Security compound in a long line formation.

I directed our new arrivals to lay under their assigned bunks to avoid any violent confrontation with the riot-clad police, as well as to minimize the unpleasantness of detonated tear gas that would surely precede the incursion. Minutes later, the entire Maximum Security compound and surrounding area was engulfed in a thick layer of yellow CS gas haze. (CS are the initials of a chemical compound used as a riot control agent.)

The haze transformed itself into a thick fog in Reception, igniting panic among the new arrivals. As I dashed out I was thrown to the floor and trampled by a dozen or more prisoners also desperately trying to flee the building. Several of them fell on me as they were overcome by the thick gas.

Struggling and gasping for air near the surface of the floor, I broke free, crawled down three steps of the front door porch and to the ground outside. That's when I realized my left shoulder and the ribs on the left side of my body had sustained some sort of injury. Also, when I raised my head in an attempt to gain a better view of where the gate might be I was immediately overcome by CS gas.

All soldiers are intimately familiar with what CS Gas does to the respiratory system. During Chemical Warfare Training, every Basic Training Recruit is required to endure a painful session in a locked gas chamber with the stuff. Inside, with the DI's (Drill Instructor) blessing, your gas mask must be removed to allow the full misery of exposure to CS grenades. It is not uncommon for the DI (usually deaf) behind his gas mask to demand the Recruit's full name and serial number, and have to repeat the information.

It took about ten minutes to feel my way out to the gate Jim Connell left unlocked, a distance of no more than thirty or forty feet. Throughout the first ten minutes of my odyssey I heard the screams of prisoners and the muffle commands of the military policemen shouting through their gas masks as wood, glass, metal and chunks of cement and asphalt rained down on them.

My challenge was to successfully low-crawl through the hundred yards of hostile maximum security and Intensive Training prisoners who had broken out.

My eyes burned constantly and tears poured down my face. My nose would not stop draining mucous, and I gagged non-stop. After an eternity, suddenly and unexpectedly a slight breeze hit the facility. The breeze permitted me to get on my feet and sprint, half blinded, toward the riot MPs. It was during the sprint that I felt the sting of a baseball-sized piece of asphalt penetrate my right calf. I fell right at the feet of a fellow MP who firmly pressed the bayonet on his M-16 rifle on the middle of my back.

After a short exchange of identities I was handed off to an Army medic. Fortunately, I sustained no major injuries, just a series of cuts, bruises and perhaps a slightly deflated ego. I owe my escape that night to SP/4 Jim Connell who had the presence of mind to leave that gate open for me.

The protocol under such circumstances actually required all gates to all compounds to remain locked.

Property sustained damage and numerous injuries to both prisoners and military police were recorded, but there were no fatalities. Lessons learned from the August, 1968 LBJ riot had been effectively applied. The ordeal lasted less than six hours.

That was it.

The next day I requested to see Captain Fortenberry and again asked to be transferred to a Military Police line unit, which he again flatly refused reminding me, "I already told you it ain't gonna happen. You will remain right here for your entire tour. No transfer!" The First Sergeant added his two cents, by warning not to "even think about bothering the Captain or me with this again!"

Within the span of the three months in Vietnam I was involved in several physical altercations with prisoners. Confrontations that required great restraint on my part not to seriously hurt or kill anyone. I did not want a repeat performance of my experience at Fort Riley. Long Binh Post came under several rocket attacks, but I hadn't even touched a rifle or pistol since I arrived in-country. To add insult to injury, within days of this incident, the First Sergeant was handing out Bronze Stars like candy to the administrative staff for their actions in the riot. All of whom were comfortably outside the facility during the entire disturbance.

My patience was all but gone. What the hell was I doing here, and how was I going to get out of this insane asylum?

14

Command Sergeant Major
William Wilkinson
18th Military Police Brigade

I stewed in this quagmire for several days. There had to be a way out and it finally dawned on me, there was. Roadblocks had befallen me before. I by-passed the chain-of-command with letters to decision-makers in California and Washington D.C.— and got immediate results. Now, I quickly drafted a letter to the Commander of the 18th Military Police Brigade detailing my reasons for requesting a transfer to a line unit. I made no secret about my intentions of transferring out of this place with some of the guys in my hooch.

Within a week, the Commander, a "full bird colonel" directed his Command Sergeant Major to meet me.

A Command Sergeant Major is the Army's highest enlisted rank. The position confers enormous authority. Staff officers are wise to avoid conflict with Sergeants Major.

It was early afternoon when the company clerk told me to report directly to the commanding officer. A thousand thoughts danced in my head as I threw my uniform on and, once again, proceeded to Captain Fortenberry's office. I saw the First Sergeant with Captain Fortenberry talking with a Command Sergeant Major. There was disdain in the face of the First Sergeant. I immediately assumed I was "in a world of shit."

A smart salute to Captain Fortenberry followed with

"Specialist Bogison reporting as ordered, sir." Fortenberry returned the salute and said, "Command Sergeant Wilkinson from Brigade would like to speak with you."

"Bogison. Let's go in here. Captain, I would like to use your office" where he directed me to sit in the captain's chair. He sat in a folding chair in front of the captain's desk. This was the first time I was treated like a respected guest by a high ranking superior. What a switch.

720ᵗʰ MP Battalion Photo: C SM William J. Wilkinson 720ᵗʰ MP Battalion -18ᵗʰ Military Police Brigade

Sergeant Major Wilkinson was a rugged, stocky-looking career Army professional. His jungle fatigues were starched, boots spit-shined, and his dark short cropped hair was graying along both sides. The man was old enough to be my father, and by the lines in his face and his no-nonsense demeanor he demonstrated immediately that he was not just any old time-serving lifer. This guy was alumni from the good war, WW II.

The conversation started with, "The colonel has asked me to look into your situation here. I've read your 201 File. I know you wrote your senator to volunteer for Vietnam service. Now that you are here, why are you requesting a transfer? And what happened to the chain-of-command? You do know what that is don't you?" "Yes sir, I do." I replied somewhat nervously, now that I really felt I had stepped into it. I responded, "After carefully explaining that no one in my chain-of-command would consider my request I resorted to writing a letter to somebody who might." That response caused the sergeant major to chuckle and ask, "All right son, what do you want?"

I explained that I enlisted in the Army to be a military policeman, not a baby sitter. I told him that my patience in dealing with prisoners was growing thinner by the day, particularly inside the wire. I added that I feared, given the right circumstances like the one I experienced during the recent riot, that I might seriously harm or kill someone. I reiterated that I did not want to repeat the experience I had back at Fort Riley.

The sergeant major was studying every word that came out of my mouth. He never interrupted me. He just studied me intensely, silently.

He nodded his head up and down and then said something to the effect, "Okay. I'll tell you what. I am going to ask you to try to do something for me. I will arrange for you to be reassigned to something outside of the stockade and your First Sergeant will send you to something having limited contact with prisoners. I want you to just try this and see if the change in environment is a workable solution to your problem for one month. If at the end of that month you still want a transfer, then we will look into that. Does that sound fair enough for you?"

Not exactly what I had in mind. But it was something. Like the good soldier I liked to think I was, I replied, "Yes Sergeant Major, that's fair enough."

But deep inside of me, I said, "No, God damn it! I want out of this insane asylum. Now!"

Walking out of the company office I saw the First Sergeant was not happy with all this attention on this personal fiefdom. What is in store for me now, I wondered. Back in my hooch, Tom Bacon and Jim Connell instantly asked me what had happened. I told them. Jim said something to the effect, "Well Bog, I'll bet Top (Army slang for First Sergeant) will have something real slick in mind for you now. Maybe tower guard. Those guys are outside the wire. I wouldn't be surprised if they play that one on you."

Exhausted, all I said was, "No shit. That would be about right. Thanks, Jim. I'll sleep on that." And then I just fell face first onto my bunk. Within seconds, the drone of those fans coupled with the garbled conversations of voices talking over the sounds of rock and roll, Motown and country music, put me into a deep sleep.

15

"You Number One GI, Bogie-san."

S leep didn't last long. The same company PFC as before came back to irritate me again an hour later. This time it was the First Sergeant who ordered my presence. Half asleep, I walked back over to the Company Office and reported. His Largeness was seated and leaning back in his chair, hands behind his head, boots on his desk. "Well, Bogison, I have found something I think that even you can handle. At 1700 hours you will check out a .45 (automatic pistol) two loaded magazines, a deuce-and-a-half and meet with Tam here in front of the company office."

Tam was head hooch maid responsible for the dozen or more hooch girls assigned daily to provide laundry and clean-up services in the company area. It would be my responsibility to load these women into the truck each evening and drive them to their respective villages.

Bright and early the following morning I pick up the women where they had been dropped off. After transporting them to the company area I was to report to the First Sergeant. I was a bus driver without a bus. Just a truck driver loading passengers like cattle.

Concerns? I had a few.

Driving a truck without a radio around Biên Hòa in the hours of darkness is crazy enough, but being armed with only a .45 caliber pistol was beyond stupid. When I asked the First Sergeant, "How about an M-16 (automatic rifle) to go along with that pistol," he answered, "No. You don't need an M-16. A .45 will do. You ain't gonna run into any Zips out there." Zips were the enemy.

There was no further discussion and the meeting ended. "I don't want to hear any more about it. Get out of here, and don't forget to report to me tomorrow morning after you bring the mama-sans to the company area." The older Vietnamese women were commonly called mama-sans.

What had I done to myself? Maybe this was payment for jumping that god-forsaken chain-of-command. This had to be some kind of retribution.

At 1700 hours, armed with my .45, and seated in my truck near the front of the company office, Tam hopped up onto the side step of the passenger side door and tried to stick her head through the window, but the large cone-shaped hat she was wearing wouldn't let her. After several unsuccessful tries she loosened the chin strap and pushed the hat back and asked, "Are you 'Bogie-san'? I show you where we go. I go home last. You get me first in morning." When I opened the door for her to get in, she said, "No, no. I sit in back with Mama-sans. I tell you when stop."

This would be interesting. I drive this loud diesel powered truck, occasionally peek into the side view mirror and try to understand Tam's broken English and dodge and weave in and out of the sea of Biên Hòa traffic.

I hadn't yet driven a jeep in Vietnam but now I am going to drive this monster truck making a dozen or more stops without killing some fool on a bicycle, a moped, a motorcycle, a rickshaw, a midget car or, God-forbid, one of those Vietnamese five-ton trucks built with spare parts transporting a hundred passengers.

It was all beyond interesting and a huge challenge the

instant I drove out of the main gate of Long Binh Post and onto the streets, alleys and dirt roads. I quickly learned the rules of the road and answers to all those questions ringing in my head. Courteous driving was non-existent. The biggest and the fastest wins the right of way. There are no rules of the road. You drive and give way to nothing. Everybody and every machine seemed to just naturally move out of my way.

And if I stopped suddenly, scores of motorcycles and mopeds traveling only several feet behind my behemoth would have to do the same.

Tam would yell, "Bogie-san! Bogie- san! You stop here. You stop here."

Wherever "here" was, I stopped. Traffic behind me stopped and then immediately merge into traffic off to my left. No sooner had I stopped when the mama-san — standing on the back bumper while clinging to the rear tailgate with both hands — jumped off and walked in the opposite direction. After each mama-san jumped clear of the truck, Tam said, "You go now Bogie-san." Sometimes adding, *"You number one GI, Bogie-san,"* meaning on a scale of one to ten, one being the best, ten being the worst, Bogie-san was good.

My final stop came in Tam Hiệp, a hamlet just outside Biên Hòa. Tam jumped off and yelled, "Bogie-san, you get me same-same here tomorrow before sun," meaning same place before sunrise. The process seemed simple enough although driving in and out was spooky. Early the following morning, I began my trek into the darkness and into the less traffic-congested roads to where I found Tam waiting for me on the side of the road.

As she climbed onto the tailgate and scrambled to the front of the bed of the truck she leaned toward the driver's window and greeted me with, "Choy Duc, Bogie-san" and began barking out directions for the next stop. I never did find out what Choy Duc means. The whole routine took just under an hour. After breakfast I met with the First Sergeant, as directed. Near the company office I noticed the First Sergeant standing in the doorway talking to four prisoner trustees and pointing his finger in my direction.

Three of them were holding eight or ten green empty sandbags, and one of them actually had empty sandbags wrapped around both of his hands.

I knew precisely what this meant and I remember muttering to myself, "You gotta be shitting me." But the First Sergeant wasn't "shitting me." But, in fact, he was. Literally.

16

The Honey Wagon

Among the first and most vivid memories for anybody who served in Vietnam were the plumes of black and gray oily smoke funneling from the ground into the sky and forming dark clouds. Viewed from any direction revealed anywhere from one to half a dozen such clouds during daytime hours. And the smell filled the air by their production of a truly unfamiliar and unpleasant stench. The average nose could easily identify some components as coming from burning oil or gas.

The other mysterious element was human waste. There were no flushing toilets in the Vietnam I was in. The bathroom, or latrine in Army vernacular, on most firebases ranged from nothing more than a wooden outhouse that provided anywhere from one or two seats, to larger and more elaborate facilities retaining as many as a dozen or more round holes drilled out on wooden benches.

Fifty-five gallon steel drums cut into half barrels were positioned directly below. Affixed to the outside wall of the latrine was a rectangular hinged door fashioned to open upwards from the ground to facilitate the exchange of barrels. Consider use of these facilities coupled with the plethora of digestive disorders associated with common diseases in that part of the world, dysentery and jaundice to name a few. These barrels often spilled over with horrific sights and smells.

Before I could speak, the First Sergeant bellowed, "Ah Bogison. You will take these four trustees and hit every latrine within sight of this Company. Every 'shitter', every one. These men know where they are so just go where they direct you. Then go out there (pointing at some mystical location) and burn the shit. When you are done with that, go out and make a second round. That'll take you most of the afternoon. Then take the mama-sans home. This you will do every day. Clear?"

"Clear," I replied.

As I turned to walk away he grabbed me by the arm and muttered, "Ah, no alcohol for the trustees, just ten minute smoke breaks. They are still serving their sentences. Is that clear?" I glanced back at him nodding my head and said, "Yes First Sergeant." What the hell did I do to myself? I had literally stepped into a world of shit.

I directed the four to follow me to the truck parked a short distance away, when one of the guys asked if this was my first run on the Honey Wagon. "Is that what you guys call this detail? The Honey Wagon?" I asked. "Yea man, you know Sugar! Sugar! Like the song." He was referring to a fairly popular song at the time performed by a pop band called "The Archies." The lyrics went, "Honey, Honey . . . Oh Sugar, Sugar . . . you are my candy girl . . . and you got me wanting you." It was funny and appropriate for the detail we were stuck with.

To this day, when I hear that song I chuckle to myself. Three white guys and one black, none of whom were really bad. The two white guys were finishing up six month sentences for smoking dope. The white and the black guy had been intoxicated and insubordinate to an NCO. All too common a tale, unfortunately.

Off we went into the land of shit. The first stop had over a dozen seats. Six empty half barrels sat waiting attention. Two guys jumped off the truck clad in their make-shift sandbag gloves, removed the barrels and poured the contents into one or more of six empty half barrels. The process was repeated until all the barrels were emptied. The partially filled half barrels were handed off to two on the bed of the truck. The team switched roles at each stop. As I watched them go through this miserable routine I was glad. Glad it was them and not me having to do it.

When the six barrels on the truck were full, I headed towards the all too familiar black and gray smoke clouds in the distance, far and away from any company or headquarters area.

Our objective was a fairly large open area within the confines of Long Binh Post, pot-marked with dozens of hand-dug pits roughly six to eight feet in diameter and up to about four feet deep. Scattered about were five-gallon olive drab gasoline cans.

And we were not alone.

Poor bastards from other units came and went. Some unloaded their catch of the day into empty pits while others fueled pits from the gas cans and set them ablaze. As I would learn, there is a correct protocol to successfully incinerate shit. Any old accelerant won't work well enough to make the stuff disappear. Somebody probably spent time and research to conclude that it required a formula of two parts diesel and one part gasoline to produce the best results.

Sometimes, a ratio of three-to-one was needed depending on the amount of the waste and its consistency, and the experience of the shit-burner. I was astonished to learn that you could not just pour the formula on the target and expect to do the job. No. One or more guys would have to methodically and painstakingly stir the accelerant formula thoroughly into the soup with sticks and shovels before setting it ablaze.

All this bestowed a new and truer meaning to the terms "stirring shit" and "shit stick." No surprise that they called this place the Shit Field.

I cannot accurately describe the stench.

After two rounds of several dozen stops, the guys would wash down the truck bed with buckets of water and mops. I usually marched them back to the trustee hooch and reported to the First Sergeant. But not always.

Defying orders from the First Sergeant, I would make a quick stop at an EM Club (enlisted man's bar) to buy a couple of cold beers for my guys. They earned it. In two short days I mastered the ins and outs of collecting, transporting and burning shit. Finishing the detail early allowed the First Sergeant to send me off to all parts of Long Binh Post and Saigon to scrounge building materials, tools, and other essential supplies that the Company R&D (Research and Development) sergeant needed for maintenance and building projects.

It was during this particular aspect of my assignment that enabled me to cultivate a significant number of contacts with NCOs affiliated with Quartermaster (Supply) and Transportation Units (land and sea) along with the rest of what we commonly referred to as "in the rear with the gear."

These trips taught me some unwanted insights into the lucrative business of the "Black Market."

A Black Market, despicable in principle and all but ignored in practice, most often centered on the exchange of household items found in any American supermarket, and openly sold on the sidewalks of the larger Vietnamese cities, and along dirt roads of the villages and hamlets between them. Most disturbing to me were hundreds of US military supplies like jungle boots, jungle fatigues, socks, blankets, field first aid pouches, ammo pouches, tactical flashlights, rucksacks, toiletries, canteens, helmets, C-rations, cartons of American cigarettes, compasses and field binoculars to name just a few.

Virtually everything supplied to our military except arms and ammunition. All for sale to anybody willing to pay or trade. Why would a GI pay $20.00 for a new pair of jungle boots (a hefty sum back then) for something he was issued for free?

In contrast, the local Vietnamese bar owner, barber, or mechanic (when switching roles for their Viet Cong membership later in the day, to set booby traps or raid firebases) had plenty of use for these things. I could have made a small fortune for myself dealing in the Black Market. It just wasn't in me. Besides, every dollar made in this way was an investment in killing US military personnel. Might as well hold hands with likes of Jane Fonda.

It didn't take long to grow weary of the assignment. As previously indicated I did not travel 10,000 miles from home to baby-sit problem soldiers, pick up shit and burn it, or transport short women to and from work during the hours of darkness.

Unbeknownst to me, my world was about to change.

Early one dark morning about the fourth week into the assignment, on my way to pick up Tam. Traveling in my beast at about 30 miles per hour, I was literally jolted out of my seat when I heard a loud ping and the sound of glass shattering somewhere near my arm, which was resting on the open driver's side window. Simultaneously, I felt a faint brush of small hard objects cross my left forearm. Less than a second later I heard two distinct gunshots that seemed to come from somewhere in the darkness, just ahead and off the road to my left.

It didn't take much to figure out what had just happened. I'd just been ambushed. Instinctively, I stepped on the gas and frantically patted my arms, chest and face expecting to feel blood somewhere. But there were only small shards of glass on my chest and legs. The windshield showed no damage and neither did the passenger or rear windows. Nothing.

I started to question what had just happened. I was down the road a mile or so when it dawned on me that maybe I should remove the .45 pistol from my shoulder holster and put it between my legs. That's when I felt a small metallic object on the seat between my legs, burrowed near my crotch. A slightly deformed copper-jacketed projectile that looked like a .45 caliber bullet. No mystery now, not at all. Some son of a bitch had tried to kill me.

But how did this bullet cause all these small shards of glass? Another mile down the road and the gravity of what had just happened hit me like a fierce arctic wind. I found myself shaking uncontrollably. It was right then that I questioned my worthiness as a soldier. I loathed any possibility of being a coward and as a consequence, I took several deep breaths and forced myself into a calmer state.

Approaching Tam's hamlet I noticed a convoy of military vehicles spearheaded by elements of the 720th Military Police Battalion traveling in the opposite direction, towards Long Binh Post. A glance at my oversized side-view mirror and immediately showed that it was completely shattered. Mystery solved. The bullet meant for me had struck the mirror. As I learned many years later investigating homicides, bullets and their trajectories are often unpredictable and sometimes defy logic. Logical or not, this bullet ended up way too close for my comfort.

I continued picking up all the Mama-sans and after dropping them off in the company area I reported and explained how the driver's side view mirror was damaged and presented the deformed projectile. The First Sergeant responded with little more than a nod and suggested that some irresponsible or drunken GI or ARVN (South Vietnamese Soldier) must have been the cause. During his convoluted explanation I remember asking myself, "What? Has this buffoon been drinking his bathwater or am I in another dimension?"

The sooner I got out of this place the better. I still have the deformed bullet.

Immediately after my meeting with the First Sergeant, I walked over to the 18th Military Police Brigade Headquarters and requested a meeting with Sergeant Major Wilkinson.

He was out touring battalion tactical areas and fire bases (Fire Support Bases) assigned to the 720th. I left word that I would like to meet with the command sergeant major at his earliest convenience. Jumping this chain-of-command was risky business and it was starting to become a habit with me. In fairness, the Command Sergeant Major Wilkinson had in fact told me to contact him if I still requested a transfer. I reasoned that I was not really jumping any command chain.

Besides, I had fulfilled my side of the agreement as it had been just over four weeks since our meeting.

It was in this period that the Army decided that I was up for promotion to "buck" sergeant. I was required to report to an oral board comprised of several officers and senior NCOs. Certain that my chances for promotion were slim, particularly in light of recent events, I was astonished to find that the ranking officer on the board, a captain, was concerned why I had turned down the opportunity to go to the West Point Preparatory School, Fort Belvoir, Virginia.

I can't recall my response exactly, but said something to the effect that I thought the war in Vietnam would be over before I graduated. They all just glanced at each other. I was also surprised to hear the other officer, a first lieutenant, jokingly say, "I see you received a traffic citation just before you enlisted, for a projection in excess of thirty-six inches protruding from the trunk of your car. I'll bet that was a surfboard, wasn't it?" All the while I asked myself, "What don't these guys know about me?"

Obviously, the lieutenant was from California and a surfer himself. He was impressed with himself for guessing correctly. I had been cited twice by the Los Angeles Police Department for stuffing surfboards in the trunk of my car, once in 1966 and again a year later. I left the interview believing that I would remain a SP/4.

17
The Promotion

Two days later, about mid-morning, I was driving the boys to our next latrine stop when I recognized one of our company clerks in a jeep going in the opposite direction honking his horn and waving his arms. I pulled off the road to stop and heard the jeep's tires screech to a halt, followed by the familiar sounds of a gearshift grinding into reverse. The clerk — whom I never cared for — directed me to report to Captain Fortenberry, immediately. Again. He could not or would not provide any further information.

This had to have something to do with my request to speak with Command Sergeant Major Wilkinson. But the instant I reported to Captain Fortenberry he said, "Bogison. You've been promoted to Specialist 5. I guess that makes you somebody."

"Specialist 5, sir?" I asked. "Yea. A Spec 5, with a 95C MOS. You are a specialist in Military Police Physical Security, therefore you are an E-5, an NCO, just the same as a buck sergeant. That's all, and standby, somebody from Brigade will be here shortly to talk to you. Get out."

I walked out of the company office and stood outside, bewildered. Promotion was an unexpected surprise and a good thing, but a Specialist 5 stuck with the horrible MOS of Physical Security was not good. Mixed emotions set in, but only briefly as I spotted Command Sergeant Major Wilkinson walking towards me.

"Bogison. Got your message. Sorry I missed you. Let's walk for a while. Congratulations on your promotion. How's it feel to be an NCO?"

I do not recall how I replied to him, but I am certain that it was respectful. "Okay, you tried it and you still want out is that right?" he asked and I replied that I did. "Well, I can send you anywhere in Vietnam. Quy Nhõn, Vũng Tàu? Got any preferences or places you think you could fit in? "No sir. Just anywhere I can do the most good. Anything besides stockade duty. Like I said before Sergeant Major, I didn't come over here to babysit a bunch of misfits. I came here to be a part of the war effort as a military policeman."

"Well, that's good enough for me. Within the week you will receive orders assigning you to a military police company in the 720th Battalion." As he shook my hand, he said, "Good luck Bogison. I'll be seeing you." As he walked away, I kept telling myself that it wasn't a dream. I was actually going to be free from having anything to do with stockades. I would be assigned to a real military police unit doing real police work, which was why I enlisted into the Army in first place. I just couldn't believe it.

The First Sergeant had already replaced me and assigned some poor sap to pick up the mama-sans and run the Honey Wagon. My new-found position as an NCO on the food chain got me out of details but it also came with more responsibilities. Now, instead of picking up cigarette butts, scrubbing pans or cleaning equipment I was supervising PFCs and Spec 4s performing work details. Never really forgot where I came from, I chipped in. I never asked anyone to do something that I wouldn't do.

I had witnessed my fair share of arrogance among those chosen to lead and direct others and vowed never to be like them. Lead by example and not to be afraid of getting your hands dirty was a principle I learned somewhere early in my life and it remains with me to this day.

Sergeant Major Wilkinson was true to his word. Within three days I received orders assigning me to B Company, 720th Military Police Battalion, just about a mile down the road. It was mid-December and my orders directed me to report on December 21, 1969. It wasn't a R&R (Rest and Recuperation) area like Vũng Tàu or Quy Nhõn, but it was a military police company and that suited me just fine. During the week, Al Drever, now Sergeant Drever, met me in my hooch.

Al was assigned to the 300th Military Police Company maintaining security on the Saigon Docks.

We had corresponded with one another when he left Fort Riley earlier that year. I ran into Al on one of my trips to Saigon while he was assigned to a guard shack near the waterfront. It was good see to see him and he congratulated me on my promotion and getting out of LBJ. He was scheduled to "ETS" (Expired Term of Service/Honorable Separation) out of the Army sometime within the next few weeks.

A "short timer" now and pretty excited about getting out of Vietnam and into civilian clothes back in the "World." Everybody stationed in Vietnam referred to the US as the "World." As far as we were concerned, Vietnam wasn't in the world. It was in a world of its own.

Leaving the 284th Military Police Company was easy and I didn't look back. At least not right away. On the 21st of December with orders in hand and my duffle bag over my shoulder I began the trek to B Company, 720th. I actually felt pretty good during my walk. I tried to anticipate what my new duties might be: road patrol, convoy duty or maybe just walking a beat somewhere.

As I approached the B Company office a lot of unshaven guys clad in mud-stained, torn camouflaged fatigues, bush hats and carrying all kinds of assorted weaponry came in sight.

Camouflaged fatigues were generally issued to special

operations people like the Green Berets and LRRPS (Long Range Reconnaissance Patrol.) Infantry units wore standard olive drab jungle fashions, the kind I was issued.

Who are these guys?

Affixed to the Command Post wall was a large green placard that read:

Command Post Company B
720th MP Bn
Bushwhackers

"Bushwhackers." Hmm. What does that mean?

The company clerk took me to see the First Sergeant who sat at his desk examining 201 files. First Sergeant Hardin Collins was a fit-looking man in his mid to late thirties. A strict disciplinarian, I later learned, with a penchant for getting just about whatever he

720th MP Battalion Photo: L-R: First Sergeant Hardin Collins receiving salt pills from Sergeant Angelo Torres during a Battalion Sweep.

wanted.

Looking up from his desk he studied my name tag sewn above my right breast pocket, and said, "We've been expecting you, Bogison. Welcome to B Company. Heard a lot about you. You are just what I need right now. I understand you don't take a lot of shit from prisoners. Is that right?"

He caught me off guard. What kind of response did he expect? Without much thought I stammered, "Only when it was necessary, First Sergeant." He grinned and said, "Well, I guess it must have been necessary back at Fort Riley." He referred to the Campbell incident. I didn't respond. "I have a lot of problems with the "snuffies" in 3rd Platoon, he continued, "You'll do." Snuffies in the literal sense meant soldiers who were replaceable, disposable, expendable.

Not a flattering title to throw around as one was constantly being reminded how many ways a soldier could get "snuffed" in Vietnam during training. Words like *snuffed* or phrases like *"He bought the farm"* were common among drill instructors and veterans who served in Vietnam. It meant you were dead.

"I'm assigning you to the 3rd Platoon as a squad leader. Go to supply and see Staff Sergeant Joyner. He'll get you squared away with your gear. The 3rd Platoon just got in from the field this morning to get fed, showered and resupplied. You'll be going out with them tonight."

Get my gear, coming in from the field, going out with them tonight? What the hell did that mean?

My mind racing, I blurted out, "Sir, excuse me, what kind of gear am I going to need?" "Yea, right," he answered. "You will be going out on a reconnaissance and ambush mission. Your platoon has already been in the field for the past four days and nights. They're coming in to be resupplied then heading back out for the remaining two days left in this mission. The 1st Platoon is still out there and the 2nd is off for the next two days."

He could have hit me in the head with a hammer and I wouldn't have felt it. I was numb. I said something to the effect, "You mean I'm going to lead a squad of men out there when I don't even know where I am going or what the hell I am doing? This is a military police company?" and with a slight chuckle he said, "Yes. That's what you are going to do. This is B Company. We are combat infantry military policemen. Every man out there is a military policeman. They will show you what to do and you'll catch on, just like they had to. Sergeant Mintec is your platoon sergeant. You report to him."

And out of my mouth flowed, *"You gotta be shitting me."* With a deeper chuckle, he said, "No, God damn it. Now go get your gear. I'll check with you when you get back two days from now. Just do what they tell you out there. You'll be all right."

The company clerk pointed at one of the four 3rd Platoon hooches and apologized for not having an NCO room available for me. Not that I knew it, but NCOs rated a private living space. The least of my concerns. I was used to living in a building with dozens of men. I entered what I thought was the 3rd Platoon hooch and was greeted by the only inhabitants, a Mexican guy and a white guy at the opposite end. The Mexican guy had his left arm in a sling and a bayonet in his right hand. The white guy was on crutches with one of his legs wrapped in a cast.

"Hey, amigo! Why are you here? We don't like sergeants. Especially new ones. My friend and I had a little disagreement and we decided to shoot each other. We are amigos now. My "carnal" (Spanish slang for brother or close friend) and me are going home tomorrow. You better be real careful now."

Great.

I just left one insane asylum and here I am with a couple of loons who think that shooting each other was a good way to foster friendship. I was pissed and this little exchange filled me with rage. I simply did not have time for this. As calmly as I could, I asked, "Is this the 3rd Platoon hooch?" to which the white guy relied, "Fuck no, this is the 2nd Platoon." The Mexican chimed in with, "Is the little sergeant lost?" while waving his bayonet." That was it.

I dropped my duffle bag and as I closed the gap between us responded in loud and ominous tones, "All right, you! You're gonna look real fucking stupid with that toad sticker shoved up your ass, not to mention that after I break your fucking right arm and shove it down your throat so far that you won't be able to shit or throw-up. And you, Mr. One Leg, you wanna go home tomorrow hobbling on one leg or on your fucking back? Now where the fuck is the 3rd Platoon hooch?"

The Mexican dropped the bayonet on his bunk and pointed with his right finger. End ordeal. The next hooch over. I never saw the pair again.

The 3rd Platoon hooch was littered with muddy backpacks, canteens, and web gear on every bed and all places in between. Web gear is best described as heavy-duty canvas-type suspenders attached to a wide, heavy-duty canvas belt. Assorted pouches were affixed to both items. About midway in the building PFC Rellis lay on his bunk reading a book. He instantly got up and asked, "Can I help you?" Where could I find an empty bunk?" I asked. Rellis — from Sacramento, California — had the job of platoon truck driver. He recently rotated out of the field. An available bunk was found. The platoon was at the armory cleaning weapons.

I dropped my duffle bag on the bunk and met with Staff Sergeant Joyner at the Supply Shack. Joyner, from New York, was a typical Lifer. A smooth talker and very shrewd operator in appropriating and misappropriating military supplies. He was also an excellent source of information. Handing out my gear Joyner

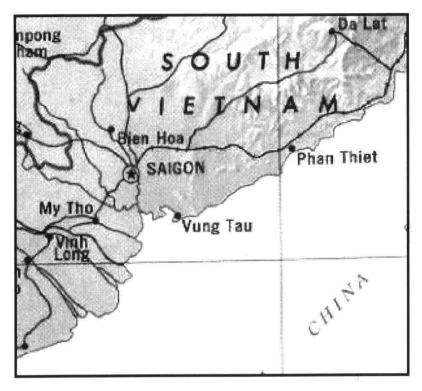

B Company Tactical Area of Responsiblity (TAOR) was, roughly, around the words "Bien Hoa" on this map — North and NorthEast of Saigon.

enlightened me on what B Company was all about.

B Company comprised three reconnaissance and ambush platoons with the task of seeking out and destroying Viet Cong or North Vietnamese Army units within a twenty-two square mile Tactical Area of Responsibility (TAOR) outside Long Binh Post and Biên Hòa. Each mission generally required a six day/six night trek into swampy rice paddies and flooded jungle adjacent to the Đồng Nai River. The Đồng Nai ran north and south and flowed into the South China Sea and served as a major Viet Cong supply line.

It was not uncommon to remain in the field for as long as ten to twelve days, depending on the mission our platoons were ordered to complete. A platoon was three six-to-eight man squads, three squad leaders, a platoon sergeant and occasionally a 1st or 2nd lieutenant platoon leader. Every squad had an M-60 machine gunner, an M-79 grenade launcher operator and a radio telephone operator commonly referred to as the "RTO."

It was not unusual to see some men carry a variety of personal-preference weapons comprised of rifles, machine guns, shotguns, automatic pistols and revolvers in lieu of the M-16 rifle.

A fourth tactical element — the PBR (Patrol Boat Riverine) Platoon was manned by B Company personnel working with the 458th Transportation Corps. PBRs and their crews provided fire support for the ambush platoons and maintained security along the Đồng Nai and its tributaries, intercepting Viet Cong movements. Initially, PBR operations were reserved for the US Navy. The 720th was among the US Army's first units to be delegated with this assignment. In essence, B Company had its own navy.

A PBR is depicted in the popular but ridiculous Hollywood movie starring Martin Sheen, "Apocalypse Now." We had about eight boats along with a contingent of smaller craft called "Boston Whalers," or "Skimmers." Whalers were powered by 70/80 HP outboard engines and used to transport ambush platoons to and from their drop-off locations, in lieu of helicopters.

The men assigned to the reconnaissance and ambush platoons were referred to as "Bushwhackers." It made sense now. Bushwhackers. What did I get myself into? No point sticking blame on Sergeant Major Wilkinson. I did tell him to send me where I could do the most good. But even in my wildest thoughts I couldn't have figured on this.

Gear in hand, I met Staff Sergeant Mintec. Third platoon was cleaning weapons at the armory. Mintec was a stocky guy in

Staff Sergeant Mintec, taking a break: "Watch him (Greg Thompson) and do what he tells you. Your rank doesn't mean shit."

his late 20s and looked career Army. He was wiping down a long-barreled shotgun when I introduced myself. Studying me briefly, he told me that I would take over 2nd Squad and, pointing to SP/4 Greg Thompson said, "He knows what to do out there. Watch him and do what he tells you. Your rank doesn't mean shit.

Experience and know-how keep people alive and he's got it. Once I think you have it, you'll take over but until then let Thompson direct your squad. Clear?"

With a quiet sigh of relief I replied, "Very clear." Mintec then had me join him in the mess hall for a hot meal where he rattled off an endless list of the DOs and DON'Ts in the bush. My head was spinning with the effort to absorb every word. The conversation ended with Mintec reassuring me that I would be snapped into shape sooner than I thought. It was an immense relief to know that in at least one aspect of my new life I was only responsible for my own dumb ass and not for seven or eight other guys.

A typical six-day mission required a riflemen to carry 75/85 pounds of equipment and ammunition. The backpack itself would generally contain an entrenching tool (small shovel), a metal mess kit along with two to three days of C rations consisting of seven or eight assorted canned foods, a full body plastic poncho, a black plastic inflatable one-man-raft, a camouflaged blanket, four to six pounds of C-4 plastic explosives, two or three Claymore mines (anti-personnel devices each containing approximately 1.5 pounds of C-4 along with several hundred feet of time fuse).

Also attached to the backpack were two green (friendly contact), two red (enemy contact) and three Illumination Parachute pop-up flares, along with three M-79 Grenade Launcher, HE (high explosive) rounds or three Canister rounds. These were 40mm HE rounds (grenades) or 40mm Canister rounds (shotgun type).

The web gear each man carried also had a first aid pouch, two canteens of water, ammo pouches, up to six fragmentation grenades, two smoke grenades, between 200 and 300 rounds of M-16 ammunition in bandoleers containing 20 round magazines, and two one hundred round belts of M-60 machine gun ammunition. Every man also carried a three foot long machete, a kabar knife, a bayonet in a scabbard, compass, a side arm (optional), and perhaps a book or deck of cards.

Last but not least came his choice of rifle, machine gun or shotgun. In addition to most of the above, the RTO carried the PRC-25 radio which weighed approximately 25 pounds.

Squad leader's gear added an L shaped olive drab flashlight with a red colored lens, and a small laminated map of the 22-square mile Tactical Area Of Responsibility.

I met Greg Thompson in the 3rd Platoon hooch. A thinly-built, quiet guy from Phoenix, Arizona. I assured him of his authority over deployment of the squad. He was to disregard my

720ᵗʰ MP Battalion Photo: SP/4 Greg Thompson.

rank and that I was there to learn, not direct. He didn't say much. Just an acknowledgement. "Don't wear any deodorant and don't use an aftershave. They can smell that shit out there so don't leave them a calling card. Just stick close to me. Oh, and don't mess with the dog or get near it. He'll have you for lunch. He's an attack dog and the only guy he respects is his handler."

Each ambush platoon had an attack dog and handler assigned from the 212th Military Police Sentry Dog Company.

I sat on my bunk. Senses of sight and sound fine-tuned to the conversations among all these strangers, carefully scanning their webbing and back packs trying to develop a method of my own for packing all this loose gear. I was a fish out of water here, and there was no hiding it. None of these guys were friendly. They considered me a liability not an asset. This mixed bag of people came from all parts of the US, some of them had shady backgrounds. Somehow, I assembled my gear in an acceptable fashion before going off to the armory to collect my weapons and ammunition.

18
First Mission

The M-16 rifle and Army .45 automatic pistol were my weapons of choice. I was intimately familiar with M-16 nomenclature and qualified as an expert with it. The .45 was no less comfortable and worn in a shoulder holster inside my camouflaged shirt. I watched others store their bandoleers of M-16 ammunition, grenades, flares, side arms and copied them. Without much thought, I slung the two circular shaped belts of M-60 machine gun ammo over my head and shoulders forming a crisscross configuration on my chest and back, like everybody else.

So I thought.

The weight of all this stuff was more than I imagined and I cringed at the thought of tripping or falling down.

It was just about sunset when everybody was geared up. In front of the company area were two 2 1/2-ton trucks fired up, waiting to take us to our rendezvous point near a place named the French Pier. When I started to climb the steps below the truck's tailgate, a hand gripped my left wrist and pulled me up and into the bed of the truck. I do not recall who it was but I was very glad that he was up there. I had serious doubts that I could have successfully accomplished the task on my own.

No sooner did we load up and sit down on the bench seats

of this open air taxi, then we were on the road. I hoped to remain anonymous and blend in just like any other body in the group.

Looking around I could see who was seasoned and — to my surprise, others like myself — who were cherries, a derogatory term applied to new guys in the bush. Deep into my own thoughts, the guy seated to my immediate right asked in a distinct New York accent, "Hey, do you know where we're going? I heard some guys talking about the French Pier place. This is my first mission." to which I responded, "You know as much as I do. This is my first night out, too."

He introduced himself as Ed Lewin from the Bronx. Ed was a big guy and because of his size he had been directed to carry the M-60 machine gun. Unknown to me at the time, Lewin was assigned to my squad as the primary machine gunner. I think we were both somewhat comfortable with each other because we had one thing in common. We were cherries.

The instant we left the main gate of Long Binh one of the sergeants barked out, "Lock and load your weapons and keep your fingers clear of the trigger. If we get hit, get off this truck fast, hit the dirt, and start throwing some lead back at 'em."

All conversations ceased.

Only the familiar sounds of the diesel engine, shifting transmission gears, the tailgate slamming against the truck as it rolled over each bump in the road, and the wind roaring by us was left.

It was just about dusk when we reached an old, multi-pillared, bullet-riddled and open-aired cement structure on the bank of the Đồng Nai River. My first glimpse of the Đồng Nai was a stretch nearly a mile wide with a fairly swift current. Waiting for us were three Boston Whaler operators seated in their boats moored adjacent to the dock at the muddy bank, engines idling. Also referred to as "Skimmers," the boats were small fiber-glassed, tri-hulled, approximately 17-18 feet in length and about five feet wide.

Each was equipped with a PRC-25 radio and armed with an M-60 machine gun mounted on a pole and swivel just in front of the operator, positioned near the center of the craft. Each whaler could transport eight or nine of us to the jump-off location.

Once we were all loaded aboard, freeboard clearance was less than a foot. This suggested that the term Skimmer was a more fitting description than Boston Whaler. After everybody was loaded, Sergeant Mintec seated in the front, said, "You new people, stick close to your squad leaders. If you should get separated don't wander. Stay where you are and we'll find you. Keep your eyes open and your mouth shut."

Seated next to me was Lewin. Thompson sat at the very rear. The three boats proceeded southbound in a column formation about ten to fifteen yards apart and just about a 100 yards away from the eastern shoreline. French Fort was several miles downriver. We were the lead boat traveling at a fairly quick pace. Our engines were more powerful than I expected. I tried to determine if being in the lead boat was a good thing or bad thing, but the more I thought about it the more I realized it didn't matter as we were nothing more than sitting ducks, anyway.

Even if the Viet Cong couldn't see us, the loud drone of the three engines would certainly help them zero in on us. I felt completely powerless and vulnerable. Thinking about who or what was watching us out there in the darkness didn't help matters. Instead of dwelling on that, I turned my attention to both shorelines. As I scanned to the east and west I could see faint silhouettes of irregular shaped vegetation on the banks.

The east revealed dozens of inlets and tributaries, heavily vegetated, each of which bent and twisted into a forbidding black abyss.

Finally, about a hundred meters north of our destination the boat abruptly slowed and the roaring engines were reduced to a low hum as all three boats slowly drifted to shore. It was almost pitch black when we disembarked. My first three steps made enough noise to cause someone ahead of me to whisper, "Be quiet!" Instinctively, and for reasons I cannot explain, my subsequent steps were taken by a slower, shorter stride into and out of the muddy morass by placing the weight of my body on the outer soles of my boots.

This resulted in the desired effect. Virtually, no noise. A dozen or more steps into my new gait moving further inland, revealed the faint features of a very small brick type structure, about twenty meters ahead. This must be it. French Fort. Then, all hell broke out.

19
This is not like the movies

Massive artillery, small arms and machine gun fire was concentrated less than hundred meters ahead of us. Red tracers passed over our heads along with the snapping sounds of small arms fire whizzing past. Illumination parachute flares ignited high above us, creating our silhouettes against the backdrop of the Đồng Nai. Instantly, I hit the ground on my stomach.

Inky one second, then everything in front of me lit up the next, revealing lines and moving shadows of foliage as the parachute flares gently descended to earth. I glanced up and behind me and watched several men scrambling to get out of the boats. Out of nowhere, several helicopter gunships referred to as "Hueys" along with the roar of a C-47 fixed-wing aircraft sprayed machine gun fire just east and south of us. The commotion all this fire power produced was deafening. Surprisingly, as it continued, the intensity of those sounds became muffled. It seemed as though time had stopped and I had been transported into another dimension. Time, as life experience had conditioned me to gauge, was now nonexistent.

Minutes, seconds were meaningless and immeasurable. I had no attachments to anyone around me and my existence in this world left me feeling all alone amid a firestorm of noise, flying metal and flickering bright lights. In an instant, all previous youthful notions of immortality I may have presumed were gone. Forever. It was only when somebody ordered us back into the boats that I realized I had been laying in several inches of water. Everybody swiftly low- crawled on all fours back to a boat.

I have absolutely no idea how long we were out there.

Time had vanished. A quick body count by squad leaders ensured that everybody was accounted for and all three boats proceeded back up river in the opposite direction very slowly, and close to shore.

Our whaler operators slowly eased us northward about a quarter mile into a small tributary and silenced their engines. There we sat in those damn boats concealed in a thicket of four foot-high reeds watching the aircraft above perform a show.

The C-47 — referred to as "Puff, the Magic Dragon" (a popular song of the era by the Peter, Paul and Mary trio) -flew in a circular pattern at about 1,000 feet pouring down a steady red flame of machine gun fire just yards from where we had disembarked. C-47s were World War II-vintage transports modified into ground assault gunships bristling with mini-guns that put a bullet every 2.4 yards in three-second bursts on an elliptical area about 52 yards in diameter at the rate of 6,500 rounds per minute. They could stay on station for hours.

My father crewed aboard earlier versions of the same aircraft twenty-five years before. Every fifth round was a tracer bullet that burned glowing red as it arced to the target. The sounds of these sophisticated machine guns produced an odd but intensely loud drone, unlike anything I had ever heard before. The two helicopter gunships no more than a couple of hundred feet above us helped to produce the same havoc with their mini-guns, simultaneously unleashing high explosive 40mm rockets.

Just as suddenly as this nightmare began, it stopped. Parachute flares burned out. Darkness returned and the only sounds left were the fading drone of departing aircraft, water lapping the sides of the boats, and my pounding heart. Minutes later small arms fire started up all over again, bringing back a couple of helicopter gunships. The pattern of activity continued intermittently for some time while we silently remained awaiting further orders directing us to an alternative location.

The ambush site had to be changed. Guys (spotters) who direct artillery and chopper crews assigned to patrol above us are briefed each afternoon as to where our ambush platoons will be each evening. The procedure is supposed to be a safeguard in preventing us from becoming victims of friendly fire. This firefight had people in our Tactical Operations Center (TOC) scrambling to find a safe place for us to set up. Of course, I didn't know any of this at the time.

At last, our platoon leader, a lieutenant, got new movement orders. Our whalers continued very slowly about half a mile up river where we disembarked in shallow water and formed a defensive perimeter about twenty-five meters inland. Lieutenant and squad leaders remained kneeling in the mud camouflaged under ponchos — a light, square piece of rubberized cloth that had an opening in the center to slip over your head. A hood covered your head — especially helpful in the monsoon season.

The garment had multi-uses: raincoat, lean-to shelter, make-shift shelter, sunshade, damp-proof blanket and whatever else that need and imagination might conjure. In this instance, the lieutenant used ponchos to conceal the red lens of his flashlight as he pointed out our positions on his tactical map.

Minutes later, Thompson tapped me on the shoulder and whispered, "Okay. We gotta move out straight ahead about a half a click in and set up. Pass the word to your left. I'll take care of the right. As soon as 1st Squad moves, we fall in right behind them. I'll go first, then the RTO behind me, then you and tell that

"60" man (Lewin) to fall in behind you. I want the RTO between you and me. And keep a distance of 10-15 feet between you and the RTO. Walk quietly. Don't fall or trip. Got it?"

Before I could respond, Thompson turned away to address the guy on my right. I wondered what the hell is a "click" and how far is "half a click?" Clearly, this wasn't the right time to be stupid by asking. Seconds later we were on the move, in the dark on what appeared to be a fairly level and straight but narrow muddy trail. I was relieved to be able to walk quietly flat-footed. However, the improvised gait soon became painful. I couldn't see but sensed that on either side of me was some sort of pond or creek. Every fiber of my being was fine tuned. Newly acquired ringing in my ears was overshadowed by the sporadic hum of mosquitoes, the faint sound of a boot sole sliding on the wet ground, and the intermittent and bizarre cacophony of indigenous creatures.

The stench of mud, stagnant pools of water and wet vegetation filled the air. The miniscule light the stars provided created a vague silhouette of the RTO in front. I heard what sounded like someone up ahead had stepped into a shallow mud puddle. The column stopped briefly and I suddenly became acutely aware of our vulnerability. As ignorant as I was on this, my first mission, I recognized that moving twenty-five men in the dark to set up an ambush was foolhardy and that we, the Bushwhackers, could easily become ambushed ourselves.

I also thought about my rifle. It got soaked in the water back at French Fort and I wondered if it would still fire. A hell of a way to go into an ambush. Twenty minutes into the trek and fatigue started to set in. Every step seemed more difficult. I was out of shape and not accustomed to carrying all this weight. Sweat poured out from my head, neck and arms.

Suddenly, the sounds of splashing up ahead caused the column to freeze in place. Someone had fallen into a body of water. Instinctively, I crouched down expecting something, anything, but nothing came. Just silence. I could almost hear myself sweating and the pounding of my heart was so loud I was certain that it could be heard by others. We remained frozen for minutes (that seemed like hours) and I was glad of it. Glad that it wasn't me who caused all that noise.

At an even slower pace, we pressed on. Instead of taking a two-foot stride at each step we now inched forward at about a twelve-inch step. Fatigue I felt earlier was now gone. My senses were focused on the ground in front of me. Finally, we arrived at our ambush site. Each man whispered to the next to crouch down, form a line ten feet apart, and told to unload our gear slowly and quietly.

During this process, Thompson tapped me on the shoulder and whispered, "Come with me. You got first watch." We crawled on our hands and knees about forty feet away to the fourth guy down the line from my gear.

There, the M-60 machine gun was loaded and set up on a small tripod with Ed Lewin on his stomach positioned directly behind it. "You guys have first watch. Anything moves out there don't fire your weapons. I'll be next to the RTO, three guys down. You get me. If you don't have time to get me use your frags (grenades) first. You should be able to get me in plenty of time. Here, look through this. It's a Starlight Scope. You see any movement, get me. I got the next watch so get me up and I'll relieve both of you. Two hours from now."

I glanced at Ed and whispered, "Well, here we are." I had heard about the scope but never received any instruction in its use and up to this point had never even seen or handled one. Several months earlier back at Fort Riley, I went to the Post Theater to see the movie "Green Berets" starring John Wayne. In the movie one of the guys grabbed this cylindrical telescope, placed it to his right eye and said something to the effect, "Let's see what starlight star bright has to see."

Now, here I was holding this thing in the dark trying to figure out how to use it. It was heavier than I imagined, maybe in the neighborhood of two or three pounds. Three inches in diameter and somewhere between twelve and fourteen inches long. As I looked through the scope I saw nothing but darkness.

The revelation came when my right index finger inadvertently tripped a metal toggle switch on the right side of the thing. This triggered a faint but high pitched tone, followed by a bright screen casting the landscape and sky in a dull light green hue. None of the shapes and forms of the objects depicted in the screen were either crisp or clear and any significant ambient light rendered the device temporarily useless.

Even the village idiot could operate this thing.

I studied the area directly in front of us, but all I saw was flat sparsely vegetated fields. I guessed we were in the middle of a large field of rice paddies surrounded by much taller vegetation in the distance. I had seen these kinds of fields along the highways in travels to Saigon and Biên Hòa. Embankments shaped in squares or rectangles sometimes as large as a football field usually containing several inches or more of water, but the ground I was sitting on was relatively dry.

As I continued to familiarize myself with the obscure objects, shapes and lines depicted before me in this green screen world, I couldn't help but wonder how many ways a guy could get killed out here without even firing a shot. Booby traps, poisonous snakes, disease, and friendly fire to name a few. My biggest fear was getting my throat slashed by an unseen foe in this darkness.

It was during these thoughts that I felt an irritating soreness on both sides of my throat. After giving it a brief thought I figured the problem was caused by the load I was not accustomed to carry.

The two hour watch went fairly quickly with nothing to report. After awakening Thompson, I silently unfolded the poncho liner, used my rucksack for a pillow, and laid down. My grenades were in a pile next to me on my right along with my rifle and bandoleers of ammunition. I put my .45 inside my front waistband. I was completely soaked and the cool night air which never got below 90-95 degrees, didn't help. As I lay there my thoughts turned to that nice dry bed I had slept in the night before back at the 284th.

I tried to sleep, but every time I started to doze off, I forced myself awake. I was too wired and really too scared to even think about sleeping. As the night turned into early morning I started to feel intermittent strange sensations all around my back and lower legs. I attributed it to my wet clothing.

By dawn, I was freezing and those strange sensations had become more than just an annoyance.

At first light, Sergeant Mintec and most of the other men were up lighting fires to keep warm and heating up instant coffee and hot chocolate in their tin mess cups. I noticed that we were set up in an L-shaped formation. First and 2nd squads were the vertical line of the L facing east, and 3rd squad formed the small horizontal line facing north. Three guys were set up about thirty yards behind us facing west towards the Đồng Nai, and four others set up facing south.

It looked to me that our ambush was prepared to intercept anything approaching us from the north or east, and the guys behind us were rear guards.

20

"No, Hoss. This is what you do"

That annoying sensation on my back and lower legs was now getting difficult to ignore. When I flung off my wet camouflaged shirt and OD green t-shirt I noticed a small worm-like thing on my left bicep. A voice behind me with a strong southern accent said, "Sarge. You got leeches all over your back. Hold on I'll get them." It was Jim Gufford, a SP/4 from North Carolina. When I tried to pry off the leech now comfortably imbedded on my left bicep, Gufford said, "Don't do that. You can't get them out that way. The best way to get these things off you is to put a lit cigarette to it like this."

He put his burning cigarette to the damned thing. Instinctively, I drew away from him figuring he was setting me up for ridicule or a stunt.

Instantly, he grasped my left arm and said, "No, Hoss. This is what you do. You can pour salt on the bastards or you can squirt some bug juice on 'em but a cigarette is the fastest way I know how to get rid of them. We got these things back home. Only difference is these guys are hungrier."

Of course he was right and as heat was applied to a dozen or more of my slimy companions, they fell off like dead flies. Gufford called everybody "Hoss."

Stripping completely naked revealed a dozen or more of the

creatures seeking shelter in the crack of my ass, my groin and my inner thighs. I could only imagine where they would eventually end up had I allowed them to explore further. One particularly nasty one managed to burrow deep into the top inside portion of my right ankle leaving a faint scar that would remain with me.

While Gufford was exterminating the little darlings I noticed that I was the only one who was gifted with this experience and asked him why.

"You must have parked your ass in the wrong place at the wrong time. We all get hit with something out here, scorpions, centipedes, snakes, ants and whatever else this place is home to. One thing you can do is get some bootlaces, wrap them around your pants from the ankles to the knees and cinch the laces tight like the rest of us. That'll keep most of them from getting into your pants.

Better get used to it. This whole damn place is swamp so you gotta check yourself a lot."

I took note of all this as we loaded aboard the trucks. Most of the guys had tightly wrapped the lower portions of their pants with laces. It made sense.

Makeshift fires I saw around me were fueled with broken sticks of plastic explosives called C-4. Wrapped in OD plastic the 3/4 pound sticks were approximately a foot long, about one and a half inches wide and an inch thick. The C-4 itself was a gritty-textured white, clay-type substance. The pliable stuff was used to blow up caves, structures, people, and anything else left to the imagination. Its most popular use was for building an extremely hot fire, fast. Lighting a match to a small piece of this stuff caused it to ignite instantly, producing a flame so hot that it would make a cold tin cup of water boil in seconds.

Half of a stick ignited could produce enough heat to comfort several wet guys standing near it.

Gufford broke off a piece, lit up, then motioned me towards him as he knelt next to the blaze swishing the liquid in his tin cup over the flame. The intense heat felt good because it penetrated through my wet clothes. Gufford stared into the flame and said, "That was some shit last night wasn't it? We could a got torn to pieces if we went any further out there." "What the hell was that all about?" I asked. "I don't know. We'll probably have to do a sweep of the area this morning to check for bodies. It's only about a click from here. I don't mind saying it. It scared the shit out of me," he replied.

"Well, you weren't the only one." I fired back. "And by the way, what the hell is a click?" I asked.

Gufford explained that a "click" was jargon for "kilometer" broken out in meters (i.e. 1,000 meters equals one kilometer) and used to calculate artillery target distances. One click meant 1,000 meters, two clicks 2,000 meters and so on. When approximating distances on an enemy position, the observer on his radio relays the measure to adjust incoming artillery to the artillery guys miles away. If the intended high explosive round was estimated to have fallen short of an enemy position, the observer would so advise to ensure that the next round was recalibrated to fall correctly.

None of us ever did get a satisfactory explanation as to what exactly occurred that evening. All I remember being told was that a platoon of Royal Thailand Rangers, our ally, had wandered into our Tactical Area of Operation, stumbled into some Viet Cong culminating into a prolonged firefight.

No other American or allied unit was allowed to enter our TAOR without prior authorization as any contact made or movement detected could easily result in lethal exchange between friendly forces. This incident appears to be precisely what happened. The Thais had no prior authorization to enter our TAOR in the first place. If they had, our platoon leaders would have been apprised of it and in this instance they had not. Had we disembarked just minutes earlier than we actually did, we would have walked directly into a kill zone between the Thais and the Viet Cong with catastrophic consequences.

Our 22-square mile TAOR was a series of rice paddies and swamps completely surrounded by the Đồng Nai River and its tributaries to the west, and the Buông River and its tributaries to the east. My new home was configured into the shape of a boot. The lower ankle and heal along the Đồng Nai bending east on the Buông to the toe, which bent north separating us from the Royal Thailand Army on the opposite side.

The familiar sound of a Huey gunship out in the distance in the eastern sky closed in towards our position, accompanied by a smaller bulbous shaped chopper referred to as a "Loach" (Light Observation Helicopter, officially the Hughes OH-6 Cayuse). The Loach was unarmed and generally ferried battalion officers responsible for assessing signs of enemy activity.

These choppers were usually escorted by a Huey gunship. In this particular instance, and routinely every morning at first light, choppers would make several passes over our position and methodically check for signs of enemy movement before our platoon made a sweep of the area checking for blood trails, footprints, or booby traps.

Dry from the fire and leech-free, I collected all my gear. Sergeant Mintec, with a group of men, interrupted my housekeeping and motioned me over to him. I was introduced to Staff Sergeant Donnie Ray Thomas, Squad Leader of the 3rd Squad, Sergeants Hank "Tiny" Fraley and Ron Snider, Squad Leaders of the 1st Squad along with Assistant Squad Leaders SP/4 Carlos Lozano and SP/4 Ed "Shakey" Marley.

Thomas hailed from Louisiana, Tiny, the biggest man in the platoon, was born in Maryland, Snider came from Northern California, Lozano from Southern California and Shakey was a streetwise guy from Pittsburgh, Pennsylvania. All were congenial and I felt humbled in their presence. These would be the men who collectively shaped me into the kind of squad leader I eventually became.

Sergeant Mintec directed us to prepare the men to meet the whalers at French Fort. He added that we would be passing through the same area that we got caught in the night before, and our orders were to conduct a thorough sweep of the place looking specifically for blood trails.

After strapping on my gear I slung the two 100-round bandoleers of M-60 machine gun ammo over my shoulders. About half way to our destination both sides of my neck were being rubbed raw. Although I tried to slide items away from my neck, little relief was gained. I couldn't dwell on this so I simply ignored the pain. I had to stay focused on the ground in front of me. As we approached the area just east of French Fort all I found were hundreds of expended shell casings.

Somebody located blood but I never personally witnessed the find. Not really knowing what I was looking for I was careful with each step I took keeping a keen eye for anything out of the ordinary that might reveal a booby trap. The Viet Cong were famous for them.

Completing our sweep, we met the whalers at the bank of the Đồng Nai. French Fort was nothing more than a very small and tall square-shaped old brick structure. The bullet ridden building couldn't have been more than 20 feet wide, 20 feet long and maybe two stories high, with several portholes on each side. Just a brick

French Fort as it appeared in late 1967 early 1968. Dong Nai River in the background. Note the lack of foliage. Agent Orange (defoliant) was heavily dispersed throughout our entire tactical area of responsibility. In 1969 and throughout 1970 the entire area depicted here was completely overgrown with thick and tall brush concealing the portholes as seen here.

structure surrounded by thick vegetation about fifty yards from the eastern shore of the Đồng Nai. I have no idea what purpose it could have served for us, or the French.

The shoreline had receded considerably. The Đồng Nai's ebb and flow to the South China Sea could drastically change the landscape. The river had narrowed to almost half its width and the twenty-foot wide shoreline we experienced the night before, had now expanded to several hundred feet.

We waded in the mud and into knee-high waters in the direction of the boats. I couldn't help think how vulnerable we were, sloshing through all this muck. It was during this phase that a black snake about two feet long swirled its way under water in front of me. Its head broke the surface. A voice shouted out, "Don't fuck with it. It's a sea snake. They bite and Oh, yea it can kill you!" I didn't need any more persuading and splashed away from the damn thing. My reaction drew laughter.

Leeches, now a deadly snake and I had only been in the field one night and one morning. By the time we finally jumped into the whalers, I was physically exhausted and tried not to show it but I wasn't really fooling any of the old timers. All the other cherries were the only ones with their upper bodies completely saturated in sweat. And it was just the beginning.

L-R: Sergeant Ron Snider, SP/4 Ed "Shakey" Marley.

SGT Ron Snider.

SP/4 Carlos "Chuck" Lozano.

L-R: SP/4 Ed "Shakey" Marley, SSG Donnie Thomas.

SGT Hank "Tiny" Fraley.

L-R: SP/4 Jim Gufford, SP/4 Robert "Crazy" Marich, SP/4 Glenn Barmann.

21
"You've got your bandoleer on backwards."

Our destination was about a mile further south to the heel of the boot, at the confluence of the Đồng Nai and Buông Rivers, where we would disembark and await further orders. Heading down river, the wind brushing against my wet body felt good, but that nagging rash on both sides of my neck was becoming raw and painful. I managed some relief when I pried the M-60 bandoleers away from my neck.

As our whalers slowed to a stop on our approach to the destination, the distance between the shallow water we were in and the eastern bank of the shoreline was over hundred yards away. Our whalers could proceed no closer. Off we jumped into knee-high water and mud for another trek. After about half an hour we reached the upper banks at the heel of the boot. It was then that Carlos Lozano approached me and said, "Sarge your neck is all raw. You've got your bandoleers on backwards. The points of the bullets should be facing away from your neck not digging into it."

He helped me remove my equipment and all I could say was, "Thanks. I won't do that again." He also reminded me to check myself for leeches for the same reasons Gufford advised me earlier. Something as simple as rotating the pointed ends of the bullets in the bandoleers away from my neck should have

December 1969, L-R: Foreground: Author, unk, SGT Hank "Tiny" Fraley, first mission disembarking from the Whalers. The reddish colored pointed ends of the bullets crisscrossed over my shoulders dug directly into my neck.

been obvious. This time there were only a few leeches to contend with.

So much for trying to remain anonymous.

We remained at the heel of the boot baking in 110 degree heat, eating C-rations, smoking cigarettes and watching hundreds of assorted shapes and sizes of sampans traveling in both directions in the middle of the Đồng Nai. Most were fishermen. American and South Vietnamese patrol boats could be seen patrolling in the area weaving around these vessels, randomly stopping and searching them for contraband.

Later in the afternoon the tide returned, swelling the Đồng Nai to its normal width, and we sought relief bathing in it.

Our C-rats were all stamped either with the year 1952 or 1960. Typically a C-ration was a small brown cardboard box comprised of a 12 oz. tin can containing some form of meat, spaghetti with meat sauce, pork, turkey loaf, meat loaf, and a poor substitute for Salisbury steak, in a long menu of selections. You only ate the stuff because you were hungry. Back in the States, any of it dumped on a sidewalk, would make you step around it.

In the same box there were, variously, a twelve ounce can containing pears, apple sauce, fruit cocktail or peaches. Peaches were preferred. Dessert was limited to a small tin of God-forsaken concoction labeled fruit cake. Two out of every case of twelve C-rat packs contained the most coveted of all the items, the pound cake. Guys would trade just about anything to get a C-rat pound cake.

In some instances they might even fight over it. A small tin contained peanut butter, jam, and crackers or biscuits. A small waterproof pouch contained instant coffee, instant hot chocolate, instant lemonade, sugar, powdered cream, some waterproof matches, two small pieces of candy-covered gum, a sponge type toothpick, small tissues of toilet paper, and a small cardboard box containing four Chesterfield, Pall Mall, Winston or Salem cigarettes.

Just before dusk, Mintec called the squad leaders together for a briefing and revealed that our ambush site for that evening would be at a place called the "Rabbit Ears," located along the Buông River on the eastern edge of our TAOR.

Contours of the shore at this particular location were marked by two similarly shaped protrusions of land resembling a pair of rabbit ears. The Buông River, about several hundred yards wide and less traveled than the Đồng Nai, ran eastward along the sole of the boot, then turned north around the boot toe area of operations. Traveling northbound the Buông intersected numerous tributaries and several smaller east-west rivers. The Rabbit Ears were positioned several clicks north of the toe of the boot.

The 1st Infantry Division, commonly referred to as "The Big Red One," was responsible for the area west of the Đồng Nai, the 9th Infantry Division, referred to as "Old Reliables," had responsibility south of the Buông at the confluence of the Đồng Nai, and the 25th Infantry Division, commonly referred to as the "Wolfhounds," along with elements of the Royal Thai Army was responsible for areas east and north of the Buông.

Just like the previous evening at dusk, we loaded into our whalers and slowly traveled east on the Buông, hugging the northern shore, then eased our way northward to the Rabbit Ears, always hugging the shoreline. Cruising at less than ten miles per hour was even more foreboding than flying at 25 miles per hour on the Đồng Nai. The Buông — sometimes referred to as the Back River — was a spooky place, and if we encountered any contact with the enemy I was told it would be on this side of our TAOR. I dreaded just sitting in these open air death traps when dusk turned to darkness.

My heart pounded, my stomach churned, and a cold chill settled over my body as I expected something bad to happen around every river bend.

Anxiety became my constant companion every time we set off on the water headed to or from an ambush site.

Finally, after what seemed like an eternity, we arrived at Rabbit Ears. On this particular evening we set up our ambush near the shoreline, directly between the lobes of the ears. Men quickly set up claymore mines in front of our horseshoe-shaped emplacement facing mainly westward toward the Đồng Nai, leaving the open end of our formation facing the Buông. Sergeants Snider and Fraley of the 1st Squad were deployed on the northern rim of the horseshoe.

Our squad formed the middle of the rim, and Staff Sergeant Donnie Thomas's 3rd Squad deployed on the southern rim.

The claymore mine was an interesting anti-personnel killing device. C-4 plastic explosive material was encased in a rectangular convex shaped green plastic case an inch or two thick, about the size of a small assorted chocolate box. A pair of scissor-like legs attached to the bottom of the device allowed it to be firmly inserted into the ground for support. It weighed a little over three pounds and contained over 700, 1/8 inch diameter steel balls.

When detonated the steel balls would fly out to about 100 meters in a 60° arc in front of the device, mowing down the vegetation and killing anything in its path up to 50 yards or so.

The mine was armed with a blasting cap inserted in the device which was crimped to an electric wire and electrically detonated by a mechanism controlled by a member of the ambush squad. These devices were arranged in various crossfire patterns about 25 yards directly in front of our horseshoe formation. With the words "Front Toward Enemy" clearly embossed on this thing even an idiot could figure out which way to point it.

I was given the 03:00 to 04:00 watch this time, as a rear guard to observe movement along the Buông, and the sparsely vegetated area directly across and east of it. We referred to this area across as Thai Territory because it was the tactical area of responsibility for the Royal Thai Army. Any movement observed from our side of the river to theirs would be forwarded via the radio to our Tactical Operations Center. The TOC Operator would then contact a Thai translator who forwarded the information to Thai Army Tactical Operations Center.

When a line of communication was established the observer, one of us, would report the location of the incursion on the coordinates of a tactical grid map. After it was confirmed that the movement reported was not friendly, the observer requested an Artillery Fire Mission, or an air strike, on the position. That was the protocol as I understood it. However, as I would learn later the Thais did whatever worked for them on their timetable. Not ours.

Laying on my makeshift bed of a deflated rubber raft, and my now filthy camouflaged blanket, I stared at the thousands of bright stars cast against a pitch black sky.

This would be the first time I had ever actually taken time to study the stars so intently. Two worlds. The peace and serenity of the night sky from the perspective of a land full of danger and uncertainty. And how did I get here, in this place, in this time? There was no mystery about that, I asked for it and there was no turning back. I reasoned that if all these boys out here with me could do it, then so could I. My body was tired and sore but my mind would not let my eyes close. Too many questions running through my head.

What if the guy on watch falls asleep? Worse yet, what if they were all killed without uttering a sound? Then what? If I fall asleep, what are the chances I won't wake up? Even worse, what if I fall asleep and start snoring or talking in my sleep.

I might give away our position and be responsible getting somebody killed. If I fall asleep, will I react quick enough to locate my .45, rifle, my grenades? Will I freeze and do nothing? What do I do if I sense a VC crawling towards me? Shoot him? Or do I have it in me to savagely stab another human being to death with my kabar knife or bayonet? Where do I go if we get overrun?

Too many questions.

"WHAT THE HELL WAS THAT?" The swamps and jungle around me were full of strange noises. There was a bird that bellowed several intermittent high pitched *boink! boink!* sounds while simultaneously making a noise that sounded like its beak or its entire head was breaking the water surface. Another bird yelled *"Re-Up! Re-Up! Re-Up!"* The Army was constantly pitching anything they could to get a man to re-enlist. A common phrase thrown back and forth among draftees and some enlistees was, "Don't give up. Re-Up." Meaning re-enlist and give the Army three or four more miserable years of your life. Another was, "Don't get pissed. Re-enlist."

Whenever this bird screamed "*Re-Up*" you could hear a few very faint chuckles among the platoon. By far the craziest of all the strange things heard out there was the Fuck-You Lizard. The lizard with a foul mouth. Joe Clemintine had told me of the strange creature that screams "Fuck You!" four times clearly discernible, in fairly rapid succession culminating in the fifth and final utterance of a slow and more deliberate, "FUCK-Youuuuuu!" Of course I found it hard to believe Pot-Head-Clem at the time, but seeing or hearing is believing.

Sure enough, Joe Clemintine was absolutely right, there was such a thing. Naturally when this particular creature decided to let loose it was extremely difficult not to laugh right out loud. Everybody had trouble keeping quiet once this guy started insulting us.

Precisely at 03:00 SP/4 Jack "Peanuts" Cortez, an M-79 Grenadier from New Jersey, tugged at my right arm to take over his watch as the rear guard. Cortez had just turned 18 and was one of the smallest guys in the platoon. He was a crack shot with the M-79. Back home he worked in a cigarette factory. As I low crawled to my position some 15 to 20 yards away from the rest of the platoon, I felt the ground get wetter and soggier the closer I got to the shore of the Buông.

Obviously, the river was swelling. Within the first five or so minutes into my watch, the area I was in was inundated with several inches of water. I had to reposition myself half-a-dozen times several yards further away from the shore to avoid lying in water and making noises. As I scanned the river and the Thai Territory on the other side, I could just barely make out the contours of some of the vegetation.

I didn't know it at the time, but I would later learn that elements of the VC and the NVA (North Vietnamese Army) were often spotted all around this area by all of the ambush platoons.

About half-way into my watch I saw several illumination artillery rounds burst then expel bright parachute flares into the sky several miles to the north and east, emanating from Long Binh Post, followed by sporadic machine gun fire.

Apparently, there was an attempt by the VC to breach the wire or something spooked the guys in the perimeter bunkers. It couldn't have been too significant as the entire ordeal only lasted maybe a minute or less.

I was relieved promptly at 04:00 by SP/4 Glenn Ward, who hailed from Hobbsville, North Carolina. Ward, 25 years-old, was among the oldest men in the platoon. He spoke with an unusual southern dialect, foreign to even those from other parts of North Carolina. I would learn some valuable lessons from Ward as he was an accomplished outdoorsman and a valuable source of information for all us city boys unfamiliar with living in this type of environment.

I remained damp, cold and wide awake lying on my wet blanket watching the sun rise just above the eastern horizon. Our squad was fortunate as we had been laying in saturated ground most of the night, while the other two squads found themselves in several inches of water. Everybody was cold to the bone and it didn't take long for the fires to start.

After removing leeches, warming up, heating breakfast and conducting a sweep of the area, Staff Sergeant Mintec called the entire platoon together and directed everyone to participate in live fire exercises with every weapon in the platoon. Mintec, Donnie Thomas, Tiny, Ron Snider, Greg Thomas, Shakey and Carlos Lozano ensured that all of us were thoroughly familiar with every weapon carried by every man. I discovered that the M-79 Grenade Launcher and I seemed to fit like a hand in a glove.

Having only fired the weapon three times back at Fort Gordon, I quickly learned that I didn't need to bother looking through the sights as I had been trained.

Cortez told me, "Just let the thing be a part of you. If you know what it's like to hit a homerun over the centerfield fence, this is the same thing. The 79 is your automatic bat and the HE (40 MM high explosive) is your explosive baseball. If you have to hit one way out into the bleachers, go for it." Made sense to me and I never forgot it. Peanuts was a good kid.

It wasn't yet 09:00 and we were all sweating like pigs when just a few hours earlier we had been wet and cold. After our live fire exercises, the whalers arrived and transported us to the French Pier where deuce-and-a-halves were waiting to drive us all back to Long Binh.

After we arrived at the armory, we dumped our gear and headed to the mess hall to get a hot meal. All of us were caked in mud and grime and we didn't smell good, either. This jungle-swamp living was for the wicked. MPs from A and C Companies dressed in their starched fatigues and spit-shined boots would step aside as we passed as though we were afflicted with some kind of scourge. Sitting down on a chair and eating a hot meal off a table was a luxury now.

Never again would I complain about mess hall hot chow. Only two days in the field and I was already beginning to appreciate the simpler things in life.

22

"Things are tough all over..."

After chow we returned to the armory and thoroughly cleaned our weapons and gear. It was then that I noticed most of the web gear, camouflage fatigues and boots these guys were wearing were worn, ripped or frayed. There was a shortage of socks, t-shirts, shorts and even underwear. I found this odd and asked why they weren't being issued replacement gear and clothing. Someone in the group shouted, "Don't you know? Things are tough all over and nobody gives a shit!"

After the usual cold shower and shave, I went over to see Staff Sergeant Joyner in supply to get some answers. All Joyner could tell me was that he got just about anything except boots, web gear and camouflaged clothing. He had an abundance of ponchos, bush hats, regular fatigues and heavy field jackets but nothing essential for these guys to use or wear in the field.

After trying to grasp the reasoning behind this explanation, I told Joyner to throw all the excess field jackets, bush hats and regular fatigues onto the bed of a deuce-and-a-half so I could do some negotiating with other supply depots. Bush hats were a hot item for all those in the "rear with the gear" guys as they were all but impossible to get unless you were assigned to an infantry unit.

Standard issued regular fatigue pants and shirts were always in demand. Field jackets were useless for our people as they were too cumbersome to pack and carry, but on those cool 80-85 degree rainy monsoon nights the rear echelon boys considered them a luxury. I knew because I had been a rear echelon guy just three days earlier and given anything to have one.

Armed with my .45 and a fully loaded M-16, off I went in my 2 1/2 ton beast loaded with trade items of assorted shapes and sizes.

After stops at the Biên Hòa Air Base, the Ton San Nhut Air Force Base and several other well-stocked supply depots on Long Binh Post, I parked the truck directly outside our 3rd platoon hooch. The bed of the truck was loaded with hundreds of assorted sizes of new combat boots, camouflaged fatigues, t-shirts, underwear, socks, web gear, first aid kits and whatever else I deemed was needed. The commotion I created backing the truck up to the sandbags just outside caused the men to come pouring out.

The instant I opened up the tailgate, I yelled, "Have at it. Things are tough all over. I guess somebody gave a shit!"

The mad scramble that followed was reminiscent of children opening up presents on Christmas morning. At that instant I felt that I was one of them. I was to most, but not everyone.

L-R: SSG Fred Pazmino, Unknown, SSG Joyner, SGT Ron Snider, SSG Donnie Thomas.

Our platoon was off for the next three days. Not off, as the Army never allows you to just sit around and do nothing.

The men were restricted to Long Binh Post and assigned various details involving trash pick-up, commonly referred to as Police Call, filling sandbags, replacing sandbags, discarding sandbags and something called Beautification of the Company Area. This required a sergeant supervising four or five guys armed with rakes to neatly scrape the dirt, remove weeds, and comb the gravel sidewalks so that the area looked nice and pretty.

Between supervising details I spent time with Squad Leaders Donnie Ray, Tiny and Ron learning how to read tactical maps, call in fire missions, how to properly set up ambush sites and reconnaissance missions. There was a lot to know and not enough time but I was learning what we were actually supposed to do out there. It was pretty simple really. We were not to be seen or heard. We go out for six nights or more at a time and just observe and report. We would engage an enemy as a last resort only if and-or-when they should happen upon us.

We were not designated to aggressively seek out the enemy. We were to let them seek us and then destroy them. In other words, we were put out there as bait.

I learned that you never open fire with small arms on a force until after claymore mines or grenades were detonated. This made sense as rifle and machine gun fire produce flashes and the noise they produce telegraphs your position. Grenades and mines don't, they just explode leaving no trace of how or where they came from, thus confounding the enemy, at least initially. Fire control and discipline were stressed.

No rock and roll automatic firing. Three to five round bursts from every rifleman was emphasized. Ammunition was the lifeline. I learned to plot artillery and have coordinates adjacent to our pre-scheduled ambush site ready to call in an immediate fire mission just before we jumped off to our ambush site. I was given Army handouts describing the nomenclature and weaponry used by NVA Regulars and the VC. I was taught how to set up booby traps with grenades and C-4 plastic explosives, and what to look for when encountering a VC booby trap. The list of topics was endless.

In Vietnam, everyday brought with it new lessons on how to survive. Some lessons came at a heavy price.

Foremost among all the things passed on to me was the unwavering belief in taking care of the men we were entrusted to lead. Their safety and welfare was the central theme. With so much responsibility riding on my ability to be a good squad leader, I wondered if I was over my head and not up to the awesome challenge. When I openly questioned them about it, Donnie Ray said, "How do you think I learned to do this? None of us were infantry trained. I learned it from Ron. He got here before I did. He took me aside and taught me."

Tiny chimed in and said, "Yea, and I learned it from both Ron and Donnie." "And I got it from the guys that got here before me," added Ron. These men commanded a lot of respect and I wanted to be one of them.

23

Christmas in the bush: "You're being watched, man."

Our platoon spent Christmas Eve, Christmas, New Year's Eve and New Year's Day out in the boonies while Bob Hope spent the holidays entertaining troops at Long Binh and at dozens of fire bases throughout South Vietnam. The "Boonies" was synonymous with field, bush and the jungle. Memory of sitting out there on Christmas Eve is indelible.

Like everyone else, I was wet, miserable, and homesick. One night between Christmas and New Year's Eve, I was wide awake on my back somewhere on the Back River, wet, cold and in fairly deep thought when I felt the cold sharp blade of a kabar firmly against my throat and the barrel of what I believed was a .45 pistol against the middle of my back. I was jolted but did not react.

I knew straight away that this was somebody in our platoon and not a VC. I would never have known what hit me if it was a VC as I would have been killed instantly.

Against my right ear, whispered a voice, "If you are CID, you are a dead motherfucker."

I guess I must have been feeling somewhat sorry for myself at the time because I really didn't give a damn, at least at that moment. As I slowly turned my head the blade started to break the skin of my throat, I whispered back, "Go ahead. You would be doing me a favor." As the blade slowly retracted from my throat and as the pressure of the object on the small of my back subsided, the stranger said, "You're being watched, man."

And then as quickly as it started it ended with him slithering off in the darkness. I don't think he expected that kind of a response and to be quite frank, neither did I.

Sometimes I have found that I even surprise myself. I never turned to see who it was but I did give a damn and no, the man would not have done me any favors by slicing my throat or blasting me with his .45. I damn sure didn't want to die out there. Not that way.

The Criminal Investigation Division or CID was the investigative arm of the US Army. Because of increasing reports of drug abuse among Army personnel, the CID would infiltrate certain units to flush out and arrest the "heads" (drug users) from the nonusers. This was very serious business. Paranoia concerning CID agents infiltrating military units was rampant. In reality, they were spread pretty thin and engaged in a multitude of investigations involving crimes other than narcotics.

Each branch of service had its own investigative arm. Just like police agencies in major cities tasked with investigating murders, rapes, robberies and the like, the various military branches were tasked with similar responsibilities.

Lying there, I reasoned that I must have come on too slick when I managed to acquire all those needed items in a matter of only a few hours when the company supply sergeant couldn't get them at all. Obviously, in some minds this new sergeant from nowhere must be a plant. How else does this stranger get these things unless he had some kind of juice with some outside help? The reasoning made sense, however it never occurred to me that I would be suspected of working for the CID.

Now, in addition to dealing with survival issues in the bush, I would have to prove to these guys that I am not what they suspected me to be. And soon.

Excluding the previous incident, our six-day mission over the holidays was uneventful. We witnessed another spectacular night show put on by the fly guys in their choppers mowing down and blasting some position over in Thai Territory. The ground was still wet, the nights were still cold, the mosquitoes were hungry, the leeches still invaded our bodies, and the Re-Up Bird along with the lizard with the foul mouth still mocked us.

There were new and even stranger animal sounds emerging from the swamp and jungle in the form of snorts and guttural exchanges. Imagination conjured up wild thoughts. When jungle creatures made noise, it was usually a good indication that no humans or predators were among them. Conversely, when the noises stopped an eerie silence set in, and a cold chill set inside me. Simply put, noise generally meant we were safe. Silence generally meant something ugly could be out there, somewhere.

I was adapting to my new environment and all of my senses were becoming fine-tuned with each passing day.

I experienced a boost in my ability to see sharper images of moving objects and a wider span of my peripheral vision. Hearing was enhanced. I could quickly distinguish between the various odors of the jungle floor and swamps from the scents of man and beast. As the days passed, every fiber of my being was adapting to survive in this hostile environment.

One evening our platoon set up near the base of Hill 15. All the trip flares and claymore mines were placed.

Later, several guys on watch heard what they believed was some kind of movement beyond our perimeter. As was the protocol, no shots were fired and silence was the order. Generally, if a noise was heard and it was determined to be movement, a grenade would be tossed in the direction of the disturbance.

In lieu of tossing a grenade, the platoon sergeant might

order up an artillery fire mission on the suspected target or direct a series of illumination rounds (parachute flares) in an effort to identify the threat.

In this instance the noise was dismissed and no action taken. The following morning we were all dumbfounded to learn that our perimeter had been breached. It was Bill Parker from North Carolina who discovered that some of our claymore mines had been repositioned and pointed towards us. The little bastards who pulled this off were pretty brazen and stealthy.

They obviously had some inside information about how we did things. Usually, the platoon sergeant or the platoon leader would determine which morning of the 6-12 day mission the platoon would engage in what was commonly referred to as the "Mad Minute."

The term, coined by infantry guys, was an exercise in which an entire squad, platoon or a company would unleash all its weaponry, rifles, machine guns, claymore mines, grenades and flares as a training exercise in simulating a real ambush.

This particular exercise was called off by Staff Sergeant Mintec as a precautionary measure on the possibility that the noises heard the previous evening may have in fact been VC movement. Had we not been blessed with the leadership and seasoned experience of Staff Sergeant Mintec that morning, a fair number of us would have been killed or maimed by the destructive force of our own claymore mines.

24

"Now, don't screw up."

After completing my third mission - and much to my surprise - Sergeant Mintec determined that I was ready to assume my role as Squad Leader of 2nd Squad. His second tour in this place was over and he was rotating back to the States before the end of the month. I had no say in the matter as his absence created a shortage of sergeants. My intense on-the-job training was over.

Primary responsibility would be focused on the safety and welfare of the men I was directed to lead. Any concerns I might have about my own welfare would be secondary. Anyway, there was no time to deliberate. 2nd Squad was my world now, whether I wanted it or not. I thought to myself, "Now, don't screw it up."

SP/4 Ed Lewin, who I referred to as Lew, was paired with Doug Bischoff as primary operators of the M-60 machine gun. Bish was a big, soft-spoken guy from a small town in Michigan. Bish and Lew, along with Tiny, were the biggest guys in the platoon. Jack "Peanuts" Cortez would be my M-79 man, along with SP/4 Glenn Ward as the carrier of the Laws Rocket Launcher. Richard Bias from a small town in Ohio was our mine sweeper.

Stan Galonski from Los Angeles, a guy we called "Gomer" who hailed from a small town in West Virginia, along with a streetwise blonde-haired soldier I will call "Specialist B" — from Pittsburg, Pennsylvania — were assigned riflemen. Greg Thompson remained as my Assistant Squad Leader and John Main from Anchorage, Alaska got the RTO job. I couldn't depend on

Specialist B as he was constantly finding excuses to avoid going out in the field with the rest of us.

It interfered with his black market business which involved the illegal sale of American products to shady Vietnamese and Chinese black marketers in Biên Hòa and Saigon.

I didn't trust him and after several weeks I had First Sergeant Collins remove him from the platoon.

About mid-January 1970, our platoon was directed to set up three separate ambush sites with three squads, several hundred meters apart, along the western shoreline of the Buông, directly east of Hill 15. Before dusk and still several miles from Outpost #6 on Finger of the Land, my squad and the 1st Squad were directed to proceed on foot in a southwesterly direction to our ambush site. Arriving shortly after dusk our mission was to intercept any vessels travelling north or south.

Donnie's 3rd Squad would initially accompany us on foot. After dark his squad — along with Tiny's squad — would deploy in several sampans (small, shallow draft fishing boats) southbound on the Buông toward the 1st and 2nd Squads as bait. Our objective was to lure into the open VC observers concealed in tunnels they had burrowed into the banks of the eastern shoreline.

1st Squad passed us without incident, disembarked and quietly deployed with the rest of us several hundred yards apart. Donnie's squad was positioned at the southern end, Ron Snider's 1st Squad was at the northern end. My squad was in the center. Directly east of our position and across the Buông was a well-known Viet Cong stronghold in Thai Territory.

Within minutes, all of us were pinned down by massive small arms fire from two directions across the Buông. Illumination artillery parachute flares accompanied with heavy machine gun fire (.50 caliber) from the north and east by a known Thai Army outpost, and intense small arms fire from the south and east directed the fields of fire predominantly on Donnie's position.

Donnie and Tiny reasoned that we were mistakenly identified as VC or NVA by elements of the Thail Army patrolling the opposite bank. Repeated radioed requests for a cease fire by the Thais proved fruitless. Communications between our respective Tactical Operations Centers were stymied by a language barrier.

Consequently, sporadic small arms and heavy machine gun fire, accompanied by intermittent incoming 81mm mortar fire pounded our positions throughout the entire evening and into the early morning hours. Donnie, Tiny and the 3rd squad was virtually cut off from the rest of us and had to endure the brunt of the ordeal.

Just as dawn broke, Jared Kelley from Kentucky, manning the M-60 machine gun in Donnie's squad, observed three armed VC approaching from the south on a trail west of his position. He immediately advised Donnie. Donnie wisely directed the entire platoon over the radio not to fire on them reasoning that a communication breakdown still existed with the Thai Army. Any overt action on our part would likely direct more accurate fire on us from our ally.

The three VC moved cautiously westward and away from the area. Fortunately, nobody was killed or wounded during this nightmare. During a debriefing days later it was determined that the three armed VC were among a larger force that had observed our ordeal from afar and that in all probability the VC deliberately tried to lure us into a firefight. Had we engaged them, the massive artillery and small arms fire we were taking from the Thais would have helped them in zeroing in on our position. So much for allies. We were lucky.

Hill 15, Author standing, SP/4 Doug "Bish" Bischoff sighting-in the M-60 machine gun, SP/4 Rich Bias spotter.

SP/4 Stan Galonski heating up a can of C-Rations with an ignited piece of C-4 plastic explosive for a hot meal. Turning a cold can of C-Rations hot generally in less than 45 seconds.

SP/4 John Main, RTO-M-79 Grenadier.

L-R: SSG Donnie Thomas, SP4 Rich Bias, SP/4 Radcliff, Unk, far right, SSG Mintec, far back, SP/4 Bob "Crazy" Marich.

L-R: SP/4 Klemm, SP/4 Richard Radcliff, SP/4 Glenn Ward.

"Rabbit Ears" L-R: Author, SP/4 Ed Lewin, SP/4 Stan Galonski, SP/4 Greg Thompson, SP/4 Jack "Peanuts" Cortez.

25

Johnson, Hemke and McArthur

In the early evening hours of Saturday, January 31, 1970 our platoon was positioned on Hill 15. A hill is identified with a number according to its height in meters. However, Hill 15 was much higher than 45 feet. There were steep grades all along the southern and eastern slopes. Any high ground was strategically advantageous for us or the VC, and Hill 15 had a commanding view of our TAOR.

A major battle was fought for this hill during a Post-Tet attack directed at Long Binh Post, almost a year earlier. The hill was defended by several squads of B Company Bushwhackers against a sizeable force comprised of NVA and Viet Cong. The twelve hour battle ended when B Company successfully resisted the assault and held on. B Company sustained several wounded having inflicted scores of dead and wounded among the enemy. The place was spooky and littered with unexploded ordinance and booby traps, particularly along the hill's southern slope.

Just humping into the place was hazardous to your health. Fresh in our minds was the death of a squad leader and several severely wounded men who had been struck down by booby traps at this very place a little more than six months earlier.

As darkness settled in we heard panic and pandemonium on the radio among the three squads of the 2nd Platoon calling for help. Proceeding to French Fort in their Boston whalers, the wake from a passing South Vietnamese Patrol Boat threw most of the men - heavily laden with equipment-to be tossed into the river. At the same moment, Sergeant Ralph Takenalive initially reported small arms fire directed towards their position.

The melee resulted in the disappearance of SP/4 David Johnson, PFC David Hemke, and PFC Robert McArthur. After several frantic hours of searching the shores and waters of the Đồng Nai with the assistance of the PBR Platoon, hopes of finding the trio vanished and the search was terminated.

As for us, we all wanted to jump off that hill and help find those boys. There was absolutely nothing we could do. Moving a platoon on foot in the dark was foolhardy. Moreover, with artillery and air units already dialed in with their pre-designated coordinates, delivering high explosives in and around our position would be just as reckless.

I remember feeling helplessness turn to silent rage sitting on that hill. At daybreak, everyone assigned to B Company was ordered to participate in the search and recovery of our missing comrades. About mid-morning the following day, the distorted and bloated body of one of the men was recovered on the opposite side of the Đồng Nai, a little over a mile south of French Fort. No one knew for sure which of the three it was. Advanced stages of decomposition had already set in.

The other two men would be recovered days later, face down adjacent to the vegetation along the bank on the opposite side of the river, two miles south. They were impossible to identify. I remember witnessing men of the 2nd Platoon placing their bloated bodies into body bags on the muddy shoreline. Sadly, the three casualties had only been in-country about a month. How do you explain this to the mothers of these boys? Nine months of pain and twenty years of hope, all gone in an instant.

I recall watching all three of them getting their field gear from Staff Sergeant Joyner just a few weeks earlier, and wondered if they would be assigned to our platoon.

At the memorial I was glad that I never knew them. It was easy for me but not for the guys who knew them. Bob "Crazy" Marich, a rock and roll drummer from Detroit, had a particularly hard time dealing with it. Johnson and Crazy were in the same Advanced Infantry Training Company (AIT- Military Police School) back at Fort Gordon, Georgia.

SP/4 David Allan Johnson 24,
West Lafayette, IN

SP/4 Robert Lamar McArthur 20,
Chattanooga, TN

Rice Barn aka Delta-Delta SSG Ralph Takenalive depicted as "2" along with unk members of the 1st Platoon which included Johnson, Hemke and McArthur.

SP/4 David Lee Hemke 20, Apollo, PA.

26

"Well, Let's light 'em up."

A round the first week of February, my squad set up along the bank of the Buông just below Rabbit Ears. We were to report any movement on the river. 1st and 3rd Squads set up a half-moon formation to ambush any movement directly behind us. It was on my watch in the late evening hours under a dimly lit moon when I couldn't believe my eyes. On the opposite bank about 100 meters away, on a plateau maybe ten feet above the shoreline, I saw three silhouetted human forms setting up some portable launching pads to send 122mm rockets towards Long Binh Post.

What surprised me more was their carelessness in trying to accomplish the task in partial moonlight, on a plateau, silhouetted against the faintly lit backdrop of Long Binh Post.

The VC were infamous for building crudely-built bamboo pads to launch their rockets into American firebases throughout South Vietnam. The methodology was simple, target accuracy was poor, but the devastation to life and limb within a 100 yards of detonation was deadly.

You immediately knew when you were on the receiving end of these flying monsters because they threw off a loud, continuous whistle from about midway into flight to just seconds before impact. The unmistaken sound at least warned you that something terrible was coming your way, allowing just enough time to hit the ground face first. Mortars were different.

Even if you were in a position to hear the thumping sounds of one of these explosive devices being spit out of its tube, you still had no idea when or where the thing was going to land. Regardless, if your name was on any of these things, there wasn't a damn thing you could do.

I was beyond stunned. Night after night I heard all kinds of things far and near, sometimes even what I swore were whispered voices in Vietnamese, but I never saw anything.

This time it was different. I didn't hear them scurrying about, but clearly watched as three live bodies prepared to deliver a deadly payload. I immediately shook Main and directed him to give me the microphone to the radio, then I called Donnie and apprised him of what I had witnessed. Within seconds he was next to me, confirming the activity for himself. Instinctively, we covered ourselves under a poncho and illuminated a tactical map with my dimly lit red-lensed flashlight and quickly determined what we believed to be a close six-digit coordinate position.

As Donnie grabbed the microphone he said, "Well, let's light 'em up." Reporting the activity and the coordinates via the radio to our TOC Operator, Donnie requested an artillery fire mission consisting of 105/155mm high explosives. Word was passed for the platoon to lay low in an effort to avoid any possible injuries from debris or shrapnel as the target area was only a 100 meters away.

As we impatiently waited for our special delivery to arrive from the 9th Division artillery guys miles away at a place called Bearcat, we watched helplessly as the VC lit the fuse to the rocket. Within seconds the thing left the ground towards Long Binh Post. The familiar whistling sound was followed by a flash of light in the distance, then a loud explosion. Long Binh was hit but exactly where was anyone's guess.

Growing more concerned, Donnie requested an ETA (estimated time of arrival) of the fire mission. It looked like the VC were packing up and leaving.

We were wrong.

These guys were not packing up at all, they were scrambling to set up a launching pad for a second rocket. No sooner did the guy on the other end of the radio say "Standby!" then we heard several faint thumps of outgoing artillery rounds, immediately followed by the familiar jet-like noise of projectiles screaming through the air.

Milliseconds later, deafening explosions created a storm of mud, water, and dirt debris all around us.

I quickly peered over the rice paddy dike I lay in — really a stupid thing to do — and saw the three VC run away in an easterly direction. We were fifty yards off target. The rounds landed between us and them and directly in the middle of the Buông. I yelled at Donnie to "drop 100 and unload." Donnie immediately yelled into the radio, "Check your fire. Go 100 short." Within seconds a flurry of artillery rounds danced all over the Buông's eastern bank sending more debris flying in every direction.

Then silence.

We couldn't see much change in the landscape when it all ended but were confident that we had hit our target. I don't think anybody slept for the remainder of that night, too wound up. I was also concerned that our fire mission might have given our position away leaving us vulnerable for an unpleasant encounter with VC lurking somewhere out there, to our flanks and rear.

We remained vigilant until daybreak. As the morning sun rose, I scanned the landscape and noted that it had changed considerably. Scores of freshly uprooted brush, large sections of torn high grass, fallen trees, piles of dirt, and pieces of tree branches, large and small along with dozens of crater holes were scattered everywhere.

I could not imagine anyone getting out of that place alive. We would never truly learn the fate of the enemy trio as we were forbidden to cross into that area. Sweeps conducted by the Royal Thai Army that morning revealed blood trails, but nothing more. We reported two more sightings of VC setting up rocket launching pads in the same general vicinity between February and April using the same tactic. Again, there were blood trails but no bodies.

How these people could be so careless in some aspects and so elusive in others was beyond me.

27
Man vs. Land

Fear of getting killed is a given, after all you are in a war. Each soldier will process the reality differently, but the common denominator uniting us all is fear. Other misgivings come in play when war is made immediate and personal, waged directly in a hostile environment. Setting up ambushes and deploying men in reconnaissance operations through swampland and flooded jungle creates an additional dimension: war between the man and the land.

A host of poisonous creatures indigenous to this part of the world were on hand to greet us day or night. Snakes of all varieties including python, cobra and a small green thing we called the "two stepper," (bamboo viper). Word had it that if you had the misfortune of getting bit by one, two steps later you dropped dead. Poisonous centipedes and fat black scorpions appeared out of nowhere.

Mosquitoes would constantly scream in your ears and ants, leeches and insects of all sizes and shapes hungry for our flesh and blood. Rats the size of cats were found gnawing on the toes of our boots. Land crabs, assorted reptiles large and small scurried around and on top of us as we tried to sleep. And the thought of a crocodile snuggling up next to you could keep anybody from falling asleep.

Nasty interactions with the land were routine. Early one

evening our platoon had just set up its ambush site somewhere next to the Đồng Nai south of French Fort. We unfolded our ponchos to set up makeshift beds. Suddenly, and almost in unison we began whispering profanities of all types. My left foot and lower leg were on fire with pain. The guys next to me were experiencing the same misery.

Instinctively, all of us made a mad dash to the river to alleviate intense burning, stinging sensations on the assumption that soaking our lower extremities in water would somehow help.

There was just enough daylight for me to see that the entire boot on my left foot and the pant leg was now darker in color and appeared to have a life of its own. Ants! We had unwittingly parked our butts on a huge ant farm. Thousands of them produced increasing doses of pain with each passing second.

Initially, sloshing in knee high water did absolutely nothing to rid these things from our bodies. The water appeared to not even affect them. It was only after removing the boot, the sock and constant brushing against the lower leg and pants that eventually made these little monsters go away. As for the boots, we had to thoroughly soak them underwater. I knew that we made enough noise to attract unwanted attention from anything out there, but the pain was so intense that I doubt anybody could have contained themselves any better.

So, another cold, wet night made extra miserable by that ant farm. Swollen feet and legs along with hundreds of visible bite marks came in view the next morning. Lucky for us, this was our sixth and final night for the mission. Pain and swelling slowly subsided over the next week.

On another night we set our ambush position somewhere east of Buffalo Shack, home to a number of domesticated water buffalo. The place was located a considerable distance away from the Đồng Nai in a relatively dry area. Nonetheless, in the early morning hours of the following day, lying on my poncho, a cold stream of water trickled slowly down my neck, along my spine and into the crack of my ass.

So much for dry places. The Đồng Nai's ebb and flow into the South China Sea miles away was truly unpredictable. We experienced many nights like this, setting up in a relatively dry position only to be jolted out of a light sleep and inundated in several inches of cold water.

Nearing dawn, I had started to assemble my C-4 fire when I noticed that Donnie was laying on his back, in several inches of water with an unnatural looking creature about the size of a small dinner plate outstretched and comfortably occupying his entire face. As I rushed over to get a closer look, Donnie was slowly lifting his right hand towards his face. Just before his hand reached his upper body, I said, "In case you are wondering, it's a land crab, Donnie."

As he grasped the thing and flung it off into the surrounding water we both started laughing uncontrollably, as did those who witnessed it. Nobody was immune from these kind of things.

On any given night, somebody got bitten by some kind of insect. It seemed that something, a mosquito, an insect, would feast briefly on the lips of some poor sap who had dozed off. The following morning you could clearly see the effects of these encounters by the abnormally large, disfiguring swelling. One swollen upper lip was humorous. Both lips exploded to three times their normal size was hysterical.

Generally, the swelling subsided within a few hours but the relentless badgering by everyone not afflicted with this temporary condition could be brutal. Names like Bimbo Lips, Platypus Lips, Duck Lips, or Pregnant Lips were awarded to the hapless victim.

Rich Bias was a frequent victim of this phenomenon. Apparently, the little devils were fascinated with him. The jokes only got larger as those who laughed the hardest would invariably succumb to the very same harassment they had dished out when they got the Large Lips Syndrome. As for me, I was fortunate to have only been cursed with this condition once and only on the lower lip.

A guy reached out one night to adjust the tripod of the M-60 machine gun he was assigned and inadvertently placed his hand on a poisonous centipede. The burning sensation and intense pain that followed was accompanied with an immediate swelling of his hand and a severe case of nausea. In another incident, a guy had just laid down on his poncho when he was stung on an arm by a scorpion. Severe nausea and swelling immediately set in.

And then there was the time Tiny took off his fatigue shirt and hung it on a fence post. When he slipped his arms into the shirt several hours later, a large fat scorpion that sought refuge in the shirt stung him on the shoulder. These were serious health issues that required the victims to be immediately evacuated by helicopter to the nearest field hospital. Generally, those who fell victim to these encounters required several days of hospitalization and a week or so in recuperation.

On each mission, the 212th Military Police Sentry Dog Company provided one Sentry/Scout Dog and his handler to accompany us.

The K-9 was usually a male German Shepherd, highly trained to sniff out enemy movement. These dogs could not be approached by anyone other than its handler. Whenever anybody in the platoon got too close to the dog, he let you know that your presence was not wanted. Everybody kept a safe distance. Reality was belied by the unconditional love and respect evident between the handler and his dog.

Early one evening our platoon was about to disembark from our whalers just north of Rabbit Ears. First to jump out and onto the shore of the Buông was our K-9. The animal managed to scramble from the muddy shore and several feet into the short-cropped grass when he was bitten on the leg by what some later claimed was a bamboo viper.

The dog and its distraught handler were immediately "dusted-off" (military jargon for being transported by helicopter) to a field hospital. There were conflicting accounts as to the status of the dog. I understood the dog died in the chopper. Others maintained that the dog survived.

The land was a hostile environment and just as eager to bring you harm as were the men we were hunting.

28

"I'm up. I got the point."

S ometime in February when our platoon finished setting up an ambush south of French Fort and darkness had set in, the TOC operator directed us to move 1,200 meters east to the vicinity of Rabbit Ears. Somebody blew it. The area we had newly secured was designated to be a free-fire zone for artillery and air strikes. Immediate evacuation of the area was directed. Remaining would be lethal.

It was bad enough having to silently retrace our steps, locate and carefully disarm our claymore mines and booby traps, but then they threw another curveball at us. No Boston Whalers were available, which meant that we would have to hump the distance across swampland, rice paddies and some high grass in the glow of a full moon. A perfect recipe for the ambusher to get ambushed.

Grunts, groans and utterances of blasphemy quickly waned as the serious business of packing up and preparing for this unwanted journey set in.

My squad was selected to lead the platoon. I never asked any of my people to do something that I wouldn't do myself, so on this particular night I designated myself point man. Walking the point or being directed to take the point was dangerous. Point man scouted ahead of the entire platoon. He was the eyes and ears for everyone behind him. He was also usually the first to be spotted by the enemy and more often than not, the first to trip a booby trap or among the first to be struck down in an ambush.

Bravado had nothing to do with the decision, it was my turn in the barrel and I was scared, almost stiff. I said nothing more than, "I'm up. I got the point." I felt my body shaking with fear but I had the presence of mind to realize that if I continued talking any further, my voice would tremble.

Telegraphing any form of fear on my part could be contagious among others. Besides, what little ego I had left told me that I could never gain any respect from these guys if I couldn't follow through on doing the same things I asked of them.

Off I went into the darkness about twenty meters ahead of everybody. 1,200 meters is less than three quarters of a mile. Not all that far, but in terms of silently walking with over 75 pounds of gear on your back while trying to avoid making any noise in mud, water and thick brush is taxing. My mind worked in overdrive and I was further bombarding it with a laundry list of do's and dont's:

- Check the ground in front of you for trip wires.

- Try to avoid walking in water.

- Don't fall.

- Look straight ahead.

- Don't forget to look up.

-Point your rifle wherever your eyes scan.

- Stop and listen to the jungle talk.

- Don't rush.

- Forget thoughts of home.

- Stay focused.

- Look to your rear to make sure you are not too far ahead of the platoon.

- Don't get lost.

- Use your peripheral vision.

- Don't get complacent.

- Don't be too cautious.

- Don't slap the mosquitoes pestering your ears.

- Don't stand, crouch down low to the ground while scanning and listening.

This thought process was never ending.

When humping to various places on all previous missions, day or night, a sense of loneliness set in. I think everybody experienced some form of this. Despite the fact that I was in the company of 25 to 30 men, I felt alone. Occasionally, when I wasn't wondering whether my next step would be my last, or whether some VC sniper had me in his cross hairs, I found some solace when I turned my thoughts to Lorraine, and what I was going to do when I got home.

Now, walking point added a new dimension - isolation. Not the time or place for hopes or dreams of any future. Just the here and now. No time to even think about what I did or didn't do just seconds earlier. That was past. All that existed was the moment. Time was nonexistent.

As the Buông River and our new ambush site came into view I felt reasonably comfortable with my performance. The platoon was still behind me, I hadn't gotten lost and most importantly we had managed to avoid contact with the VC. No sooner had these thoughts crossed my mind when I felt my whole world crumble. I fell directly into a hole that was barely wider than my body, and what I reckoned to be seven or eight feet deep.

The Viet Cong were famous for firmly planting poisoned, razor sharp bamboo sticks or metal objects, protruding several inches from the sides of these holes. The tips of the protrusions were usually dipped in animal or human urine and feces. At the very bottom of the hole they buried larger razor sharp-tipped stakes pointed upwards, or an explosive device triggered by the falling weight of an unsuspecting victim. Instantly, I knew I was in big trouble.

The only way I can put this experience into words is to describe it in the various mental and physical stages as I perceived them at that moment.

As I slid into the abyss, I felt cold water but no slicing sensations or pains to my face, stomach, arms, elbows or the outer portions of my upper and lower legs. The instant I accepted this, a temporary sense of relief set in.

Relief turned to fear as my thoughts wondered about the evil that awaited me at the bottom. As my feet hit ground, my fears of being blown out and vaporized disappeared. There was no explosion, only silence. Instant relief was followed by fear about my lower extremities and what pain I should be feeling from the bamboo stakes. At this instant I realized my head and body were immersed in water. All concerns about my feet and legs vanished. It had come to this. I was about to die not in battle but by drowning in this godforsaken mud hole.

Fight or flight, and in this situation it was both as terror and adrenalin kicked in. I spread my legs and dug my feet firmly into the sides of the hole and started scaling upward while scratching, clawing and pushing my way with my left hand and a firm death grip on my rifle in my right hand. I slowly inched myself upwards in the muddy morass with every ounce of strength I had. All the while my hands and arms extended above me were still immersed in liquid and my capacity to hold my breath was about to expire.

I truly believed that I was going to die and listed as just another MIA. Lorraine, my family and friends would never know how or what happened to me. The Army would tell them that I am missing in action, by unknown means and presumed dead.

I knew that the instant my squad determined I was missing, the platoon would conduct a sweep of the area in a frantic effort to find me. I also knew that panic and pandemonium would set in just as it did with the 2nd Platoon when Johnson, Hemke, and McArthur were declared missing. Now, my actions could very well cost the lives of others.

I figured the only way my body might be recovered was if someone were to fall into the same hole and land on top of me. In milliseconds a half-dozen other scenarios raced through my head but I was determined not to die, not here, not this way. I have absolutely no idea how long I remained in that waterhole, probably only seconds. I clearly remember that when my hands and arms finally broke the surface into the cool air I inhaled and swallowed an entire mouthful of water.

I pulled myself from the hole and managed to squelch much of my choking noise, coughing and the uncontrollable gagging that followed.

As the platoon caught up to me somebody whispered, "Was that you?" to which all I could reply was, "Yea, I fell into a hole." I still had my M-16 Rifle, and virtually all of my gear.

When we reached our ambush site minutes later, I realized that I lost my bush hat and one of my fragmentation grenades was missing. Despite the 80 degree evening temperature, I stripped off all my clothes for warmth.

I prayed that we wouldn't make any contact. I couldn't imagine running around in the jungle during a firefight with no clothes. The night was no different than any other regarding sleep. However, I never thought that one day I would be laying on a jungle floor, at night and naked. Visions of every crawly creature known to man occupied my mind the remainder of the evening and throughout the early morning hours.

At daybreak, I was smothered in leeches. They obviously preferred me over the muddy hole they had been living in. I never even felt them. I had been lucky, again.

29

"Where the hell am I?"

About a week later, our platoon set up at the southernmost end of our TAOR near the shore adjacent to the confluence of the Đồng Nai and Buông. An unseasonably cool evening created an eerie, thick white fog to rise several feet above the warmer jungle floor. I had seen this phenomenon in a World War II movie, "Bataan" starring Robert Taylor and George Murphy. The story centered on a handful of soldiers and sailors ordered to hold a vital bridge in the Philippine Islands to delay the advance of Japanese invading forces at the onset of World War II.

One by one, each character in the film was killed. The closing scene depicted the last man firing a .50 caliber machine gun scanning his eyes over the eerie white fog and shooting at dozens of Japanese soldiers low-crawling under the fog then jumping up rushing towards him. The last scene of that movie left an indelible impression on me when I was a youngster. Years later here I was, in a jungle under a thick layer of that same kind of eerie fog.

Concern was quickly deferred by rising river waters just yards away from us. In short order, our ambush site was drowned in several inches of river water. We were all dead tired from conducting lengthy daytime sweeps of jungle and swampland the previous two days, and now the reality of having to lay down and doze off in cold water was not comforting.

One by one, each of us silently broke out our black plastic inflatable one-man rafts and began the tedious effort of inflating them manually by blowing air into the small porthole. Blowing up these things silently took just about ten minutes and was painfully tiring.

All thoughts about fog and damp clothing quickly disappeared as exhaustion set in. My thoroughly drained mind and body craved comfort and laying on this soft air mattress was instant gratification. And then it was good night, Irene! I fell into a deep sleep.

Next thing I was conscious of was being jolted awake, my left arm and part of my left shoulder submerged in cold water. Frantically, I reached under the water for my rifle which I always positioned to my immediate left. It was not there. My fragmentation grenades, ammunition belts, pop-up flares, smoke grenades along with my compass attached to my web-gear I always positioned to my immediate right, were not there either.

Trying to suppress panic from setting in, I took a deep silent breath, slowly exhaled and then began assessing what kind of situation I was in. My watch read 04:00. In disbelief, checked and rechecked the time at least a half a dozen times. I repeatedly asked myself, "How long have I been here like this? Where the hell am I? Where is the platoon, and do they know I am missing?"

Getting separated with no rifle, no grenades or knife had become a recurring theme in my nightmares. But this was no nightmare. I was comforted slightly knowing that at least I still had a loaded .45 pistol with two 7-round clips affixed to the shoulder holster I never removed from my person. Nonetheless, I was in a very bad situation.

Instinctively, I knew that I could not lift my head up above the fog. I also had to remain completely silent. My platoon, wherever they were out there, would have to assume that any noise I might make would cause them to react — with violence. The same could be said for any VC.

I nervously laughed at myself thinking, so much for the navigational class I practically slept through back at Fort Riley regarding the use of the stars as a compass. After all, that was grunt and Navy stuff. What purpose would it serve a military policemen assigned to military facilities and cities?

I did recall the instructor saying that the North Star could be seen somewhere inside the Big Dipper. Straining to get an occasional glimpse through thinning portions of the fog passing above me and trying to locate the elusive North Star, I sensed my mattress floating gently on a slow-moving current. I grasped some vegetation and the movement stopped.

A gentle current moved through my fingers confirming what I thought. I must have simply floated away on my air mattress as the tide from the Đồng Nai and Buông River swelled.

But where? How far? More importantly, what direction could this current have taken me from the rest of the guys? I didn't have any answers to anything and gazing at what stars I could see didn't provide any solution, either.

05:00 now, still dark and a full hour consciously into this predicament I managed to maintain a death grip on the vegetation, preventing me from floating even further away. I lay there, intently listening and waiting impatiently for someone or something that might move my way. A string of "what ifs?" began racing through my mind. What do I do if somebody comes upon me? Do I shoot him with my .45 or do I strangle him? Either way, it will make noise. What if it is one of my own guys and I shoot him? So what good is my gun?

The more I thought the angrier I got with myself. I simply couldn't believe that I could have allowed myself to get so comfortable and so complacent. I swore to myself that should I survive this stupid and totally unnecessary living nightmare that I would never pack an air mattress again, and I would always carry a compass. It was during this process that I realized the water running between my fingers and the vegetation I clung to, was telling me something.

The direction from which the current was flowing against my hand would have to be west, from the Đồng Nai, or south from the Buông.

Which one produced the stronger current? Of the two, the Đồng Nai was the largest and flowed directly into the South China Sea some 30-40 miles away. Its current, I reasoned, had to be coming mainly from the west. I figured that if I silently pulled at the vegetation against the current in a westerly direction with about a 45 degree turn to my left I would theoretically be traveling in a southwesterly direction towards the confluence of both rivers.

If.

Switching positions on the raft from back and to stomach was time consuming as movement was measured in inches. Sudden movement caused noise. The same was true as I began my trek toward the shore. I had to slowly and silently grasp, then pull on the short-cropped vegetation just above the surface of the water with my left hand while simultaneously pushing the vegetation and mud about eight inches below the surface with my right hand.

Approximately 20 minutes into the journey I started questioning the logic of my decision in spite of the fact that I was making some progress, albeit very slowly. What if I was incorrect in my assumption that moving against the current put me in the right direction? What if the current was misleading? What if I am proceeding toward the VC?

Maybe, I better stay right where I am. The first thing I was told by Donnie and Ron Snider was to stay put if I ever got separated from the platoon. Besides, it would be light soon.

I remained, on my stomach clinging to vegetation waiting for light of day.

Nearing 06:00 the darkness waned with the faint light of day and that eerie thick fog was beginning to dissipate. Uncomfortable from laying on my stomach, I was still reluctant to move or stick my head up for fear of getting it blown off. However, just as my patience was about to give out, I heard several garbled voices and familiar grumblings along with some profanities from what I knew were guys in my platoon somewhere close by and in front of me.

Slowly, I moved from the raft into the water and knelt on my knees, then peered just above the vegetation in front of me.

There they were just ahead, about 50 yards away, burning C-4 fires for heat laughing and joking among themselves. As I straightened my upper body I noticed that Jim Gufford was about 30 yards away off to my left and several other guys off to my right about 50 yards away. Then several more guys popped up about 30 yards just ahead. Apparently, I wasn't alone after all. I sure would like to have known that I had company out there all night. Suffice it to say, lessons were learned.

From that time on, I always carried several compasses. One on my web gear and another in my pants pocket. I never even thought about sleeping, not even a wink in the field ever again. And as for that blow-up rubber raft. Well, I gave it to a Vietnamese kid named George, at the Rice Mill in An Hoa Hung Village where we often set up during the day to be resupplied. I had been lucky, again.

L-R: SP/4 Jared Kelley, SP/4 Klemm.

30

The new Lieutenant

Time moved along as one mission ran into the next under the leadership of a platoon sergeant and devoid of any officers. Sometime in February, three days or so into our mission while being resupplied at the Rice Mill (or tactically referred to as "Delta-Delta"), all that changed.

Approaching the wooden and steel bridge across the Buông to the Rice Mill below were the familiar sounds of an American jeep shifting into higher gears, from the village of An Hòa Hung. As the jeep came into view, it crossed the rickety bridge and slid to an abrupt stop creating a cloud of dust in front of the platoon. The passenger, a rather heavy set, dumb-looking 2nd lieutenant fresh out of Officer Candidate School jumped out as the jeep sped off. He was clad in newly issued OD jungle fatigues, new boots and brand new web gear, nothing even close to resembling the camouflaged gear the rest of us were issued.

Lieutenant Scott (not his real name), introduced himself as our new platoon leader. He hailed from a small town in Ohio and fashioned himself as some kind of bad-assed guerilla fighter with novel ideas on how to set up ambushes.

As I came to understand, the platoon looked on any new guy with suspicion. It was not uncommon for men to be transferred from one ambush platoon to another. People would rotate out of the field as new replacements filled in. Leadership changes were scrutinized even more carefully, especially officers.

The lieutenant immediately called a meeting with Donnie, Tiny, Ron and me. It was brief. He decided to cede his authority to Donnie and the three of us for the remaining three nights of our mission, and added that he only wanted to observe. None of us expected this.

Briefly, perhaps for only a few minutes, I thought maybe, just maybe, my first impression of this guy was off. It wasn't. Immediately after dropping his gear this goofy-looking overweight lieutenant began shadow boxing and throwing his body into karate maneuvers while hurling bellowing grunts as he simulated high kicks with his feet. Donnie, Ron, Tiny and me sensed a problem with him immediately.

The next three nights were uneventful and our new lieutenant, true to his word, participated only as an observer. However, during the daytime at our resupply staging areas, the lieutenant entertained all of us with his self-defense antics. It was almost comical if it were not for the fact that this buffoon was now responsible for the safety and welfare of our entire platoon. All any of us could do was just shake our head in disbelief and walk away.

Little did we know that this bizarre behavior was just a peek into the mindset of our new leader.

The next three days were spent preparing for a new mission, along with several meetings between us, the squad leaders and our new leader. Lieutenant Scott told us that his observations during the previous three days had amply prepared him to assume command of the platoon and added that he intended to make significant changes in our tactics. What those tactics might have been were never fully revealed.

Throughout the meetings Donnie, Ron and Tiny patiently tried to educate the lieutenant on the dos and don'ts. It did not go well. Our new leader was not receptive. Donnie, always the diplomat, was clearly the most patient. Ron, "if I don't have anything good to say . . . I won't say anything at all," was obviously growing impatient. And Tiny, the least tolerant among us, glanced at all of us in disbelief as various shades of red covered his face listening to the lieutenant dismissing lessons learned and the dangers involved in setting up ambushes.

I still considered myself on the learning curve and remained mostly silent. That said, the experience I had acquired at this juncture convinced me that the lieutenant was obstinate, inexperienced, and dangerous.

31

"Lieutenant, you've got us in the wrong place!"

O ur first night with Lieutenant Scott in charge was, exasperating. The whalers dropped us off several hundred meters south of French Fort just before dusk. From there, the platoon had to surreptitiously trudge 500 meters through a series of rice paddies and open areas, while maintaining a southeasterly direction along a tree line where we would set up our ambush facing the same open area we just passed through.

Customarily, and this was no exception, we travelled in a linear column always maintaining 15-20 feet of open space between each man. The lieutenant determined that he could guide the point man to our destination without assistance, followed by Donnie leading his squad, followed by me and my squad with Ron and Tiny and the 3rd squad to the rear.

I was not familiar with this particular destination, but right from the onset I sensed that we were not proceeding in the right direction. My compass confirmed it. We were heading almost directly eastwards and stopping much too frequently. Each time the column stopped, everybody instinctively hunkered down on the assumption that the point man had made contact with the bad guys. Then nothing.

Getting darker by the minute plus constant delays created a gut-retching ordeal for everybody.

The column stopped again, except this time we remained motionless for more than just several minutes.

Ron and Tiny made their way towards me and Tiny whispered, "Bog, what the hell is the hold-up?" "I don't know but I don't like it. Maybe we better find out." I whispered back. Ron, Tiny and I then headed towards the front of the column.

As we by-passed the 1st squad and approached the front of the column, I heard Donnie loudly whispering, "Lieutenant you've got us in the wrong place! We can't stay here. We need to be over there!" He pointed at a small tree line a couple of hundred meters directly south of us. I don't recall exactly who said what but Donnie prevailed and we arrived at our proper location.

And none too soon, for within moments of our arrival we could hear the incoming 105s pound the area we had just passed through. All thoughts about our fearless leader were confirmed. The man was a proven buffoon and dangerous.

3rd Platoon avoided another catastrophe and, fortunately got through. Another uneventful night.

Next morning the entire platoon was buzzing about our new lieutenant as we trudged through several miles of rice paddies and bush to Rice Mill for resupply. As squad leaders, we received an earful from just about everybody. Some of these guys were talking about eliminating the problem all together by "fragging" the man.

Fragging meant planting a grenade next to him and blowing him to pieces. And some of these guys were serious.

Donnie, Tiny, Ron, and I curbed further talk on that subject. I should add, the four of us had no intention of subjecting our people to any form of military justice by reporting it. The men had reason to be upset. Lack of sleep, miserable living conditions, canned shit for food and the constant fear of getting killed can bring out the worst in people.

There were city boys like Bob "Crazy" Marich who was just that, crazy. Guys like Shakey, Peanuts, Lewin, and Patrick Palmateer from Los Angeles were openly critical about anything associated with authority. Gomer and mild-mannered Kentucky boys like Jared Kelley, Jerry Perry and Delton Propes along with North Carolina boys Ward, Gufford and Parker were more restrained. Thompson, Lozano, Bish, Bias, Galonski, Main, Mike Ambrose from northern California, and Rich Radcliff from Columbus, Ohio remained mostly silent. Throw in a guy like Lieutenant Scott in the equation was a recipe for disaster.

Boys assigned to B Company were a mixed bag. Some were reassigned from other units as replacements. Most just caught the luck of the draw and received orders to this outfit. Others, men who had pissed off their commanding officers or senior NCOs, were sent to B Company as a disciplinary measure. No one as I recall, ever volunteered.

And then there were fools like me, displeased with their current assignment, and freely pulled into the unit like cattle to slaughter. The overwhelming majority never had a clue as to the true nature of what was in store for them when they reported to B Company. Everybody had a variation of the same experience I had on my first day with First Sergeant Collins.

One thing was clear, at least to my thinking. Don't mess with these guys.

L-R: SP/4 Bill Parker, SP/4 Jerry Perry, SP/4 Glen Barmann, SP/4 Carlos Lozano, SP/4 Ed 'Shakey' Marley, SP/4 Jared Kelley.

L-R: SP/4 Jerry Lee Perry, local village girl, SP/4 Rich Radcliff.

*SP/4 Mike "Ambi" Ambrose standing in an Artillery hole--**ours.***

Rice Mill aka 'Delta Delta' L-R: SP/4 Doug "Bish" Bishoff, 'Max', SP/4 Ed Lewin, SP/4 Jared Kelley, SP/4 Bruce Zirk standing, PFC Patrick Palmateer-top.

32

"Lieutenant, my guys aren't going up the south face of that hill!"

We arrived at Rice Mill exhausted and hungry. I was always amazed at how satisfying a can of mystery meat smothered in a greasy brown sauce on a twenty-year-old cracker could be after slogging several miles through rice paddies, mud and brush in sweltering heat.

Later that afternoon, word had it that we were ordered to set up our ambush atop Hill 15. After a refreshing dip in the slimy green waters of the no name river/tributary adjacent to Rice Mill, I propped myself on the ground with my back against the trunk of an old tree. No sooner did my eyes close when I was interrupted by the sound of boots walking towards me.

Glancing up, I discovered the lieutenant standing over me. Our eyes met and he squatted down on one knee in front of me. Immediately, I suspected something disturbing as I had hardly even spoken to the man since his arrival.

He looked directly at me and said, "Your squad is on point tonight. We won't be using the whalers to transport us. We're going to hump to Hill 15, arriving there at dusk. It'll take us a couple of hours to get there and we'll be approaching from the south. Be ready to jump off in an hour. Questions?"

I was stunned at the stupidity of his plan and equally astonished by my spontaneous response as I exclaimed, "Lieutenant, my guys aren't going up the south face of that hill! The southern slope of that place is littered with booby traps and live ordinance. The engineers haven't even cleared it yet. What are you, nuts? My guys aren't going. Not that way!"

In an instant I had disobeyed a direct order and inferred that the man was mentally unstable.

I recognized the seriousness of the dilemma at once. Before he could respond, I added, "Look, Lieutenant, the southern slope of that place is deadly. You can't expect a platoon to go stumbling up that hill in the dark. None of the other ambush platoons would even consider trying it in daylight. We lost a couple of guys less than a year ago to booby traps on the south slope, and that was during daylight hours.

There's a history, not to mention the twelve-hour battle for that hill by our guys back in February of last year. These men will do just about anything you order them to do," I paused.

"But not this. And I wouldn't blame them. We'll go to your Hill 15 from any direction, but not from the south."

His face flushed with anger. He was flabbergasted. All he seemed capable of was to just stare at me with disdain. Breaking the unnerving silence, I suggested, "Lieutenant, you should run this by Sergeant Thomas."

As he stood up to turn away, he exclaimed, "You know, that was a direct order I gave you, don't you?" "Yes sir, I do." I replied, as I watched him walk towards Donnie who was seated in the shade, on the dirt and leaning against the wooden wall of the Rice Mill about thirty yards away. I watched the lieutenant squat down in front of Donnie and studied the interaction between them closely while straining my ears to catch an occasional word or two.

I didn't have to hear anything as Donnie's facial expressions and gestures spoke volumes. It was clear that Donnie was trying his best to diplomatically challenge the lieutenant's thinking. Ultimately, Donnie succeeded in convincing the lieutenant that the platoon should be transported to Hill 15 by Boston Whalers and make the ascent from the west, at dusk.

Why he had decided to confront me with his grand plan before discussing it with the platoon sergeant made no sense. The platoon leader generally confers with his platoon sergeant before issuing movement orders to a squad leader. Besides all of that, why me? I had less time in the field than Tiny or Snider. Regardless of the whys and wherefores, it wouldn't be the last time.

We approached Hill 15 from the west that evening without incident. As was our routine, the three squads formed up in a horseshoe configuration directing our field of fire in a southerly direction, downward and along the entire southern slope of the hill with my squad sandwiched in the middle. If the Viet Cong or North Vietnamese Army were to probe or infiltrate Long Binh Post several thousand meters away to our backs it would be here, on this hill, that we could expect to intercept them.

Dozens of small rivers and tributaries emanating from the Đồng Nai and Buông crisscrossed our TAOR. A maze of water routes that facilitated enemy penetration virtually at any place on the map. Several hundred meters directly below us was a major water thoroughfare used by the Viet Cong. Consequently, Hill 15 was frequently occupied by one of the three B Company ambush platoons at any given time of day or night, rain or shine.

Rice Mill referred tactically as "delta-delta" in the Village of An Hoa Hung.

Buong River intersecting Hill 15 left (North) and Little Hill 38 right (South).

33

Aiming Stakes and Vectors of Fire

I cannot accurately recall the chronological order in which some of these events occurred. I am reasonably certain that within days of the incident on Hill 15, our platoon was directed to stage an ambush in the vicinity of the Heel of the Boot.

Again, as was our routine, at dusk we set up claymore mines and booby traps some thirty to forty meters out in front of us. Booby traps are crude but effective early warning devices, and lethal when properly positioned along routes of travel. We used transparent fishing line to string a trip wire roughly six to eight feet in length, less than a foot above the ground and firmly attach to a tree trunk, the base of a larger bush or a rock.

The other end of the line would be tied to the loosely secured pin of a pineapple grenade. When the wire is tripped, the grenade would detonate four-to-six seconds later.

Everybody became expert in deploying devices like this, and did so in a stealthy and timely manner.

My squad completed the task as darkness set in. I had just finished assigning the men to various watches for the night when the lieutenant approached me with ropes and small sticks in his hands. Pretending not to notice, I turned away slightly and knelt down to spread out my gear. I was hoping he would pass without stopping but I knew full well that he wasn't just passing through.

As he drew near my peripheral vision sensed the urgency of

his steps. It suggested that he had something special in mind for me.

Standing above me briefly just as he had done back at Rice Mill, on bended knee, he said, "Bogison, we are going to try something a little different tonight. Get your guys to take these ropes, and string them out about thirty to forty meters beyond your position, and attach them to these stakes. You will be forming 30-degree angle vectors of fire for each man in your squad. In other words, each man will be responsible for maintaining his own individual kill zone within that thirty degree vector."

Not one to be too shy when confronted, I again found myself flabbergasted, but only briefly. During the seconds in which to fully comprehend the complete insanity of his idea, I responded with words to the effect, "If I understand you Lieutenant, you want me to gather my men, have them string these white ropes out in front of our position, drive these stakes into the ground, forming 30-degree vectors of fire. Is that right?" "Yes, you got it." he replied.

"Right now. In the darkness. Pounding stakes into the ground while dodging any booby traps we have already set up out there. Is that right?" I fired back. "Well, you will have to redeploy your claymores and grenade traps first, of course." he responded. I then asked some very pointed questions which I had hoped would cause him to rethink.

"So, Lieutenant, we engage the VC. Cortez, my M-79 man is hit and knocked out of the fight. I have no grenade launcher in my squad because all the other guys are concentrating solely on this 30-degree vector of fire they are assigned. That leaves a serious gap in our defense. A 30-degree gap. Who covers Cortez's field of fire?" I snapped sarcastically.

With a puzzled look, he retorted, "Don't you understand? These are overlapping fields of fire."

With absolutely no diplomacy or any trace of patience I firmly stated, "I am not going to ask my guys to go there in the darkness, remove and redeploy the claymores and booby traps they have already set up. Then pound stakes into the ground so that every VC within a square mile of here can come over just to test your theory on kill zones. Go over to the platoon sergeant and sell him on this. I am just a squad leader responsible for the lives of eight guys. You sir, are preventing me from doing this."

Without a word in response, he stood up and walked towards Donnie's Squad forty meters away.

No stringing of white ropes, no pounding of stakes and no 30-degree vectors of fire that night. Donnie's diplomatic mannerisms saved the night, again. No more Lieutenant Scott either. Somebody, somewhere in the battalion figured he was better suited for something else. Every now and again in life, some fool will come forward ready, willing and very committed to acquiring some form of self-aggrandizement at the expense of others.

Lieutenant Scott was that kind of man. Many years later, I discovered the best possible description of our leader in William Manchester's "Goodbye, Darkness." He characterized the intelligence of an incompetent officer he served under in his Marine Battalion during the Pacific Campaign in World War II as "within the confines of that 3rd rate brain, a 2nd class mind was trying to surface."

April 1970, Grave Yard adjacent to the French Fort. Rear L-R: SP/4 Glenn Ward, SP/4 Ed Lewin, Author, SP/4 Doug 'Bish' Bischoff Front L-R: SP/4 Wilber 'Gomer' Martinmoss, PFC Patrick Palmateer, SP/4 Jack 'Peanuts' Cortez.

34
Of Pigs and Men

It was dark that night. Not uncommon but always a concern, particularly on top of this desolate patch of rock and gravelly red soil we called Hill 85. Nearing midnight, gazing at the stars I sensed something out of the ordinary. I wasn't alone. I saw the faint silhouettes of others raise their heads and crane their necks. The usual sounds of the jungle and swamplands below had become silent. Then, a voice slightly louder than a whisper uttered a short, clear phrase in Vietnamese.

The voice appeared to come from directly below us. I immediately crawled toward our machine gun, thirty feet away. A litany of questions raced through my head. Bad ones. Gomer was on watch. Was he asleep? Was his throat cut? Have we been infiltrated? How could these little bastards be so careless and fail to maintain silence?

Gomer was very much awake and alert. He was lying in a prone position, behind the M-60 machine gun, his right finger on the trigger and at the ready. We exchanged glances and quickly scanned the black abyss below.

Nothing.

Seconds later, Donnie was pulling on my leg and directing me with hand signals to meet him several yards behind Gomer. In an exchange of whispers Donnie asked, "What do you think? Have we got zips out there? Those voices came from your way, right?"

I remember saying, "I don't know, but that wasn't some damn bird or that Fuck You Lizard." To which he retorted, "Get your pitching arm ready to throw a couple of frags out there. If they're out there, the frags will flush them out. If we hear anything I'll pop a flare so we can get a fix on'em. Then the whole platoon can open up."

"Discipline," he emphasized. "Tell your people, no firing unless I shoot a flare. We don't want to give away our position if there is nothing out there. Throw one long and the second one short. Got it?" I nodded, then scrambled into my web gear and grabbed two baseball grenades.

I preferred the round baseball grenade over the old WW II oval "pineapple." The M67 baseball grenade weighed just under a pound and could be thrown much further than its older cousin the Mk2 WW II grenade which weighed a half-a-pound more. I directed Main who was already prepared to transmit coordinates for a fire mission to pass the word of our plan to the rest of the squad.

Less than a minute elapsed from the time we first heard the voice to my glancing back at Donnie awaiting his hand signal to throw the first grenade.

My entire being was consumed in a clash between the forces of fear and a mysterious feeling of calm.

Fear, in the physical sense that I was experiencing intermittent tremors in my lower extremities, coupled with concerns of fumbling the killing device now firmly gripped in my right hand. Calmness, in the metaphysical sense that I just knew I would effortlessly hurl this device the distance I used to fire a baseball from shallow right field to home plate.

Fear and failure competed with that serenity and over control of mind and body. Calmness won out.

The instant Donnie gave the go-ahead, I stood up, pulled

the pin from the grenade, released the arming lever (referred to as the spoon), held the device for one second then chucked the thing with a supernatural feeling I had never experienced in my life before or since. I threw this thing higher and further than I ever thought possible because when it detonated four or five seconds later it hadn't even hit the ground.

Out in front of us the flash of the aerial burst released an earsplitting blast that caused me to instinctively dive back on the ground. A midair explosion of metal fragments is more deadly than one detonated on the ground.

Seconds later I tossed the second grenade about twenty yards in front of Gomer, where it rolled down the hill and exploded with far less intensity then the first. Then silence followed by more silence. No rustling of brush, no telltale signs of insect or animal and no voices. Just nerve-racking silence and the pounding of my heart.

Whatever was out there remained a mystery. A meticulous sweep the following morning at the base of the hill revealed no discernable signs of movement or blood trails. But for those of us who heard the voice there was no doubt. The VC were out there. Recent discoveries of underground tunnels adjacent to some of the riverbanks within our tactical area fed into the theory that these little bastards could simply vanish into the earth below us.

Perhaps this was the answer to our mystery. Or as some suggested, maybe it was just an animal grunting. On an evening several months earlier, 2nd Platoon was alerted to noises coming from the southern slope of this hill. They destroyed virtually every living thing on the slope with small arms fire and claymore mines. A sweep conducted on the following morning netted them a freshly killed wild boar. They rewarded themselves by roasting it over an open fire.

Apparently, the typically tough meat associated with this

particular species of hog was tenderized by the overabundance of ball bearings from the claymore mines, and lead projectiles. Was it really just a pig that caused us all that consternation? Who knows?

35
Another innocent casualty of war

March, 1970 during the late afternoon hours found our platoon walking a trail to an ambush site near Buffalo Shack. Somewhere up ahead in the column I heard a loud explosion which caused all of us to hit the ground. Within seconds came the screams of several Vietnamese, and what sounded like people running in shallow water. Seconds after that, shouts of, "Booby trap! Somebody stepped on a booby trap!" passed from one man to the next all the way down the column.

It was SP/4 Bruce Zirk, a mild mannered, blonde-haired native of Wisconsin designated the point man from Donnie's squad who witnessed the event. Just yards away from him, a young girl harvesting rice in the family paddy had inadvertently stepped onto an unknown type of explosive device. Pandemonium let loose in the girl's family and her neighbors, along with the screams of terror from children nearby.

As the rest of the platoon gathered near the rice paddy, I saw Zirk along with Main and others lift the girl and carry her to a clearing near the village. Donnie, Ron or Tiny had already requested a dust-off for the child. As I got closer to the girl I estimated her age to be about 11 or 12. Her injuries were horrific. The device, whatever it was, had nearly severed her body in half at the lower torso. Her face was ashen, her body lifeless.

Within minutes the unmistakable sound of the medevac

touched down, the girl was placed on a stretcher and lifted into the bay of the chopper accompanied by her mother and father. Several days later we learned that the girl died before arriving at the field hospital on Long Binh Post. It is my recollection that this incident occurred near or at Buffalo Shack. Others insist that it happened near Rice Mill. Location is irrelevant. It happened.

36

"Sergeant Snider got hit!"

I don't recall precisely when or where we were on an evening early in 1970, but we had just finished setting up our claymore mines on the slope of a hill. Our squads were positioned about a 100 meters apart.

On occasion, our missions required the entire platoon to split into three squads, each one deployed in a different position within an entire grid on the tactical map of our TAOR. One grid on the tactical map is 1,000 square meters.

For example, Donnie and Tiny leading 3rd squad could set up 100 to 500 meters north of my position, while Ron and Carlos leading 1st squad might set up 100-500 meters south. Naturally, the entire platoon was far more comfortable when we were deployed as an entire unit comprised of three squads. It didn't take much reasoning to figure out that planting 20 to 30 of us at a given location would be far less productive in luring VC then, say striking a squad of six or eight guys.

I'm sure all of us knew that we were nothing more, nothing less, than expendable bait.

Suddenly and unexpectedly, silence was broken by a faint popping noise immediately followed by the familiar hissing sounds of a pop-up flare flying erratically (and directly) over us. It twirled abruptly skyward, about a hundred feet. The discharge that followed produced a shower of green star clustered flares that gently fell over our position.

Pop-up flares are aluminum tubes roughly the size of the red flares emergency personnel place on the road at the scenes of traffic accidents. About a foot long and two inches in diameter, they are activated by striking the cap sharply against the ground or slapping it with an open hand.

A small rocket launched out of the open end reached a height of about 200 feet, then burst into a shower of burning red or green star clusters, or as a parachute flare to illuminate the night. Infantry units fired a green flare to identify their location as friendly during air strikes, meaning "We are the good guys." Green star flares meant friendly, red star flares signaled that the unit had made contact with the enemy.

Unaware of the whys and wherefores to explain the incident, coupled with the bizarre trajectory, stunned everyone. Seconds later, somebody screamed, "Sergeant Snider got hit!" which begged the question, "How?" We weren't engaged in an exchange of small arms fire and nothing suggested that anyone had tripped a booby trap. The squads were positioned a considerable distance apart so all I could do was monitor the radio and wait for some explanation.

Within a minute or so, Donnie advised that Ron had inadvertently dropped a pop-up flare on the ground in front of him. The device discharged striking him in the face. A dust-off was radioed in and within minutes approached our position. Ron was transported to the field hospital at Long Binh. Snider was very fortunate as the flare had glanced off his cheek, which probably spared him from losing an eye.

To our great relief Ron was treated for a superficial wound and soon would recover.

❧

37

"Now remember this! The concussion can be just as dangerous as the stuff itself!"

Early in the field, Tiny and I were directed to meet with Top in the company office. During that meeting First Sergeant Collins told us that we had volunteered for some special training.

"You guys get to learn how to blow things up. I'm sending you boys to Explosive Ordinance School. It's the same training you would receive at the Redstone Arsenal."

I had heard of Redstone Arsenal. It was located somewhere in Alabama. This was where they put combat engineers through a long course on all aspects of explosive ordinance. "That's a 16 week course, Top," I blurted out. With his all-too familiar grin accompanied with his usual sarcasm he said, "I know that, Goddamn it. We don't have the time to put you boys through a sixteen week course. You are going to learn everything you need to know in three days at Cu Chi from the engineers of the 25th Infantry Division."

He continued, "From now on, when one of your snuffies comes on a suspicious hole in the ground, instead of just throwing grenades in it, you two will be our experts on the proper way to blow the damn things up. Then with all that knowledge you boys are going to teach your snuffies everything you know."

Tiny and I exchanged a quick glance then turned our attention back to what Top was saying. "Got it?" he barked again, but before either of us could utter a word, he said, "Good. Report to Sergeant Alley at 0:600 hours tomorrow morning here. He'll get you a jeep and tell you where to report. Now, both of you get out of here. And for Christ's sake listen to what they are telling you, God damn it!"

As ordered, the following morning Tiny and I gathered our M-16s, our .45's, several bandoleers of ammunition, a couple of grenades and made the twenty mile trek to Cu Chi. The drive between Long Binh and Cu Chi was not a particularly safe one. Desolate and forbidding, the road weaved among acres of a densely populated rubber tree plantation owned by the Michelin Corporation.

From both sides of the roadway as far as the eye could see there was nothing but neatly lined mature rubber trees, a favorite for a VC ambush of military convoys, day or night. The firebase at Cu Chi was primitive in comparison to the huge complex we were accustomed to at Long Binh. This place had numerous manned bunkers with a heightened sense of security among the men. You could feel it.

The sights and sounds of a half-dozen or more Huey and Cobra helicopter gunships were constantly crisscrossing the area overhead, and the men assigned here were clad in steel helmets, OD sleeveless flak jackets and armed with M-16 rifles, and bandoleers of ammunition slung over the shoulder.

Flak Jackets were green sleeveless vests with heavy metal plates sewn between layers of nylon.

Our first day of EOD training was conducted inside a tent. We got the basic details of all the Do's and Dont's of handling C-4, and appropriate C-4 uses in the destruction of tunnels, booby traps and enemy strongholds. The rules were fairly simple. One foot of ignited smokeless time fuse, equivalent to the arced distance of the tips of an opened pair of pliers ("crimping tool"), produced approximately one minute of time before burn out.

One end of the time fuse is carefully slipped into the hollow end of a thin silver metal tubular blasting cap, approximately 2 1/2 inches in length and 1/4 inch in diameter. Next, the hollow end of the blasting cap is crimped to secure the time fuse. The other end of the cap is crowned with a small powder charge. The small charge in the blasting cap had enough destructive force to blow a hand and fingers to pieces.

When the ignited time fuse meets the capped end, the 3/4 pound stick of C-4 detonation results in tremendous destruction. A foot of time fuse allows the soldier to distance himself by 100 meters to a safe zone. Two sticks of C-4 and two feet of time fuse allows two minutes to walk to the safe zone 200 meters away, and so on.

Safe zones were designated as distances reckoned to be free of lethal flying debris and the effects of concussion created by the detonation. Our primary instructor, a seasoned Staff Sergeant, constantly drilled into our heads, *"Now remember this! The concussion can be just as dangerous as the stuff itself!"*

Profound words, indeed. And prescient.

The last couple of days were conducted in the field with a platoon of infantrymen patrolling an area several clicks outside the wire. One booby trap was discovered adjacent to a heavily travelled dirt trail. The device had about half a stick of US-made C-4 loaded with rusty nails stuffed inside a C-ration can. Spoon and blasting cap came from a grenade, also of American manufacture.

The device was placed on a small bush next to the trail. Detonation would have occurred when a passerby tripped a fishing line six inches above the ground. On the third day, a "spider hole" (camouflaged entrance to an underground tunnel) was discovered by the point man at the base of an old tree. Booby trap and spider hole were blown up in place. The tree was obliterated with six sticks of C-4. Our three nights spent inside the wire were not so entertaining.

Two attempts to breach the wire of the base camp were thwarted by the guys manning the perimeter. However, just preceding these attempts, the local Vietnamese talent managed to slam several mortar rounds into the base causing the entire compound to remain on alert. Fortunately, nobody was hurt.

Now that Tiny and I were certified in the art of blowing things up we were eager to put our new knowledge to work. From now on, anytime anybody in the platoon stumbled upon any suspicious object consisting of — but not limited to — vehicle parts, discarded tires, piled up debris, freshly covered-up depressions in the ground or any suspected entry to an underground tunnel, we wasted no time in blowing it up.

Within several weeks most of the platoon was intimately familiar with the use of plastic explosives. I had become quite comfortable with the stuff. Actually, too comfortable. Give young men an opportunity to blow things up and they often develop a tendency to resort to childhood behavior. I was no exception.

For instance, somebody in the platoon had spotted freshly chopped vegetation at the base of an old tree. Meticulously, the pieces of brush was removed to reveal what appeared to be a freshly dug hole large enough to accommodate a small person's access to an underground tunnel. It was my turn for the destruction detail so I directed Peanuts and Crazy to assist me. I determined that eight 3/4 pound C-4 sticks would result in the total destruction of tree and entryway.

Generally, each man carried between four and six sticks of C-4 on every mission. Without hesitation, I handed the two men four sticks and told them to bundle eight sticks, while I attached the blasting cap to an eight foot time fuse.

Assuming all was in order, I directed the insertion of the blasting cap, leaving me to prepare to ignite the opposite end of the time fuse with a manual igniter. The igniter is a small tubular plastic device which is activated by pulling a pin.

As we confidently strolled away from the tree towards the safe zone 800 meters away, I couldn't help but chuckle to myself thinking this was much like a Looney Tunes cartoon when the Roadrunner outfoxes Wylie the Coyote. The VC were always setting up some kind of booby trap to blow us up and here we were reversing the situation. Seconds later I remember Crazy saying something to the effect, "Well, if any VC are in there, that should send the sons of bitches to their ancestors!" which caused all of us to break out into uncontrollable laughter.

As laughter faded, looking at my watch I estimated that I had ignited the fuse five minutes earlier and we were about 500 meters into our stroll.

I asked Peanuts, "How much C-4 you got left? "None Sarge." he replied. "How many did you have?" I asked. "Four sticks," he answered. "How much you got left Crazy?" "None Sarge. I gave all mine." "And how much was that?" I barked. "Four sticks. Is something wrong, Sarge?" he asked nervously.

I don't remember our exact exchange but reasonably certain I screamed, "Run for your lives!" which we did. Crazy's four sticks, plus four sticks from Peanuts plus my four meant a dozen — instead of the eight sticks as planned — were about to blow.

The safe zone was not 800 meters away. It was 1,200 meters away. We had to make the distance of six football fields in high grass and shallow swamp in less than seven minutes.

The last thing I remember is looking over my right shoulder, seeing a great white flash, and then an invisible force I had never experienced before or since, picking me up and throwing me head over heels into the air with the words, "Now remember this! The concussion can be just as dangerous as the stuff itself." No shit! I never even heard the explosion.

On my back and looking into the sky, I actually thought I was dead and rising up into the great unknown. But only for a second or two. When I looked to my left I saw Crazy about fifteen feet away, on his back, facing in my direction, and to my right about twenty feet away Peanuts lay on his stomach, lifting his head which was turned my way and facing in the opposite direction.

After a lot of "You, all rights?" and "What?" and "What did you say?" it finally dawned on the three of us that we were all deaf. And we remained that way for the rest of that day and into the next. I am thoroughly convinced that this particular incident is the causal factor for the constant ringing in my ears that I have endured every day of my life since. I estimated that we were about 200 meters short of reaching the safe zone when the concussion reached our dumbasses. Once again, I was lucky. We all were.

Lessons learned? Several. No longer would I assume anything. Every time something had to be destroyed, I checked and double checked the number of sticks of C-4 put in place. I always conducted a dry run of the assignment by walking the necessary distance to the safe zone, timing the walk and counting the steps on the terrain itself. I ensured that there was always enough time fuse in terms of feet and minutes proportionate to the number of sticks deployed.

Finally, as an added precaution I used one foot more of time fuse than was necessary to reach the safe zone.

&

38
Misadventures at French Fort

Hand grenades were another fun toy with which bored young men entertained themselves. There were several types, and everybody had their favorite. The pineapple fragmentation grenade was contoured on the outside with odd sized squares and rectangles having the appearance of a pineapple. They were thrown like a miniature football. The fragmentation baseball-sized grenade was smooth and round. And then we had the standard oval shaped fragmentation grenades without any patterns.

Regardless of preference, all were lethal. It wasn't uncommon for somebody in the platoon to boast about how far they could toss these things, or how accurate he was at hitting a specific target.

When the platoon became restless awaiting arrival of our whalers back to the company area after an extensive sweep of the area adjacent to French Fort and having determined the area was relatively free of Viet Cong activity, we experienced a moment of adolescent immaturity. It never takes much for a group of young men to answer the call of a challenge.

Someone suggested he could accurately lob a grenade onto the top of the flat roof of French Fort, roughly from a distance of a throw from second base to home plate. The challenge did not long go unheeded.

Within seconds the familiar sound of (grenade) spoons being released and half a dozen fragmentation grenades arced their way towards the target. Five fell short, evidenced by the unmistakable pinging sound of steel hitting brick. Everyone scattered and hit the ground face first, with dread visions of little pieces of hot metal slicing through exposed body parts.

When the crescendo of explosions subsided, silence hung in the air followed quickly by the sound of a dozen hands patting bodies to check for wounds. Then came a mix of blasphemous rants followed by laughter. Fortunately, no one was hurt. As for the grenades, only one found its mark, with each participant fervently claiming ownership.

The missions demanded daunting logistical challenges. Transporting an entire platoon on the waterways was not an easy feat for our Boston Whaler operators. Between mechanical breakdowns, low tides and manpower shortages, it wasn't uncommon for the platoon to be split up into five man squads and a sergeant left stranded at the pickup point for hours at a time.

Several weeks after the aforementioned incident and at the same place, four Boston Whalers — each with capacity for only six men — arrived on station to ferry the 26-man platoon. Two men were out. Snider and I volunteered to remain behind. We determined that our time separated from the rest of the platoon would be less than an hour. As we sat near the bank of the Đồng Nai staring out at French Fort behind us, Ron and I joked about the bad throws the guys had made with their grenades at the Fort several weeks earlier.

We continued our mockery of the incident and eventually figured putting a grenade on top of the structure would be a relatively simple task, given our years of experience playing in Little League, Babe Ruth, and high school baseball. Armed with six grenades each, we figured on an easy one-toss attempt. It was not to be.

Mystified by our failure after three attempts each, we wisely decided to cease and desist for fear of attracting some unnecessary attention from patrol boats or possible enemy forward observers.

Stuff we hadn't thought about before we concocted the idea.

Within minutes of making that wise decision we heard the familiar drone of a South Vietnamese patrol boat idling in our direction. We had literally put our lives unnecessarily into a very hostile situation. Concealed among thick foliage adjacent to the bank of the river, Ron and I together - and without uttering a word - dove onto the muddy bank, face down. We remained motionless hoping and praying all the while that no trigger-happy sailor had a grip on the boat's .30 caliber and .50 caliber machine guns.

Laying there in silence for what seemed like an eternity, I thought again what a ridiculous way to get killed. The Army would label it "friendly fire" with no logical explanation. How would you explain it? Two idiots huddled behind greenery hiding from a friendly force?

Flinging our hands in the air in an abortive attempt to identify ourselves could be just as lethal. Fortunately for us, the familiar and welcoming sound of the 70-horsepower whine of the Mercury outboard engine of an incoming Boston Whaler caused the South Vietnamese patrol boat to vacate the area.

Naturally, as squad leaders we never related the story to any of our people. At least, not when we were sober. Given the same set of circumstances, and had I been manning a machine gun on a patrol boat rushing to the scene of unexplained explosions, I would have, in all probability sprayed the area with indiscriminate machine-gun fire. We were lucky.

Had the Boston Whaler not appeared at the precise moment that it did I am reasonably certain that an entirely different, and very negative, scenario would have emerged.

⁂

39

High School Geometry—The American Civil War—Muck & Shallow Water

Anytime our platoon was directed to occupy an area within the eastern portion of our tactical area everyone remained in a high state of readiness. If anything really ugly were to happen, it would be here.

This was sometime in early February after having set up an ambush site mear the Rabbit Ears, on the previous evening. The following morning we learned that the whaler crews were experiencing mechanical problems. Only two skimmers were operational. This meant that transporting our entire platoon to the next staging area would take much longer to complete.

If anything could go wrong, it would. As early morning turned into mid-day the waters of the Buong River separating us from the Thai Territory on the opposite side had receded so severely that movement by way of any kind of watercraft was impossible. The ebb and flow of hundreds of tributaries adjoining the Dong Nai River were subject to the temperament of the South China Sea, some 40 miles to the south.

The only option left us was to wade through roughly 100 yards of muck and shallow river water to reach the opposite bank. This state of affairs left us — Greg Thompson, Ed Lewin, Doug Bischoff, Gomer, Crazy Marich and me — stranded, cut off from the rest of the platoon and devoid of any logistical support. Left there in the open with no freshwater or C-rations, baking in 100° plus temperature.

The circumstances did not sit well with any of us. We were in for the long haul. We knew that this situation would last a very long time.

As for me, I was relatively comfortable with the fact that it was daytime and we had what I estimated to be about a 500 meters of unobstructed view behind us to the west, and about another 500 meters of observable open space to the east, into Thai territory. I also had access to air and artillery battery support available from nearby Bearcat fire base.

I was reasonably confident that our chances of making any contact with the VC was minimal, at best. That said, several things concerned me. In the event we were to make contact with a superior force I had to be certain of a plan to evade and escape. I was very familiar with the terrain, the landmarks and hazardous areas directly west of Rabbit Ears but totally unfamiliar with the Thai territory east of us.

Additionally, I was uncertain as to what the approximate distance was from our position on the west bank to the opposite side of the Buông River. In the event we made contact to the west and forced to retreat across the muck into Thai territory, I needed to estimate the distance to a tree line several hundred yards away.

It was at this exact point in time in my life that all those miserable geometry courses I had to repeat two and three times during high school summer sessions would actually be put to use. I also recalled reading a book when I was in the 10th grade in the Granada Hills High School library about a Northern soldier during the Civil War telling his commanding officer how to calculate the distances of river crossings without having to ford them.

I remembered repeatedly reading the explanation of how he did this, and it sounded plausible. However, the concept wasn't really clear in my mind until this moment. The young soldier had studied engineering prior to the war. I recalled that his commanding officer and staff had a critical decision to make: (1)

cross the river with no knowledge of the distance to calculate the time necessary to link up with another regiment or, (2) take a known road to a bridge and risk being detected and ambushed.

This is what the soldier proposed to the officer: He considered the height of his body while rigidly posed standing, as one side of a triangle. While retaining this pose on the bank of the river before him he aligned the forward brim of his hat towards a tree stump on the opposite side of the river. In doing this the soldier determined that he had formed an angle between the forward brim of his hat and the tree stump.

Further, he recognized that he had formed a 90° angle with his body while standing perpendicular to the ground. Having established the rigidity of his body as the side of the triangle, coupled with the 90° angle formed by his perpendicular stance to the ground and the angle he produced with the brim of his hat to the tree stump, he formed an imaginary triangle.

He then performed an about face. Which is to say, he made an abrupt 180° turn in place, causing him to now face directly in the opposite direction.

Once positioned, he aligned the forward brim of his hat to a large rock not too far away but directly in front of him. The angle he formed with the brim of his hat on that large rock remained at the same angle he had formed when he aligned it to the tree stump. He then counted the paces it took him to walk from where he was standing to the rock.

After converting the number of paces into yards, the soldier confidently reported to his commanding officer the yardage his regiment would have to travel to the stump opposite.

When his commanding officer questioned the validity of his estimate, the soldier explained that the geometrical theorem supported the proposition that when an angle (brim of hat), a side (the soldier's standing body), and an angle (the perpendicular 90 degree angle of the soldier's standing body to the ground) of one triangle equals the angle, the side and the angle of another triangle, in that sequence (angle-side-angle) both triangles, are deemed to be equilateral triangles.

The commanding officer heeded the soldier's advice, crossed the river and on arriving at the tree stump discovered that the distance was determined to be precisely what the soldier had told him it would be.

Here, in the blistering heat on a God-forsaken piece of ground adjacent to a dirty little river in an obscure part of a war-torn country, geometry and a US Civil War story I could not fully comprehend just six years earlier, made complete sense. Somewhat excited about my new-found discovery, I sprung to my feet and immediately applied the same principles to my current situation.

I stood rigidly at the bank of the Buông River facing east into the Thai Territory while aligning the forward brim of my bush hat to the base of the tree line on the opposite side.

Becoming somewhat complacent in the excitement of this revelation, reality began to sink when I paced off nearly 400 yards directly west of our position and determined that this was the distance our platoon would have to travel to reach the tree line deep in Thai country. I was separated from the remainder of my squad, alone, and shuddered at the thought that my actions in determining this calculation could get me killed. At a minimum I needed at least one man to accompany me during the 400 yard trek.

Complacency is deadly and I should have known better. My return trip to the squad was conducted far more cautiously.

40

"You've got movement coming your way!"

Returning to the squad I saw that our situation was taking a toll on everyone. "Crazy" Marich was unusually quiet. Greg Thompson, who seldom talked, appeared to be in a sour mood sitting at the edge of the river with his back turned away from the rest of the group. Bish, seated on the ground next to Lewin, was staring at the ground in front of him and speechless. Gomer was seated next to Lewin on the opposite side. He was usually quiet and reserved but the scorn on his face suggested some kind of anger brewing. Glancing at Lewin, I saw the same expression.

I had learned a great deal about human nature and how men interacted with one another when placed in a hostile environment back at Long Binh Jail and at Fort Riley. Something suggested to me that during my absence some kind of dispute had occurred. The atmosphere was foul and like a time bomb, ready to explode.

Seconds later my suspicions were confirmed when I heard Lewin and Gomer exchange heated words, which instantly progressed from insults to threats, then escalated to both men jumping up and Gomer reaching for his M-16 rifle and Lewin grabbing ahold of his M-60 machine gun. Just as the two were about to point their respective weapons at each other, I stepped between them clutching the barrel of Gomer's M-16 rifle with one hand, while grabbing one of Lewin's arms with the other.

I cannot recall as to what I may have screamed, suffice to say the incident was terminated.

Acknowledging the fact that these men were at that breaking point, I directed all of them to pick up their respective weapons and fire indiscriminately at targets of their choosing along the bank on the opposite side. I reasoned that this activity would alleviate some of the stress and divert their attention and their anger.

After several minutes of incessant gunfire the mood of the men changed considerably for the better. As for Lewin and Gomer, they settled their differences with an uneasy truce. Privately, I was proud of myself and temporarily basked in the belief that my spontaneous intervention in the incident provided an immediate resolution.

So much for self-congratulations. There was no time for it. Minutes later a far more serious crisis was brewing as the urgent voice of John Pedemonte, a former 2nd Platoon Bushwhacker, bellowed out of the radio from our tactical operations center loud and clear, "You've got movement coming your way!"

Movement! What did that mean? Where? How many? I had far too many questions on my mind before I could respond. Outwardly, I clearly remember putting on a good front but inside I felt like every internal organ in my body was about to create an unpleasant surprise in my pants.

Nonetheless, Pedemonte advised that Popular Forces commonly referred to as PFs (South Vietnamese militia fighters) had spotted a platoon-sized Viet Cong patrol proceeding directly towards us, approximately 500 meters west of our current position.

Good God! I thought to myself, I was out there just minutes earlier.

We immediately gathered up our gear and set up a skirmish line behind and along the muddy river bank. I took the radio and made sure that a distance of no less than 15 yards separated each man down the line. There was no time to set up any type of early warning devices in the form of booby-traps or claymore mines. It didn't matter, anyway.

We didn't have C-4 plastic explosives or claymore mines as they were all transported along with the rest of the platoon. Earlier in the haste of decision-making, I volunteered to remain in this position with these five men. It never occurred to me that I should have conducted an inventory of the assorted types of equipment I might, in fact, need. But this was no time to reflect upon what I should have done.

The reality of the situation was simple. We were six men armed with one M-60 machine gun, five M-16 rifles, several .45 caliber automatic pistols and twenty-four hand grenades, along with several smoke grenades, about to face 20 or 30 Vietcong guerrillas.

We had between 20 and 25 minutes to prepare for the inevitable. That estimate was predicated on my recollection of the time and distance it took me to make the return trip back to the squad, some 400 yards west to east. My heart pounded and my mind went into overdrive when it suddenly dawned on me that I had probably created this situation. All the fireworks we produced minutes earlier pulverizing the opposite bank of the river with gunfire must have drawn their attention.

It was also during this thought process when I grasped that during our demonstration of firepower we wasted a significant amount of ammunition. Lewin chewed up between 100 and 200 rounds of M-60 ammunition with his machine gun and Thompson. Bish, Gomer, and Crazy each burned up at least four magazines of their M-16 ammunition.

As I rattled the math in my head, I figured 18 rounds in a 20 round capacity magazine times 4 equals 72 times 5 men equaled 360+200 M—60 machine gun rounds equaled at least 560 rounds wasted. How ironic, in that the lead of 560 bullets buried in the muck of an obscure riverbank having served as a resolution for our internal row now could affect the balance between life and death in a real life-and-death conflict. I asked myself at least a dozen times, what the hell have I done?

In the midst of all this decision-making I had the presence of mind to request (via radio), air support in the form of helicopter gunships to proceed at map coordinates directly west of us. Our call sign for this particular mission identified us as "Savage Thieves 2." Each mission the platoon was designated a new and carefully constructed call sign phonetically difficult for the Vietnamese to pronounce. The consonants S and T were among the most difficult for the Vietnamese to enunciate properly in the English language.

The carefully selected call signs were designed specifically to detect enemy deception if the VC attempted to disguise themselves as Americans in order to communicate misinformation and mischief over the radio. Savage Thieves was our platoon call sign. The number 2 meant the 2nd Squad, my squad. My request was acknowledged and I was advised to expect an ETA of 10-15 minutes for the gunships to arrive on station.

It was a waiting game now, and once again all sense of time became nonexistent. Studying my tactical map, I memorized the six digit coordinates of our position. I reasoned that if our air support was delayed, and we found ourselves overwhelmed by a superior force with no other option than to retreat into Thai Territory, I could direct a fire mission of high explosive artillery rounds directly on the pursuing VC.

As a last resort I thought this might buy us some time to seek refuge in that tree line, but I prayed it wouldn't come to that. God only knows what could be waiting for us, that is if we could make it there at all.

Sooner than expected, and according to my watch less than five minutes after my request for air support, I heard the familiar and welcoming sounds of helicopter gunships emanating somewhere out of the north and east approaching our position.

Less than a minute later three 25th Infantry Huey helicopters flew directly over our position at treetop level as the pilot in the lead chopper greeted us with a smart hand salute and stated over the radio, "Okay, Savage Thieves 2, got you spotted. Understand you got some bad guys down there. We're here to talk to them the only way we know how. Any other requests from you Savage Thieves?" "No sir. But if you spot any movement I sure would appreciate you boys giving us a direction of travel. Can't thank you enough for getting here so quick," I responded. "No sweat. You call, we haul. Stand-by you Savage Thieves. We'll let you know what we got," he replied.

The three gunships continued their flight westbound in wide arcing patterns slowly fading out of sight, but not out of earshot. The constant drone of the distant helicopter blades was interrupted sporadically by the sound of helicopter machine guns (mini-guns) and rocket fire. After each cycle of gunfire I grew more confident that we were going to be alright.

I can't speak highly enough about these helicopter guys as they were always there whenever we needed them the most.

After what I reasoned was a meticulous aerial sweep conducted by the air crews of the several square miles in front of us, the now familiar voice of the pilot over the radio said, "No confirmed movement noted Savage Thieves 2, but for good measure we plowed up several suspected shelters among some high brush along the tree line about a half a click (500 meters) west of your position. Two of us will be heading back to Cu Chi. Your TOC has requested that one of us remain in the area until you people are picked up. So excuse us if we make an occasional buzz (flyby) over you. Good luck Savage Thieves 2. Nice doing business with you."

Staring in awe as two of the Hueys crossed directly over our position heading for their home base, I keyed the microphone of the radio and simply said "Thanks," as I watched them disappear from sight. The tightness in my chest, the pounding of my heart and the nausea in my gut subsided as an aura of calmness slowly took over my entire being.

It was a moment of sudden insight, a revelation about team bonding, abiding friendship forged in war. I was profoundly indebted to these guys and to John Pedemonte who dispatched them, understood our situation and for his insistence that a chopper remain on station until we were picked up.

Several hours later the river regained its normal flow of water and two Boston Whalers arrived to transport us to the staging area with the rest of the platoon. Had the gunships not arrived when they did, I am uncertain as to what fate might have befallen us.

Two months later I was transferred to the PBR (Patrol Boat Riverine) Platoon. B Company had its own Navy. In time, we rescued one individual and retrieved ten passengers and crew of a 25th Infantry Division Huey gunship that crashed into the Dong Nai, near Bien Hoa.

I snapped this photograph minutes before receiving the information about movement in our area while stranded at the Rabbit Ears. F to B: Crazy Marich, Gomer, Doug 'Bish' Bischoff, Ed 'Lew' Lewin, Greg Thompson.

41

"God damn it! I'm awfully damn sorry about that, Ward!"

Revisiting these experiences 40 years later I often wonder how we didn't end up killing each other through carelessness or misadventure. It wasn't uncommon to hear of somebody in the company handle a weapon poorly resulting in an accidental discharge. One fine morning the platoon was afoot in a single column formation on a trail entering a Banana Plantation. It was during these walks, or humps, as we called them, that complacency in various forms large and small, easily became a dangerous distraction.

Large, in the sense of total disregard for personal safety and the safety of others. In effect, allowing yourself to spiral into blind apathy. Small, in the sense of finding yourself intermittently daydreaming of home and loved ones. As our column entered the hamlet associated with the Banana Plantation, a snapping sound whizzed past my right ear, instantly accompanied by the familiar sound of an M-16 rifle report.

Instinctively, everybody dove into the ditch adjacent to the trail. Fortunately for us, the ditch was not booby-trapped with explosives or thickly embedded with razor sharp bamboo sticks, as was often the case. Seconds later voices rang out shouting, "Friendly fire! Friendly fire! Anybody hit? Anybody hit?"

No casualties this time. Somebody had accidentally flung his rifle onto his right shoulder and had managed to hit the trigger with his thumb, having neglected to put the firing mechanism in the safe position.

On another occasion, our platoon prepared to clean weapons at the company armory after completing its six-day mission. Open trays of gun oil, cleaning solvents and assorted rods, brushes, rags, gun parts and live ammunition littered the steel table tops and concrete floor.

Concentrating on cleaning my M-16 rifle, I was startled when a shot rang out immediately followed by groans and a litany of obscenities directed at the guilty party. The offender in this case had inadvertently pulled the slide back on his loaded .45 automatic pistol with his right finger on the trigger, while pointing the barrel down at the concrete floor. The weapon discharged. The copper-jacketed lead projectile struck concrete and shattered into small shrapnel that entered the lower extremities of no less than three men nearby.

Fortunately, no serious injuries were sustained.

People like me from the city were not as proficient regarding the care, discipline, and nomenclature of the assorted weaponry at our disposal as were the boys from the rural South. For instance, I qualified as an expert in marksmanship with the M-14 rifle and the M-16 rifle. But I recognized that our country boys were all excellent marksmen and extremely capable in every aspect of every weapon in our arsenal. More so than me. Understandably so, as all of them were experienced game hunters back home.

I was not immune to bouts of apathy myself, and fell victim to an avoidable incident and the humbling experience of learning a hard lesson. Early one morning when five of us were being transported by Boston Whaler, three of us laid our rifles down in the boat with the barrels protruding slightly forward, and above the tip of the bow.

As the whaler eased into the bank of the river adjacent to Rice Mill, the tip of my weapon barrel dug into the mud. When

Ward - seated just ahead of me - jumped ashore I scrambled to retrieve my rifle. I grasped the weapon by placing my right finger on the trigger, somehow striking the safety lever with my thumb and shifting it up one click, from the safe position to the semi-automatic fire setting.

The sequence caused my rifle to discharge a single round into the mud adjacent to Ward's left foot. He immediately protested, "God damn, Bog! I need that foot!" to which I yelled, "God damn it! I'm awfully damn sorry about that, Ward!" To say that I was shaken by the incident is an understatement. To my great relief Ward, the consummate southern gentleman, assured me that the entire episode was an accident and that as far as he was concerned it could have happened to anybody. I never forgot what Ward said to me that day and for that, I hold him in high esteem.

42

"Well, so much for those iodine tablets."

Sometime in early March, 1970 I found myself stranded again somewhere south of Rabbit Ears in the company of my squad, plus Jerry Perry and Rich Radcliff from Donnie's squad. Perry was seriously unwell. Two-thirds of the platoon had already been transported back to the company area when the whalers developed mechanical problems.

Unlike the previous experience I endured a month earlier in this area, the ebb and flow of the Đồng Nai had little influence on this particular occasion. We could summon the assistance of some larger PBR gunboats (Patrol Boat Riverine) on station and minutes away from our location. Unfortunately, the protocol was against us. Summon, yes but only in the case of an emergency.

New standard operating procedures prohibited deployment of larger craft in the shallow rivers and tributaries bordering the eastern portion of our tactical area.

Having just completed our six day mission in the field we all looked forward to clean showers, hot food and freshwater. I had consumed the last of my two canteens of potable water a day earlier. Early on this morning I filled a canteen full of river water, boiled it over a stick of C-4 in my mess kit cup along with two US Army-issue iodine water purification tablets. It was now approaching high noon and the whaler crews were still plagued with mechanical issues.

This meant that we would remain in the blistering heat devoid of any substantial shade for the next several hours. I had never known such thirst before or since, the way I experienced it in these rice paddies and jungle. It is indescribable. I unscrewed the cap of my lukewarm canteen, placed it to my lips, then guzzled about half the contents down my parched throat, all the while hoping it wasn't a mistake. It was.

Less than 30 minutes later I managed to regurgitate every ounce of fluid and digestible food I had consumed for the past two days.

I knew this to be so because I saw bits and pieces of the ham and lima beans I had consumed from one of my C-ration meals two days earlier. I have never been so stricken with such intestinal pain in my life, before or since. An incessant series of the dry heaves followed as dehydration set in, along with a fever.

As my condition worsened, I remember overhearing conversation about calling in a dust-off for me and Jerry Perry. The next thing I remember was being carried into a helicopter — along with Perry — and feeling the gusts of wind blowing across my face and the drone of the chopper blades during the flight to the dispensary at Long Binh.

During the flight, Perry who was laying on the floor next to me, told the medic on board that he was certain it was the river water that he drank that caused him to be so sick. Apparently Perry had made the same mistake I had. After hearing Perry's remark I sarcastically said "Well, so much for those iodine tablets." Perry and I spent the remainder of that day and into the following morning in the dispensary being intravenously fed and poked with needles. We recovered during our three day break from the field.

Needless to say, I never allowed my canteen to go dry again. I never consumed another iodine-tablet-boiled river water cocktail again, and I have not and will not even consider the thought of eating one lima bean to this day.

43
Firefights & Other Confusing Things

Firefights were generally discouraged. At least, that is how it appeared to be during the latter part of 1969, and throughout July,1970 when our entire company was disbanded. Under the campaign title, Operation Stabilize we were directed not to be seen or heard. In practical terms, we were deployed to conduct reconnaissance and avoid direct contact with enemy forces whenever possible. All sightings of enemy movement and their respective grid locations on the tactical map were reported to the Tactical Operations Center first.

The radio operator assigned to the TOC reported the observations to Battalion Headquarters. From that point, coordination of a fire mission (artillery/mortar) or sortie of helicopter gunships and fighter jets would be dispatched to destroy the enemy. Functioning as forward observers the platoon sergeant — through the eyes of his platoon — would correct fields of fire. However, like any idea that sounds good or looks plausible on paper, success in practical application does not necessarily follow.

I recall three instances that would qualify as firefights, all of which were very brief. At a place referred to as Duck Farm, located somewhere within the interior of our tactical area of responsibility, we spent several nights laying in scads of duck waste. The place was misery personified. Stickier than mud and more slippery than ice and reeked to high heaven. The stench remained with you until you could dive into the nearest river.

Shortly after setting up an ambush one night near the trail leading into Duck Farm, we spotted the movement of several VC crouching towards our position, approximately 200 meters away.

I don't remember whether we fired first or they did. I just remember a lot of noise, a lot of snapping sounds directly over my head, bright parachute flares lighting up the sky, and an abundance of red tracers floating down range towards the intermittent flashes from the weapons being fired at us.

For me time always seemed to stand still during terrifying moments. Measuring them in terms of seconds or minutes of a clock was all but impossible. However, when the chaos ended, I thought I had a fairly clear idea of a time-frame as I checked my bandoliers of ammunition and counted how many magazines I had expended. I had shot up three magazines in fairly rapid succession and estimated that the entire ordeal probably only lasted between one and three minutes.

I also realized that I did not comply with the sensible doctrine of firing disciplined 3-5 round bursts at a specific target. In fact I did quite the opposite. I slapped in three magazines and each time I did, I indiscriminately pointed my gun down range and squeezed the trigger until all the bullets were gone. Fortunately for us, nobody got hit. A sweep the following morning left us no bodies and no blood trails for our display of fireworks the previous evening.

The second time I experienced moments of terror was at the Finger of the Land. The place was essentially just a swampy island located somewhere in the interior of our TAOR, surrounded by a series of streams and tributaries. We arrived rather late in the evening and with limited visibility there were many opportunities to make a lot of noise while setting up claymore mines, booby traps and then settling in for the night. It was obvious to everyone that we were not going to ambush anybody that night, but I'm sure everyone thought as I did, that Charlie (VC) might want to pay us a visit.

He did just that.

The incident started late at night with an eerie silence, followed by faint sounds of brush in motion and the occasional slosh of something moving through shallow water and getting nearer. Minutes later our suspicions confirmed the obvious. Somebody in the 1st squad some fifty yards off to my left peered through his starlight scope and saw walking brush about hundred yards away. Seconds later the entire platoon opened up with small arms fire, parachute flares and M-79 grenade launchers. There was no time to contact TOC or even to try to explain our predicament.

Muzzle flashes were visible but there were none of the snapping sounds made by bullets. Green tracers (used by the NVA and VC) flew mainly over the heads of the 1st squad. The whole thing couldn't have lasted any more than four or five minutes. My estimate of time was far from being a reliable benchmark. When the smoke cleared I had expended six magazines.

So much for gauging time by counting magazines of expended ammunition. However, this time I deliberately disciplined my trigger finger to let loose in 3-5 round bursts down range, and I fixed my aim directly at the muzzle flashes. Just as before, nobody got hit and a sweep next morning left us with no bodies and no blood trails. Just a lot of chewed up brush and freshly blown up mud holes.

Nighttime shot of author's platoon atop of Hill 15 checking for suspected movement below after hearing suspicious noises.

SP/4 Jared Kelley firing M-60 Machine gun during an early morning firefight.

44

"Hey Bog! Check my leg will you?"

Far and away one of the most convoluted and frightening events in my life occurred on a night in early March. Staff Sergeant Fred Pazmino was our Platoon Sergeant. Pazmino, or Paz as he we knew him, had been awarded the Silver Star for heroic action during the 1969 post-Tet battle for Hill 15. A year younger than me, he was highly respected among all the men in B Company.

My squad was positioned in the center portion of an L-shaped ambush formation behind the dikes of a dry rice paddy, just about 100 yards north of the thick and tall brush in the southernmost section of our TAOR, adjacent to the bank of the Buông. 1st squad off to my left was positioned approximately 50 yards away facing south and slightly east. "Paz" with 3rd squad, off to my right, was 50 yards to the west and faced the same thick brush to the south as we did.

We had been set up for an hour or so when noises were heard in front of us. A lot of noise. The sounds of a sizeable fighting force was trying to thrash its way through the landscape. No mistaking it. These were bad guys. There was no possibility of any friendlies in this area at this particular time.

2nd Platoon was at the northernmost portion of our TAOR. The nearest Popular Forces Compound was far to our north. Recognizing the threat, Pazmino wisely and carefully timed a coordinated fire mission via the radio, comprised of illumination artillery rounds followed by HE artillery one hundred meters to our front, in an effort to score a direct hit on the enemy as they emerged from the thicket.

I was on my stomach focusing the front sight of my rifle directly into the thick brush, impatiently and nervously waiting for the all-too familiar jet-like sounds of incoming artillery shells flying over our heads finding their mark. This time however, the sound of exploding metal accompanied by bright parachute flares prematurely — and unexpectedly — detonated directly over my squad, exposing all of us.

Glancing over my shoulder I experienced an incredible burning sensation near my left ear and temporal area. More annoying than painful, I applied pressure with my left hand then immediately reached for the radio microphone with my right hand. Firmly squeezing the transmit button, I shouted, "Paz! They're dropping shit directly on top of us. We're completely lit up!" To which he yelled back, "I got it, Bog! Get off the radio! I gotta get through to TOC!" My tying up the radio to advise him of a situation that was obvious to all was unnecessary.

Lessons learned. Again.

Sight significantly impaired by the intense light of illumination rounds, I immediately recognized that my effectiveness as a rifleman and squad leader would be compromised. Seconds later, HE rounds began dropping short, detonating between us and the thick brush prompting the various squads, including mine, to open up with small arms fire.

The constant drone of the three M-60 machine guns, automatic rifle fire, intermittent explosions from our three M-79 grenade launchers, coupled with a continual stream of our red tracers filling the air and the constant detonation of artillery HE and illuminations rounds added to the confusion.

What started out as a classically planned ambush quickly

degenerated into nothing more than bedlam. I cannot recall how long this ordeal lasted, nor do I have any memory whether we even received any hostile fire. It was just too damn confusing. Fortunately, Pazmino's rapid readjustment of artillery fire with the TOC Radio Operator avoided the inevitable: a horrific friendly fire incident.

Silence came next, but only briefly. Several yards off to my left I heard the unmistakable voice of Jim Gufford calmly asking, "Hey, Bog! Check my leg will you?" He had been hit with a thin piece of shrapnel about the size of a silver dollar which was partially imbedded in the flesh adjacent to the back of his left knee.

I immediately pinched the jagged piece of metal between my right thumb and forefinger, pulled it out and flung it over my shoulder as the damn thing was still hot. Gufford never even whimpered as I called out for the Medic, the guy we called Doc. After Doc applied a dressing to Gufford's wound, Peanuts asked, "Hey, Doc, could you check out the back of my neck?"

Apparently, Peanuts experienced the same burning sensation I had. Doc applied some alcohol soaked cloth to the back of his neck and to the left temporal area of my head. I thought nothing more of it. I never knew what Doc's name was. We seemed to always have a different Medic accompany us after several missions. I do remember that he smoked a pipe, wore black horn-rimmed glasses and never carried a weapon. He was a good man.

The remainder of that night and into the early morning hours of the next day, the entire area within the thick brush and northern bank of the Buông was pummeled with 40mm rockets and machine gun fire from a Hunter Killer Team of one Huey gunship and a Cobra helicopter gunship from the 25th Infantry Division. The sweep of the area at daybreak revealed some traces of blood but again, no bodies.

Why the illumination rounds fell short and low, directly over our position, was never explained. The error was not attributed to Paz. He was far too conscientious and experienced to have provided inaccurate map coordinates when he called in the fire mission. Miscommunication, miscalculation, or a combination of both on the part of the artillery boys was the only plausible explanation for the mishap. I was just glad nobody got seriously hurt or killed.

I assumed the shrapnel in Gufford's leg and the burning sensations experienced by Peanuts and me were caused by the detonation of the illumination artillery rounds that burst over us.

Some of the various states of mind I underwent before and during a firefight are clear. I should add that immediately after one of these adrenalin-packed melees my experience includes a fleeting but indescribable kind of euphoria. Mind and body were overwhelmed by a sea of calmness, absolute silence and solitude. This wonderful feeling — which never lasted long — was interrupted by an equally brief moment of unexpected, all-consuming chill that consumed my entire being.

Breathing fell out of sync with my heartbeat and my hands and body shuddered. I avoided speaking to anyone in an effort to conceal the inevitable tremor in my speech that followed. Several inconspicuous deep breaths later and the tremors usually faded away. Lastly, I also acquired an insatiable appetite for anything to eat, with no regard for personal preferences. Even the godforsaken C-ration fruitcake was not rejected.

In the early afternoon hours several days later, our platoon was being resupplied at an old brickyard located on the banks of the Đồng Nai, at a place we visited many times before. Outpost #1, the Popular Forces Militia Compound, was roughly 500 meters north and slightly east of us.

The yard comprised several large open air structures in which

April 1970, Top, L-R: SP/4 Stan Galonski, SP/4 Jack "Peanuts" Cortez, PFC Patrick Palmateer, Author, SP/4 Glenn Ward, SP/4 Ed "Lew" Lewin Bottom, L-R: SP/4 Wilber "Gomer" Martinmoss, SSG Fred Pazmino.

thousands of hand-made bricks were neatly stacked in four-by-six foot squares, about five feet high. Local villagers gathered river mud by hand, pouring the mud into wooden forms to dry. Small, crudely constructed brick structures resembling kilns were scattered throughout the area.

By all appearances, the brickyard and the grueling manual labor provided by nearby families had probably existed for generations. In daytime the place was teeming with the activity of scores of men and women toiling in the dirt and mud, beginning at first light and lasting until dusk. At night the place was completely desolate and eerie. Shade from these old structures gave some relief from the scorching heat. But not much.

Our presence never seemed to concern the locals. We waited for the strategists at our Tactical Operations Command Center to decide where our next ambush site would be set that evening.

Taking advantage of free time, some guys wrote letters home, others — including me — were engaged in a card game we called "Two Card Guts." Aptly, as you had to have a measure of internal fortitude, or lunacy, to assume that your second card hand would be higher than hands held by the other eight to ten guys competing for a pot that could grow as high as $300 and $400. A sizeable sum back then. Others competed and placed bets on hitting etched targets on old tree trunks or wooden posts throwing their bayonets or kabar survival knives.

And then there was Tommy Chamberlain who hailed from Maryland. Generally quiet and unassuming he was seen by many in the platoon as somewhat eccentric. He spent hours at our various resupply locations stalking and capturing small lizards with a crudely assembled stick and fishing line that had an effective noose. He either released the critters or handed them off to Vietnamese children for pets.

Tommy perfected the art of tossing a bayonet, which was not designed for throwing, by successfully penetrating targets from distances up to 21 feet away, using what he referred to as simple mathematics. Nobody could compete with him.

❧

SP/4 Tommy Chamberlain

45

"Bog, how many guys in your squad can't swim?"

As the afternoon drew to a close, villagers hastily closed their respective work stations and vacated the brickyard. Nothing out of the ordinary, except for the fact that there was still enough daylight for them to continue working for another hour or so. It was a peculiar change in routine that should have sparked our concern.

But, it didn't.

Darkness came and still no orders directing us to move out. The larger question among us was, just what form of movement are we going to be ordered to execute? Movement in darkness, under a partially exposed moon, is senseless — and lethal. Whalers with their engine drone or a hump through rice paddies under cover of darkness would be equally foolhardy. Each passing minute elevated tensions. It was in the faces of the men. I was no different, my stomach churned in knots anticipating which was worse: walk in or go by boat at this late hour?

Finally, Donnie got the word. As Tiny, Ron, and I formed a semi-circle and stooped down on one knee in front of him, Donnie — stooped with us — said, "The good news is we ain't goin' nowhere. We are stayin' right here. They told me to standby because they have some intel to pass on to us. I'll know more soon, so get your people together and set up a skirmish line (squads forming a straight line). My squad will take the center and Bog your squad will be on my left and Ron, you on my right. Set 'em up facing east, in front of this brickyard for now."

"What about the river? What do we do about our rear?" Tiny asked.

"For now hold tight. As soon as I learn more we'll break some people off and set up a rear guard," Donnie responded. Then he quickly stood up and walked away. The tightness in my stomach loosened as I stood up and walked toward my squad scattered along the bank of the Đồng Nai. The brickyard was an eerie place at night but at least we didn't have to move.

Just as I started to explain to my squad our assignment, Tiny approached me and said, "Bog, Donnie got that intel and he wants us now."

As we scurried off, I asked, "What have we got?" and Tiny said, "I don't know. I heard some of it. TOC said something about a Red Alert and it don't sound good."

Forming the same semi-circle at the same place as before, I saw the solemn look on Donnie's face in the faint light of that partial moon. It was now brighter than it had been just an hour or so earlier. "Okay, boys here's what we got. We're on a Red Alert. We got movement. Victor Charlie is all over the goddamned place." To which Tiny interrupted and asked, "What the fuck is a Red Alert?"

"Well, Tiny, I'm told it is as high an alert as you can have. We're probably gonna get hit tonight." Donnie retorted as my stomach immediately tightened to its former knotted condition. "TOC says a battalion-sized force is headed our way. The PFs out in OP #1 spotted the movement."

"A battalion! That's 400 or 500 guys for Chrissake!" I blurted out. "Yea, I know Bog and that's not all. We got no artillery or air support. All the artillery batteries are assigned to the 9th Division. They got some shit goin' on down there. Air support is working on some shit the 25th Division got into up north. We're it. We've been ordered to hold this brickyard."

Donnie explained. "Twenty-eight guys against 400. They

gotta be out of their fucking minds. There is no way we can hold this place with a platoon," exclaimed Ron. "No shit. Fuck that!" added Tiny. I was speechless.

A long silence fell on the four of us. We glanced at one another as though the other person might have a bearable solution to our situation. Silence broke when Donnie asked, "What do y'all reckon the distance is to that there island over there?" He scanned his gaze across the Đồng Nai, referring to the southernmost and largest of two islands in the middle of the river.

Normally, the islands were off limits and not within our tactical area of responsibility. Nevertheless, early one evening several months earlier one of our whalers developed engine trouble, forcing our platoon to make landfall on the smaller island. Our sweep through unfamiliar territory brought us to a small village, Cù Lao Ba Xê, a leper colony.

Residents of this spooky place were not pleased with our presence. Their political sympathies, unknown.

"Bog, how many guys in your squad can't swim?" Donnie asked. I replied, "I don't know. I never gave it a thought until now. The current is pretty strong and could possibly carry us completely away from it.

Current changes direction all the time. I figure it's a good 300 yards, maybe less. Doesn't really matter, it's better than dying here."

"Okay, here's what we're gonna do," Donnie continued. "Find out how many guys can swim and pair them up with those who can't. We'll set up all our claymores in one continuous line strung out 25 meters in front of us. Forget the trip flares, we already know they are comin.' Besides, we ain't got the time. With this moon we should be able to see them from a 100 yards out."

He continued in this vein to map a first-rate defensive strategy.

"Depending on what set of claymores they come upon first,

it will be me, Ron or Tiny that will blow them up. Then, we'll hit the rest of the claymores as needed and illuminate the area with pop-up flares after we engage. Get your machine gun crews set up in the middle of your squads. When the barrels overheat, change 'em, if you got time. If not, get your 60 crew to the river and set up a skirmish line there. If both barrels flame out toss the machine gun and the extra barrel into the nook (Vietnamese term for water) if we have to swim our way out of here."

And not to neglect the hardware.

"Tell your M-79 boys to load up with canister rounds (shotgun type 40 mm rounds containing large pellets), no HEs (high explosive 40 mm grenade rounds) because this is going to be close contact. When it looks like we can do no more here, I'll give the word and every man will take what he can carry and we'll pull back to the river and make a stand there."

"Bog, I figure Ron, Tiny and me are going to catch most of the shit. I'll need your boys Lewin and Bish with the 60 with me. When their barrels get too hot, I'll send them and a few boys back to the river bank. You'll have to set up a skirmish line there to provide cover fire while the rest of us fall back to the water. Have half of your squad fill in with the rest of us while you and the other half cover our left flank so Charlie don't out flank us from the north."

And touching on the possibility of being totally overrun:

"If I am wrong, well, y'all know what to do. Again, make sure that your swimmers are paired up with those who can't. We'll give the Zips the best we can throw at 'em while we can. We, that is, me, Tiny, and Ron will stay back with the 60s we have left. Bog, you're the California boy, you'll get these boys into the water and get them over to that fuckin' island. Carry what you can. Don't leave anything for the VC and toss everything into the nook. Me, Tiny, and Ron will jump in after we are sure everyone is in the water, then we'll all hopefully meet up on the island. With any luck we'll get out in one piece. I'm with y'all, there ain't no way we can make a stand here and come out of it alive. Now, if y'all have a better idea let's hear it."

Nothing but silence and stares followed. Donnie had it all figured, and he was right.

"All right. Good luck to y'all. If anything changes I'll let y'all know," he said as we departed for our respective squads.

This was it. I just knew this was the last day of my life.

Just a short distance from my squad my mind raced, my hearing was muffled and it seemed that my entire being was gripped in some kind of indescribable trance. I was blessed with the gift of a very powerful memory of times, events and places in my life. The memory of this event is etched more deeply than any other.

No clear recollection of precisely what I said to my squad. I do know I positioned myself with my back to the moon, revealing only the lines and shadows of my face, and that I presented instructions in a matter-of-fact, rapid-fire tone. Those all too familiar symptoms I experienced after a firefight started to emerge. My heart started to pound. Hands and body wanted to shudder. Instead of hunger pains, nausea.

If I didn't get this over with soon, my voice will start to tremble. Telegraphing any of these indicators would exacerbate our situation and add my fears to theirs. Our predicament was much larger than me. I was responsible for the life and limb of seven other guys. I managed to put on an act but feared the act would fail dismally had it been in the harsh light of daylight.

I couldn't even bear to look into the shadows of their eyes that evening. How could I even think that I could look directly into their eyes in daylight?

In very short order the entire platoon was in place and spread out thinly in a straight line spanning the distance of a football field or more, in the low-lying grass in front of the brickyard. The Đồng Nai flowed about a hundred yards to our rear. Lewin and

Bish with the M-60, along with Bias and Golansky, went to the skirmish line with the rest of the platoon. I assigned Ward and Gomer to the northernmost end of the line, facing east. Main with the radio was next to me, about 35 yards west of Ward and Gomer with Peanuts off to my left about 25 yards from the river.

All of us faced north. Three of us protected the left flank of the platoon.

All we could do now was wait. Time dragged. I experienced sporadic waves of chills and tremors, nausea, the pounding of my heart and dryness in my throat, the likes of which I had never known before or since.

Between bouts the tremors ceased. Chills and nausea faded and the pounding toned down. Being in that place and time had to be preordained. Maybe as some form of retribution. Punishment for all of those wrongdoings for which I was responsible years prior. Purgatory. An existence in limbo. The purest form of agony. No thoughts about home, Lorraine or any flashes of my entire life found their way into my mind. Just the anticipation of not knowing whether I would live or die.

I wanted this, whatever this was, to be done and over with.

With the moon at its brightest and the jungle at its stillest, there they were. Hundreds of them, about a 100 yards out and off to my right moving in a southwesterly direction directly towards us. It looked like more than a battalion.

They were like ants all over the place. As far as I could tell they moved in a southerly direction which suggested that they were headed south, towards the Buông. There didn't appear to be any movement to my immediate left, or towards Peanuts near the Đồng Nai.

It looked like no imminent threat from the north. I figured if the main force made contact with the platoon I would move Peanuts up to the skirmish line with Ward and Gomer. Main and I would remain on the left flank. Mixed feelings emerged as I am sure they also did with Main. We should be with the rest of the platoon instead of guarding the flank when the rest of the platoon was sure to catch hell.

Hell never came. Inexplicably, the entire force abruptly turned south. Watching them slowly move away from us I stayed transfixed on their rear guard as he faded into the darkness. Not a shot was fired. Not by happenstance, not by fear nor stupidity. I attributed it to the platoon's discipline.

Euphoric calm slowly engulfed me as the tightness in my stomach slackened and the pounding of my heart subsided. Like other times, it didn't last long. The reality of what had happened set in. Mild, brief episodes of full body tremors accompanied with that familiar icy chill galloped through my system.

I spent the rest of the evening and all of the following morning impervious to any thought of closing my eyes, and I crushed that insatiable hunger pang by consuming every C-ration I had. This was among the most terrifying experiences I encountered during my time in the bush. Our platoon had been lucky.

Again.

720ᵗʰ MP Battalion Photo: Brick factory-facing east-Dong Nai River directly behind it-west.

46

"Jesus Christ, knock the son-of-a-bitch out or shoot the Bastard."

Late one evening nearing the end of March we set up in a swampy area near the heel of the Boot at the confluence of the Buông and Đồng Nai. Stillness was suddenly broken by constant screams of, "Help me! Get me out of here!" followed by the sounds of a physical confrontation involving several men. Somebody in 3rd Squad fifty yards away. Only for an instant, the entire platoon believed that 3rd Squad had been infiltrated by the VC and was engaged in some kind of hand-to-hand combat.

However, that notion was quickly dashed when we heard the distinct sounds of Donnie and others trying to restrain one of our own while also trying to squelch the repeated screams that could be heard for a mile or more. Seconds later speculation ceased when somebody in 3rd Squad grabbed the radio and requested a dust-off. Donnie and those assisting him had their hands full as the muffled screams persisted, non-stop.

Not only was the platoon set on edge I thought, "Jesus Christ, knock the son-of-a-bitch out or shoot the bastard." Every Viet Cong within a square mile or more could hear it and I just knew they had to have our location dialed in on their tactical maps to drop mortars down on us any minute now.

Within minutes a chopper circled our location and slowly descended, hovering several feet above the Đồng Nai while a hunter-killer team comprised of a Huey gunship and a Cobra gunship circled above for security. The sounds of the chopper blades drowned out the man's screams as four of our guys carried him face up by his appendages and threw the poor bastard into the open bay of the helicopter.

As the chopper rose I wondered what this place was doing to us. A man breaks down and I think of shooting him. Clearly, all of us were changing in ways we wouldn't have even dreamed of before we came here. Fortunately, for us there were no encounters with the VC or their dreaded mortars for the remainder of that night, or the following morning.

At daybreak we learned that it was our medic who made the noise. It was his second mission with our platoon. He was a soft spoken, likeable black guy. Some of the guys remarked that during his time with us he told them he didn't believe in carrying any kind of firearm. Instead, he preferred carrying a kabar knife should the situation require it.

Being unarmed was not uncommon among the medics who accompanied us. Many were conscientious objectors. Their conviction was to save lives, not take them. On this mission, his last, our medic was toting an M-16 and several grenades. We never did find out what happened to him.

About the first week in April, battalion headquarters determined it was necessary to conduct a thorough three-day sweep of just about our entire 22 square mile Tactical Area of Responsibility. All three ambush and reconnaissance platoons and all of the guys assigned to the PBR and Whaler Platoon were to spearhead this sweep, with the assistance of several Hunter-Killer helicopter gunship teams from the 25th Division circling above us.

In addition, planners of the operation decided that all the "Road Hogs" assigned to A and C Companies would assist us during this sojourn into the jungles, swamps and muck. (Road Hog is a term I came up with to describe any MP assigned to a motorized vehicle). The Military Police Corps was primarily responsible for the physical security of facilities. The Corps also provided motorized town patrols in WW II-era jeeps, and vehicular convoy escort duty in heavily armed jeeps, Chrysler powered V-100 light armored tanks, and track-powered armored personnel carriers (APC) on all the highways and dirt roads in South Vietnam.

For most of the boys assigned to A and C companies this meant no spit-shined boots, no polished helmets, no clean water showers, and no warm dry beds to sleep in for three days and nights. Just hump and hump-wade in mud, streams, swamps and jungle.

Authorized use of motorized, heavily armed track vehicles, gun jeeps and the V-100s was limited as they could only penetrate a very few dry areas within our TAOR.

Ultimately, success or failure rested with us, the Mud Hogs of B Company. A couple of abandoned VC campsites were discovered in the operation, and several booby traps destroyed over the course of those three days.

18ᵗʰ MP Brigade photo: L-R: Chaplin Major Cunningham, Ed Lewin, Author.

18ᵗʰ MP Brigade Photo: March 1970 Worship Services, An Hoa Hung Village L-R: Major Cunningham, SGT Ron Snider, SP/4 Robert "Crazy" Marich, SSG Donnie Thomas, SP/4 Ed "Shakey" Marley, Unk Medic, PFC Jerry Globis, Unk Medic, PFC Markert, SP/4 Greg Thompson.

18th MP Brigade photo: L-R: Unk Medic, SGT Ron Snider, PFC Jerry Globis, SP/4 Bruce Zirk, SP/4 Ed "Shakey" Marley, SP/4 Jared Kelley.

18th MP Brigade photo: L-R: SSG Donnie Thomas, Major Cunningham.

18th MP Brigade photo: Buddhist Pagoda, L-R: SP/4 Rich Bias, PFC Markert, SP/4 Ed Lewin, Author, Chaplin Cunningham standing.

L-R: SP/4 Jon "Rookie" Purvis, SP/4 Carlos "Chuck" Lozano.

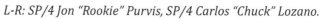

Battalion Sweep L-R: Unk, SP/4 Ed 'Easy' Aldrich, 'Doc' Unidentified Medic assigned to the 1st Platoon.

Battalion Sweep: L-R: SP/4 Ed Lewin, SP/4 Doug Bischoff.

18th MP Brigade Photo: Battalion Sweep: VC underground weapons & ammo storage bunker discovered by 1st platoon. L-R: SGT Angelo Torres, unk.

47
Rear Echelon Nonsense

After six to nine days in the field the platoon spent three days off for much needed rest and recuperation, or so one would think.

Nothing could be further from the truth. Rear echelon nonsensical chores, "details" in Army parlance, usually awaited us by order of the senior NCOs responsible for the maintenance of our company area. Details included picking up cigarette butts, litter, pulling weeds, raking the sun-baked dirt around our hooches, and of course everybody's favorite, shit burning.

As supervisors, we understood the misery our people were subjected to out in the field and made every effort to ensure that those three days inside the wire were devoid of any of the extra-curricular nonsense, whenever possible. Employing my skills of appropriating luxury items for the senior NCOs helped to relieve much of the problem.

My acquisition of a regulation pool table and an elaborate stereo system for the Company NCO lounge helped a lot, along with some very hard-to-come-by cases of Jack Daniels Whiskey among other items often eliminated the problem. Avoiding obstacles was a challenge, keeping the men restricted to the company area by order of First Sergeant Collins, with the City of Saigon only 25 miles away, was almost insurmountable.

Forging passes (allegedly signed by our captain), and

maintaining a continuous flow of luxuries to mollify our upper ranks, it enabled lowly sergeants like me to sustain a buffer between us and them. REMFs rapport was central to success. REMF as in Rear Echelon Mother-Fuckers. My skills in misappropriating military vehicles from other units, replacing their stenciled unit markings with our own designations, became second nature.

Recently acquired jeeps and trucks were presented as gifts to the more hardened REMF senior NCOS. Had I been caught in the act, court-martial would have followed, stripped of rank and sentenced to the very same insane asylum I left months earlier, Long Binh Jail. But to whom did I owe my loyalty? The Army? The system?

There could only be one answer.

It was with these former band of strangers who were now my brothers. I would bear any burden in their behalf, just as they had done for me on countless occasions out in the bush when I needed them the most.

So, what did the boys do during most of those three days of rest and recuperation? Not surprisingly, some of them were astonishingly adept in drinking alcohol. Those that smoked dope did so out of sight and — literally — out of mind. Authorized and unauthorized trips into Saigon or nearby Biên Hòa hosted gatherings of grossly intoxicated wild men sharing the company of local female talent.

Bar brawls followed by narrow escapes from local Vietnamese military police (Quan Kahns) were common. Sergeant First Class Alley was the typical 1960s Boys Vice-Principal of a typical American high school. He was always looking for anything or anybody out of place or ill-mannered that would reflect poorly on the standards of decorum of the United States Army.

He was just doing his job to maintain order and discipline. Brawls culminating in serious injuries sustained by members of other military police units, and nearby Signal Corps units, for which our boys might reasonably take the blame, were fairly common. Incidents involving throwing beer cans and sandbags at occupied motorized vehicles were among the more atypical pursuits. Lewin, Bischoff, Bias and Crazy were the usual suspects.

Breaking doors and cots and the mysterious disappearance of staff jeeps punctuated whatever we had that might fit the term, "leisure time." The boys worked hard and played hard. But there were consequences. Our escapades landed us — Donnie, Ron, Tiny and me — collectively and individually straight in the office of First Sergeant Collins who demanded an explanation. With enough experience, and there was no shortage of that, comes proficient deceit, a skill set not uncommon among the four of us.

We became exceptionally good at deflecting these issues as generally questionable. Sterner measures could also be applied, if necessary.

Three days out of the field were rarely used for the intended R&R. I generally spent the day with Donnie, Tiny, Ron or Pazmino cleaning up what messes our boys might have created, or preparing for the next 6-9 day mission. My nights were spent at the Battalion NCO Club where I sat in a corner by myself listening to some Asian band attempting to sing American songs without a pronounced accent, while I slammed down numerous whiskeys.

I looked forward to these times of solitude, in a loud and crowded smoke-filled drunken den of homesick souls. Mostly a blur as I look back on it, but a welcome place for some thinking in-depth under the influence of an alcohol infused state of mind. Perhaps also, it was a good place to feel sorry for myself.

Down time for all of us usually focused on finding release in Army-sponsored saloons, inside our own secured area. So it was when boys from the 2nd Platoon went into the Signal Corps' Enlisted Men's Club.

An exchange of words escalated into a massive bar brawl culminating in numerous injuries, including a lieutenant who sustained a broken jaw. Our platoon was out in the field at the time and could not be blamed. First Sergeant Collins immediately put the establishment off-limits to B Company.

Returning from the field two days later our boys decided they were exempt from the order. Not many drinks later another bar brawl erupted. Scores of Military Police Patrol were mobilized to bring back the peace, and First Sergeant Collins had to bail out some of us from custody.

Reporting to Collins in his office, Donnie was castigated for "Not controlling the errant behavior of the snuffies in the 3rd Platoon." Tiny, Snider and I patiently waited nearby, listening to the all-too-familiar screams of a very unhappy senior NCO. The meeting ended with Top shouting, "And anymore horseshit from your snuffies, I will personally start busting E-4s to E-3s and your PFCs to E-2s." When Donnie came out of the office Tiny said, "Guess Top's pretty pissed, Donnie."

"Yea, can't you tell? I ain't got no ass left," Donnie replied. "Get all the boys together. We gotta get' em to lay low for a while."

Quickly rounding up our people, Donnie repeated what Top had said. A brief silence. Then a flurry of grumbles. "What are we supposed to do? Hang out in our own lounge? No entertainment from any live bands? And what about all the NCOs? You guys have your own clubs with live entertainment. What about us?"

On it went, and we couldn't blame them. When the rumble waned, Donnie chimed in, "Okay, Okay. Standby while I consult with your squad leaders." Turning our backs to the crowd, Donnie said, "Can't blame em. There ain't nothin' for them to do here in the Company area except maybe get put on some bullshit details. Let's take 'em over to the NCO Club. Give 'em some of our shirts with stripes to get 'em in. We'll be in there makin' sure they behave themselves."

Unanimously approved.

Tiny handed Bischoff and Lewin a couple of his striped-for sergeant shirts. Snider gave five of his shirts to Donnie, and I added my surplus of shirts to the pile. A small overlooked detail was that all the shirts bore our name tags above the right front pocket.

After dark, we headed to the NCO Club making sure no two shirts with the same name filed past the sergeant at the door monitoring entry at the same time. The ruse worked.

The bartender was alert, and when Donnie went up to order drinks, asked, "Y'all related here?" Quick-witted, Donnie responded, "Ah. No. Not all of us. This here is my cousin. He's from the 557th MP Company. And that boy over there is just another Thomas from A Company. We are not related. Small world ain't it?" The bartender shook his head, "Yea. Recon' so."
"That was a close one. Better make sure just us sergeants go up to get the drinks," Donnie said when he returned to our table.

After several rounds of drinks watching the Philippine band on stage, somebody asked, "Hey Marich. You as good on those drums as he is?" "I'm better," Marich shouted back. "Bullshit. Go on up there and show us," someone else hollered. Before any of us could react, Marich stormed on stage and changed places with the band's drummer.

Marich was right. He was better and the crowd roared, demanding encores.

During a trip for refills, the Vietnamese girl bartender looked at my name tag and said, "Bogie-san, you have brother of you here too? I see him before." Vietnamese never missed much. "Yes, brother me." I responded quickly.

Marich's performance whipped the assembly into a frenzy.

The band's drummer was visibly impatient. Time to leave before we all got busted for creating yet another disturbance. Convinced a problem was brewing, Donnie, Tiny, Snider and I downed our drinks and herded our intoxicated Bushwhackers to an orderly exit off the premises. Donnie turned to gesture to Marich that the show was over.

No disturbance. No facing the wrath of First Sergeant Collins.

Mid-March brought changes. Donnie was near the end of his tour as was Ron. Their departure would change the whole dynamic of our platoon. Earlier in the month, Jared Kelley, Carlos Lozano, Shakey, Bruce Zirk, Rich Radcliff, and Glen Barmann were transferred to the PBR platoon.

A significant loss of some highly experienced people, which meant new and inexperienced replacements in-bound to fill the void. Losing Donnie and Ron also meant new sergeants and new headaches. During the last week of their tours, the platoon threw a three day drunken "Returning to the World party" in their honor. For Donnie and Ron, the war was over and everybody was happy for them, but we were sad to see them go. I would miss them terribly.

I soon found myself working closely with Tiny and Pazmino. Paz was a kind of utility sergeant assigned to anyone and everything that required a master in the art of infantry ambush tactics. At any given time, as the need arose, the Lifers sent him to one of the three platoons. Loss of Donnie and Ron required him to be permanently assigned as our platoon sergeant, which was very reassuring.

As for our two new sergeants, all I remember is that one of them was a black Staff Sergeant transferred from a line Military Police Company, and the other was a white Buck Sergeant from the same unit. Both were decent guys, and just like the rest of us on our first mission, in a state of shock after being placed in such a hostile and totally unfamiliar working environment.

Tiny and I were the only two seasoned squad leaders Paz could rely on to help him hold the platoon together. With it came new responsibilities. Just like those before us we had to ensure that anything we knew about fulfilling our missions had to be passed on to these babes in the woods. Self-preservation and the fate of the platoon demanded it. No time for rank, personalities or egos to interfere with the functionality of our machine, the 3rd Platoon. And just like parts of any well-oiled machine, every man's life depended on the actions and reactions of the next man.

Names recede with time, but I remember SP/4 Mike Ambrose who was assigned to my squad. Mike hailed from San Francisco and a regular military policeman earlier in his tour, near Lai Khê, attached to the 1st Infantry Division which had its headquarters in Lai Khê and which was responsible territory directly to the west of our TAOR, and on the opposite side of the Đồng Nai. Mike, or Ambi, as we called him adapted quickly to his new environment and required little supervision on my part.

All the guys in my squad took him under their wing and did the work for me. I could concentrate working with Tiny in training the new sergeants along with all of the new replacements. These people, just like me when I arrived, were vulnerable and totally ignorant of all the unforeseen hazards around them. The hard and cold facts were that new people potentially posed a danger not only to themselves but to the entire platoon. That's how I viewed it when I arrived.

It was no secret among those who served in the field in Vietnam, that if you "bought the farm" it would more than likely happen during these first three months of a tour.

Conversely, the final three months could be just as hazardous when many of us acquired an affinity for being too cautious, often questioning the tried and proven techniques that worked in the days and months preceding.

Fate is the unknown factor and cannot be discounted. However, in the final analysis it didn't matter why, where or when your number was up, you had no control over it anyway. Our job was to minimize casualty numbers associated with the "how" of it. The kill cause factor.

I think we did just that.

In early April I was now quite comfortable with my abilities as a squad leader, along with all things associated with living and surviving in the muck. I was confident in the decisions I made and believed that I could confront any challenge that came my way. As for suspicions some had about me early on, they had long been dismissed as along with my thoughts of having one of them slice my throat or having a grenade tossed at me.

I evolved into an integral part of a precision machine. Stresses remained, of course. The swamp, the jungle, the leeches and all that lived in it hadn't changed, and neither had the fear. During our three day, break Ed Lewin came strolling in our hooch with a brown Labrador puppy and asked if we could keep the dog as our mascot.

Knowing that the Lifers would probably object, I told Ed to keep the animal out of sight and have one of the mama-sans take care of it while we were out in the field and never gave it a second thought. Besides it was a morale booster for the platoon and who was I to say no? The dog was appropriately named Chocolate.

ॐ

March 1970, 3 day "Returning to the World Party" L-R: SP/4 Doug 'Bish Bischoff, SGT Ron Snider, SP/4 Ed Lewin, SSG Donnie Thomas.

SP/4 Ed Lewin & Mascot 'Chocolate'.

48

"You got two more days in the bush so get your shit in order."

Most of our six day missions allowed us to return to Long Binh Post after the fourth night for two hot meals, a much needed shower, and to replenish our supplies for the remaining two nights. Having just returned from four days in the field and still savoring a hot meal of some form of mystery meat in the mess hall, one of the company clerks directed me to report to First Sergeant Collins in his office, immediately. Now, what could this mean? It was much too soon for any of the boys to have caused a problem as they were still up to their chests in dried mud enjoying the same gourmet delicacy I was.

When I rose from my chair, I broke up the ongoing conversations by shouting, "All right! Is there anything I should know about before I go to see Top? Anything I should be forewarned about so I can prepare myself for the usual bullshit? I don't usually get called into his office unless somebody fucked up!"

Nothing but stares and silence.

I glanced around me and said, "All right!" and left the mess hall headed back to the company area. On the way, I reasoned that one of our gang must have done something really stupid. My mind raced to determine what kind of a smoke and mirrors front

I could put on the First Sergeant to buy time in an effort to find out who did what, to help me come up with a solution to whatever this problem was.

On each and every occasion these boys pulled off any chicanery we squad leaders were always informed ahead of time. This time it was different and I would have to think fast. I entered First Sergeant Collins office and approached the front of his paper strewn desk and asked, "You called for me, Top?" To which he stated as he rose from his chair glancing at me from head to toe, "Yea Bog I did. Jesus Christ, you smell like shit!" To which I blurted out, "Awful damn sorry about that Top. We spent last night at Duck Farm laying in duck shit!"

"All right, I'll make this quick so you can get the fuck out of here and take a damn shower. I'm moving you to PBRs. You'll report to Sergeant First Class Henry on completion of this mission. I got problems with the 1st Watch Sergeant, Sergeant Torres. His snuffies are about to kill him. You will replace him and he'll take over your squad. Sergeant Torres has infantry experience and served his first tour over here with a light infantry unit. He should fit in the bush better than he does on boats. You got two more days in the bush so get your shit in order."

"Do I have any say in this?" I snapped as he eased himself back into a chair. He barked back, "No, God damn it! I need your young ass to smooth this shit storm brewing out there on the water."

My mind was spinning and I was not at all warming to the new assignment. Not a good fit for me. At least, not at this particular point in time. "You realize this leaves Paz and 3rd Platoon with only one experienced sergeant out there, that being Tiny? Why me? Why not replace this Torres with one of the sergeants in 1st or 2nd Platoon?" I interjected.

As he rose again from his chair, I realized I had struck a raw nerve. The signal was clearly written all over the grimace and well-worn creases on his face.

While slowly nodding his head up and down, he calmly said, "I see. You, Specialist 5 Bogison, appear to know what's best for your platoon and for that matter all of B Company. All knowing are you? Did it ever occur to you that there are higher priorities already set in motion for this war beyond your concerns about personnel changes for 3rd Platoon? Look, God damn it! I appreciate the loyalty you have for your snuffies out there and I do find the lines of shit you come up with when these boys fuck up amusing right along with all the ill-gotten hard-to-get-shit you manage to scrounge up to bribe all of my senior NCOs."

He paused for a moment, then:

"But right now, the last thing I need is a bunch of wild snuffies entertaining the thought of fucking up one of my hardnosed sergeants. Don't have the time for such shit. You *will* report to Sergeant First Class Henry immediately upon your return from the field and you *will* get the heads of all those water snuffies screwed on right."

With no obvious sarcasm, he continued: "Believe it or not, I'm doing you a favor. In the coming days we are all going to be in for some changes. Now get the fuck out of here and do what you're ordered to do."

With a short sigh, and an affirmative nod, I replied, "Yes, sir." And as I turned to leave, First Sergeant Collins said, "Bog you know, the monsoon season is coming and you won't have to lay in that duck shit anymore either, now will you?" He was right. His view of the landscape was far and away more revealing than my worms-eye-view trying to make sense of what we were supposed to accomplish in this war.

As I passed over the threshold of the door to his office I stopped, turned and said, "You're right, Top. Thanks."

After leaving the office I spotted Paz and Tiny returning from the mess hall and advised them of my change in assignment. It was no surprise to Paz as Top had informed him of the possibility of my transfer days earlier. Tiny was none too pleased. Neither would I have been had positions been reversed. Now, Tiny would be the only remnant of stability the boys could turn to during this crucial leadership transition. I decided it would be best to advise my squad of the situation just before the deuce-and-a-half arrived to transport us to French Fort later that evening.

It was not to be.

When I entered my hooch I was loudly queried by no less than a dozen guys as to the whys and wherefores of my sudden transfer out of the platoon. I should have expected it, as nothing is ever kept secret for very long in this environment. After providing the most plausible explanation I could, I saw in their eyes that this was just another disappointing change in the contorted world in which we all found ourselves.

The well-oiled machine was evolving into one requiring too many replacement parts. Many years later, I realized that the very manner in which the Vietnam War was prosecuted produced these kinds of situations. During the first few years of our involvement in the war entire divisions, brigades, and battalions trained as units, transported to Vietnam and fought as units then returned home as units.

By 1969, those units and the dynamics associated with them were long gone. Now, it was a never-ending constant trickle of new people arriving in-country while droves of seasoned veterans returned home. The entire US military was embracing what President Nixon and his administration coined as the Vietnamization Program.

The term "Vietnamization" was a transitional program intended to phase out direct participation of all US military forces in combat operations, and passing the responsibility to the South Vietnamese military.

It was a dismal failure.

Between the guilt I felt swirling in my head about leaving the platoon and the anxiety of having to adapt to an entirely new environment on boats, the last two nights spent in the bush were perfect reminders of what I would never miss.

A welcome breeze cooled us as we finished setting up our ambush alongside the Đồng Nai River bank near French Fort. As I lay down on my filthy camouflaged blanket carefully spread out on the damp warm ground and closed my eyes, I was reminded of warm, autumn Santa Ana breezes swirling off shore, my surfboard nearby, back home at the Ventura County Line Beach.

Ebb and flow of the Đồng Nai lapping against the shoreline triggered all things good about getting out of this place alive. Like all good things, a rush of contentment did not last long. The cool breeze turned into gusts of wind accompanied by a violent downpour leaving everybody scrambling for their ponchos. By the time I got into my rubberized personal tent, I was soaked from head to toe. It didn't really matter because within a few minutes I was sitting in water a little less than a foot deep as the deluge continued for the next hour. A precursor to the coming monsoon season.

I had experienced a couple of these Asian spectacles back in December, and learned that a calm accompanied by a humid stillness followed immediately after the squalls, bringing with it clouds of mosquitoes. This time was no different, and just as miserable.

My last night in the bush was spent several hundred yards south of French Fort, not far from the spooky place where Gufford, Cortez and I were superficially wounded weeks earlier. The place was littered with empty C-ration cans unearthed from their burial sites by the downpour the evening prior. Every time we consumed C- rations in the field we immediately buried the tins and cartons a foot or so into the ground.

The reason had nothing to do with environmentalism, but to prevent the Viet Cong from repurposing the metal for shrapnel, and as integral lethal parts in the construction of booby traps.

Vietnamese were extremely adept at making something out of nothing, and we were famous for making it all too easy for them by giving them our trash. Evidently, the platoon that buried their stuff had not gone deep enough, or the conditions of this particular piece of ground were unsuited for anything to remain buried for very long, however deep the hole. I should have known that all this litter would entice creatures indigenous to the area.

It did not occur to me at the time.

Just like the Vietnamese, local insects, land craps, and all things reptilian were excellent rummagers. Within several hours of our arrival the place crawled with rats, the size of a cat. One of the nasty critters found comfort in sinking its teeth into the upper part of the canvas covered boot I wore. Both jaws clamped down just above the outer portion of my right ankle and with the determined audacity of a badger, pulled and tugged as if I were some sort of plaything.

Impulsively, I grabbed the .45 pistol from my shoulder holster and extended my right arm to point the weapon within inches of what I estimated to be the head of the rodent. Just as instinctively, I withdrew my pistol realizing that a shot could easily result in the loss of my toes or foot. More importantly, the shot would pinpoint our immediate location for any VC in the area. Not a good situation.

During the milliseconds of thought, I simply resorted to smashing the top of the beast's head with the barrel of my .45, and got the desired result: immediate release of fangs accompanied with a low pitched grunt and the sound of the thing scurrying into the darkness.

And that adventure anchors the end of my days as an infantryman.

720TH MP Battalion Photo: Author, at Observation Post 4.

49

Boats & the 458th Transportation Company

Returning from the field I had no sooner dropped my gear in the billet I shared with my platoon, when the company clerk directed me to report to First Sergeant Collins.

Collins stood in the doorway of his office, waiting for me and pointing at a nearby jeep, "Sergeant Bogison, take my jeep and go to the docks next to the Harbor Master's Tower. Sergeant Henry is waiting there for you. He wants to introduce you to the 458th Transportation Company lieutenant you will be working with on the boat barge. You know where the Harbor Master is don't you? It's that tall tower between the French Pier and Cogido Bridge."

My head was spinning. Harbor Master, what is that? Cogido Bridge, where is that? Boat barge? The 458th Transportation Company, what does that mean?

He explained that 458th personnel manned the Harbor Master Tower round-the-clock to monitor and regulate all military and civilian watercraft traveling on the Đồng Nai River. Cogido Bridge (pronounced Cojeedo) spanned the entire width of the Đồng Nai allowing vehicular traffic commuting between Saigon and Biên Hòa. The land route was a major paved thoroughfare known as Highway 1.

Not knowing that a name was attached to the bridge we passed under every time we were transported by whalers from the French Pier to our ambush sites was interesting.

As for the boat barge, I was told that all of the PBR*s* and Boston Whalers were docked next to an old ammunition barge anchored in the middle of the river about half a mile south of Cogido Bridge. All of us had seen this red wooden hut on top of the large steel barge, surrounded by moored PBRs and Boston whalers.

I was a master now in the art of road weaving and dodging people and machines at ridiculously unsafe speeds I found Sergeant First Class Henry — with a couple of people I did not recognize — on the French Pier, not at the Harbor Master Tower further down the dirt road as I had been told. I had already been exposed to Henry's incompetence during his one and only ambush mission as our platoon sergeant back in January.

Sergeant Henry was a typical lifer, nearing 40 years of age. He was not exceptionally smart, and had a penchant for jokingly acknowledging mistakes and miscalculations (and there were many) with, "I have to kick myself in the ass for that!" accompanied by deftly lifting his foot to negotiate a slight twist inward, then smartly snap the toe directly up and into his ass.

He was exceptionally proficient at it and I saw him perform this remarkable feat many times in the days to come. It brought resonance to the phrase, "A swift kick in the ass." Back in January, I remember watching the frustration Donnie had trying to teach Henry how to read a map. The man was a danger to himself and to all those around him. I was glad not to have seen him again. And here he was again.

Regardless, I was always open to giving a person the benefit of doubts I harbored. Somewhere in the process of growing up I acquired the notion, in spite of my youthful 21 years, to recognize that Sergeant Henry's incompetence as a platoon leader in the bush was, in all probability, due to his age. The daily routine of eating, sleeping, and moving great distances in these swamps and jungles was physically and mentally exhausting.

It couldn't have been very easy for a man twice the age of most of us to adapt to this environment. Particularly for someone who had not served the last 20 years of his life in the Army as an Infantry Non-Com. I approached the group with memories of Henry in the bush behind me, now eager to learn what new challenges lay ahead.

To my surprise, Henry shouted out with a warm greeting, "Bogie how's it going?" and reached out to shake my hand. For the lieutenant and the staff sergeant standing there with him it had to appear as though we had known each other for years. A glance at the 1st lieutenant made me immediately snap to attention. "Sir, Specialist 5 Bogison reporting as ordered, sir!" to which he introduced himself as Lieutenant Steinberg, and the Staff Sergeant with him as Jack Canada.

I knew better than to stand at attention saluting an officer outside the wire because doing so was an open invitation for any VC sniper in the vicinity to take advantage of killing an American officer. Trying to explain this fact seemed pointless as it was apparent that he had all the qualities associated with rear echelon personnel. Steinberg was about my age, perhaps a year older with the appearance of a preppie fresh out of college. Nothing about him suggested he was going to make the Army his career.

Canada was a lifer with no less than 20 years under his belt much like Henry. Canada was carrying a six shot .38 revolver secured in a well-worn shoulder holster he was sporting. I was armed with my standard .45 automatic pistol with two seven-round clips concealed under my camouflaged shirt, along with an M-16 rifle and a bandoleer containing five twenty-round magazines draped over my right shoulder.

Steinberg was not armed but his uniform, boots and personal grooming were impeccable. A clear sign that I was in for a drastic change, and not a good one.

It seemed that every time I got a new challenge or a new assignment I would be constantly asking myself, how in the hell did I get myself here? This situation was no different but I was determined to adapt when it suited my purposes, and nothing more. I had already demonstrated to myself and others that I was proficient at saying one thing while doing another. I reasoned that in this hostile environment the ends justify the means, and I stood by that principle in just about every decision I made.

Little did I know at the time that the new assignment would present challenges far beyond my powers of reasoning. In the days ahead, unforeseen circumstances tested the limits of my sanity, and that some of my decisions would haunt me for the rest of my life.

During the meet and greet session, the distinct and familiar drone of two powerful Detroit diesel engines powering a PBR came into view. As it decelerated to a low hum, I watched the craft gently, expertly pull alongside the pier. The four-man crew, none of whom I had seen before, moored the boat with ropes to T-shaped steel brackets fastened on top of concrete siding. Truck-sized tire fenders hung by ropes from the brackets prevented the craft from making direct contact with cement.

Steinberg directed one of the crew to remain on the pier to guard my jeep while the three of us jumped on the PBR's deck three feet below. I was to be given a tour of the boat barge and introduced to the men I would supervise. This was not my first time as a PBR passenger. Back in January, our platoon had the luxury of traveling on one from our ambush site near Rabbit Ears to the French Pier when the whalers were down for repairs.

These heavily armed, powerful boats could travel upwards of 40 miles per hour in less than 12 inches of water. They were truly a marvel of the time. Two plywood placards fixed on the either side of the coxswain's space identified this PBR as a military police vessel named *Stoned Geni*.

During the ride Henry said that I would be NCOIC (Non-Commissioned Officer-In-Charge) of the combined force of B Company MPs and 458th Transportation Company crews assigned to three PBRs during designated 12-hour watches. He explained that my crews were currently into their 5th day cycle of 10-day deployments on the Day Watch, and that on completion of the remaining five days the crews would switch over watches after a 24-hour break. Day Watch began at 06:00 and ended at 18:00, relieved by the Night Watch, and so on.

My responsibility was threefold:

1. Ensure my crews interdict and investigate suspicious watercraft activity on the Đồng Nai and its myriad tributaries in the 22-square mile boot-shaped TAOR I used to patrol on foot.

2. Provide fire support when authorized by the Tactical Operations Command Center.

3. Exercise the directives strictly within the geographical limits of the three designated zones of responsibility.

Harbor Master Tower was adjacent to the eastern bank of the Đồng Nai. The French Pier was several hundred yards north of the

Tower. (The Đồng Nai River Bridge was more commonly called Cogido Bridge.) South Patrol Area extended from the southern tip of the southernmost two islands to the Buông River, veering east along the contour of the heel and toe of the Boot, then north between B Company's TAOR to the west and the Thais Territory to the east.

Central Patrol Area extended north from the southern tip of the same island to the French Pier. North Patrol Area was the largest of the three, and extended north from the French Pier through Biên Hòa Province and several miles beyond.

Approaching the Boat Barge, I was intrigued with the PBR Operator's boat handling skill. His expertise with two forward throttles in one hand while simultaneously spinning the helm with his other hand made for a smooth transition from high speed down to a crawl. He then juggled the throttles to move the craft sideways to ease the boat against some car and truck tire fenders.

The instant my feet hit the barge, Steinberg and Henry escorted me into the red wooden shack to brief me in detail about my new job. The shack served as office, bunkhouse, radio center, tool shed, weapons locker, and spare parts repository. Below decks, the barge was an ammunition storehouse.

Steinberg was articulate in the Do's and very explicit in the Don'ts. Dos included strict adherence to the mission. There was to be with no deviation. Don'ts are too many to list.

My job was to co-ordinate the 720th Military Police Battalion mission with the unequivocal understanding that 458th personnel and equipment came under his command responsibility. Care, control and use of the PBRs would be determined by the 458th, regardless of rank.

Steinberg emphasized that "under no circumstances were the PBRs to be utilized in the transportation of Ambush and Recon

Platoons to or from their respective ambush sites!" When I asked why, he responded, "Because that is not what they are designed for! These are support craft, nothing more!"

Well, I knew that was bullshit because the Navy transported their elite SEAL Teams on PBRs all the time. I witnessed it on many occasions when we crossed paths on the Đồng Nai. Just a few months earlier, my platoon had been transported on one.

However, this was not the time for debate, so I just took it all in. Not one word from Henry, standing nearby. The message came through that I would be completely on my own with no backing. As for the whalers moored at the north end of the Boat Barge, I was advised that Staff Sergeant Tapper, recently transferred from the 1st Ambush and Recon Platoon, supervised all the personnel assigned to Boston Whaler Operations.

There were six PBRs: *Blue Cheer*, *Karen Ann*, the inelegantly named *458 TC*, *Purple Haze*, *Da Fuzz*, and the aforementioned *Stoned Geni*. All of them were second generation PBRs manufactured as Mark II weighing approximately 9 tons, 32 feet long, and with a beam of 11 1/2 feet, powered by twin 180-horsepower Detroit diesel engines, driving jacuzzi water pump jets.

Skills of the 458th maintenance guys souped-up these Detroit diesels to push our PBRs beyond the manufacturer's prescribed speed. Armament was twin .50 caliber machine guns housed in a small electric-powered turret mounted forward, and another .50 caliber swiveled machine gun aft. The gunnery suite also included either an M-60 machine gun amidships, or a .40mm automatic grenade launcher (we called the "popcorn grinder").

Altogether, the boat was a formidable killing machine.

Structurally comprised entirely of fiberglass, save a layer of 1/4-inch or 1-inch metal plate encasing portions of the operator's compartment, these beasts could easily navigate through as little as a foot of water.

After the indoctrination, Henry grabbed the radio microphone to direct all three of the patrol boats to return to the barge so that I could be introduced to the people I would supervise. In the interim, I wandered toward the north end of the barge to meet Sergeant Tapper and the whaler crews. I had crossed paths with Tapper and 1st Platoon on several occasions in the field. Warm greetings extended from Glenn Barmann, Shakey, Jared Kelley and Ed "Easy" Aldrich, (a recent transfer from 1st Platoon). Aldrich, an Illinois native and jack of all trades had transported my squad to its ambush sites during my last three weeks.

I was introduced to SP/4 Ed Santry, SP/4 Doug Newman (southern California) and SP/4 Bob Cagle, who graduated from Monroe High School in 1966, the same year I graduated from Granada Hills High School, two miles away. I attended several summer school sessions at Monroe High to repeat those revolting geometry courses I failed to pass the first or second time during regular sessions.

When the PBRs docked, more introductions were made. SP/4 Ed "Klinger" Kelleher, SP/4 Denny Taylor (formerly, 2nd Platoon) and SP/4 Swensen of the 458th Transportation Company were assigned to *Karen Ann* patrolling the south sector. SP/4 Ronald Mason, SP/4 Joseph Keene and SP/4 Chuckie Bowen of *458 TC* had the central sector. SP/4 Bruce Zirk, SP/4 Robert Lynn, SP/4 Harry Marineau and SP/4 Gary Rasmussen of 458th crewed *Da Fuzz* patrolling the north sector.

Sergeant Ed York, representing the 458th, was my counterpart. SP/5 Smith had charge of PBR and Boston Whaler maintenance. Zirk and Taylor were the only ones familiar with ambush and reconnaissance operations. Lynn, Kelleher, Marineau,

Mason and Keene were immediately assigned to the PBR Platoon on their arrival in B Company.

Lynn and Kelleher hailed from Michigan, Taylor from Illinois, Keene from Kentucky, Marineau from Missouri and Mason from Texas. 458 boys Rasmussen (Wisconsin), Swensen (Minnesota), Chuckie Bowen (Chicago) and Sergeant York (Hawaii). Another SP/4 with the 458th was "Young Jack" dubbed with the nickname on account of his personality resemblance to Staff Sergeant Jack Canada. 458 guys coined the name and it stuck, much to Young Jack's dismay.

I remember that he had all the attributes associated with an up and coming lifer, which is probably the reason he did not bide well with his peers.

Indoctrination showed me the unfamiliar terminology associated with all things Navy. The PBR operator was called the coxswain, the front of the boat was the bow. Rear was aft, right was starboard and left was port. "Coxswain's Flat" meant the immediate area within the operator's reach. "On Step" indicated the bow was raised sufficiently above the surface of the water to operate in less than 12 inches of water or travelling over 20 miles per hour. "Walking it in" referred to moving the boat sideways.

There was much to learn and no room for mistakes. I was told these killing machines cost $80,000.00 each, without the weaponry and advised that loss of or substantial damage to them by any means other than combat-related would result in severe disciplinary action. In other words, they were not be used for any kind of entertainment.

In addition to this new list of headaches, it was my responsibility to ensure that the men serving under me conducted themselves in accordance with standards set in the "Nine Rules" issued by the

US Military Assistance Command Vietnam (MACV). Nice words, undoubtedly assembled by some "Rainbow Rider" not having to interact with a native population that viewed our presence as an imposition.

NINE RULES

For Personnel of U.S. Military Assistance Command, Vietnam

The Vietnamese have paid a heavy price in suffering for their long fight against the Communists. We military men are in Vietnam now because their government has asked to help its soldiers and people in winning their struggle. The Viet Cong will attempt to turn the Vietnamese people against you. You can defeat them at every turn by the strength, understanding, and generosity you display with the people. Here are nine simple rules:

Remember we are special guests here; we make no demands and seek no special treatment.

Join with the people! Understand their life, use phrases from their language, and honor their customs and laws.

Treat women with politeness and respect.

Make personal friends among the soldiers and common people.

Always give the Vietnamese the right of way.

Be alert to security and ready to react with your military skill.

Don't attract attention by loud, rude, or unusual behavior.

Avoid separating yourself from the people by a display of wealth or privilege.

Above all else you are members of the U.S. military forces on a difficult mission, responsible for all your official and personal actions. Reflect honor upon yourself and the United States of America.

I don't think anybody who served in Vietnam ever thought of themselves as special guests, considered themselves wealthy, or expected any special treatment. Life was cheap and often short for both the Vietnamese and for us. Distrust was rampant on both sides, particularly for us.

It wasn't uncommon for the Village Chief, the Vietnamese barber that cut your hair, the Hooch Maid who polished your boots, or any of the dozens of US-paid Vietnamese service workers performing jobs on firebases throughout the country to be Viet Cong guerillas. The Viet Cong were proficient at infiltrating the inner circles of the US Military, our allies and the rank and file of the South Vietnamese Army.

Among my Don'ts were not to allow any PBR to speed along the shores creating disruptive wakes while the Vietnamese were washing their clothes, dishes or themselves. No speeding near sampans or fishing boats. Transporting civilian or military personnel not assigned to B Company or the 458 was prohibited. Steel pots (helmets) were to be worn at all times and the discharge of any weapon without the express authorization from the Tactical Operations Center was prohibited.

On and on it went.

Anyone could almost believe we were in some kind of goodwill, public relations tour on a popular river back in the United States. Clearly, the priorities were askew. The demands came with great expectations by Steinberg and Henry who expressed their confidence in my ability to maintain the necessary discipline required to fulfill the mission.

Right from the outset, I was not prepared to deliver on all of the requirements as my superiors interpreted them to be. I was determined not to acquiesce to any nonsense that would prevent me from meeting my responsibility of ensuring the safety and welfare of the very people I was entrusted to supervise. It was just too damned easy to get killed out there. I spent the first week on night watch.

There was a tinge of irony in the timing of my transfer.

My right foot was swollen enough to prevent me from slipping all of it into an unlaced boot. Cause of the swelling remained a mystery but in the tropics it didn't require much to get a serious infection from a cut or a bite. Every square inch of the country teemed with bacteria and filth. It might have been my encounter with the rat days prior.

I don't remember. I do remember that it was extremely painful and put me out of commission for anything that required extended walking or standing. My new assignment required neither. Between hitching rides on all three PBRs I spent most of my time on the boat barge recovering, in company with the radio operator monitoring activities transmitted by the ambush and reconnaissance platoons.

My task included transmitting, monitoring, and receiving information exchanges between PBRs, our Harbor Master ("Hotel Mike," in military parlance) radio operator and the Tactical Operations Center. Complex and multifaceted duties. I applied all I could muster to soak up everything related to the maintenance and operations of the boats, their weaponry, and pilotage of the Đồng Nai and Buông Rivers and the sandbars and protruding rock formations that could bring us to grief.

The subject of Sergeant Angelo Torres never came up. I did not query anyone about him or ask about rumored fragging plots. The less I knew, the better.

About my fourth night monitoring the radio, I heard small arms fire south and east of the barge, followed by requests from 3rd Platoon for an artillery fire mission and air support. The familiar voice was Staff Sergeant Laughter. My old platoon was under heavy small arms fire in the same place and at about the same time that Gufford, Peanuts and I got hit by our own artillery weeks earlier. I couldn't believe it was happening again and that I wasn't there with them.

The incident played out only about a mile away from the barge, but deploying our PBRs in support was impossible as their position was too far inland to be of any help. Fireworks lasted for quite some time. Several hunter-killer chopper teams overhead unleashed their mini-guns between volleys of artillery fire. Every minute the fracas continued concerned me. It would be the next day before I could find out what had happened, and the outcome.

That night was the longest I endured during my tour in Vietnam. But early the next morning I was relieved to learn that 3rd Platoon sustained no casualties and successfully thwarted the incursion of a sizable Viet Cong force.

Lucky, again.

My first ten nights on watch were behind me. The swollen foot finally healed. Ten straight shifts and not one visit from Steinberg, Henry or Canada suggested to me that I owned the night. About this time, I was also due for my one and only three day in-country R&R which Tiny, Lewin and I had requested months earlier.

B Company permitted every NCO and enlisted man to spend one three day, three night vacation at a designated R&R center deemed to be in a relatively safe area at or near the South China Sea. Our destination was Vung Tau, a coastal city approximately fifty miles south and east of Long Binh. Eager to hit the road, we threw together some civilian clothes, loaded into a misappropriated jeep I acquired from the nearby 557th MP Company days earlier, and with R&R orders in hand hit the road.

As I drove down Highway 1 from the main gate of Long Binh Post — and before we got too far into the motorized scene of insanity ahead of us — I asked Ed (on my right) and Tiny (seated in the back) if we had everything. We had four or five bottles of Jack Daniels Whiskey, several bottles of Vodka and a couple of cases of Carling Black Label Beer (the only brand available to us at the time). For personal protection we each carried a .45 Automatic Pistol with two, 7-round magazines and one M-16 with two bandoleers containing five, 20-round magazines.

We concluded that we had all things necessary to blow off steam for the next three days and nights, completely pickled in alcohol. After dodging and weaving away from the outlying villages of Biên Hòa, we entered the main highway south to Vung Tau. The road was unfamiliar to all of us. My travels on Vietnamese roads up to this point were limited to parts of Cu Chi, Saigon, Biên Hòa and places in between. There was no need for reckless speeding and dodging now as the amount of traffic had waned considerably. I figured that a leisurely 30 mph to our destination would put us there in 45 minutes to an hour.

50

"Hey Bog. How come we're the only ones on the road?"

Twenty minutes and two beers into our journey dawned the sobering realization that we were travelling on a deserted highway. That was when Tiny asked, "Hey Bog. How come we're the only ones on the road?" He was right, we hadn't seen a single person, vehicle, military or civilian on a route that ran through an old rubber plantation comprised of thousands of neatly lined rows of rubber trees as far as the eye could see in every direction.

Like the road Tiny and I had travelled to Cu Chi weeks earlier for our demolition instruction, this was a perfect place to get ambushed. Highly unusual to see no vehicular traffic as it was a major thoroughfare. Here we were, fine-tuned to understand that in the jungle when silence sets in danger would invariably follow. The same held true for the Road Hogs tasked with escorting convoys, only with a different kind of sensory perception. A road empty of pedestrian or vehicular activity signaled imminent danger.

The Vietnamese would often telegraph their knowledge of impending doom in subtle ways. This was the theme earlier in our narrative regarding the evening at Brick Factory when the laborers abruptly shut down their operation and abandoned the area leaving us to face an advancing enemy superior in numbers. The disappearing act was a subtle sign that suggested something ominous was about to happen.

We also learned that when the Viet Cong set-up booby traps adjacent to paths or roads, they usually left clever tell-tale warning signs for the local population. For instance, an arrangement of three stones or three sticks was often placed within several yards of the device. Our deserted highway was an obvious warning that something evil might lie ahead.

I pushed the accelerator to the floorboard to gain maximum speed on the assumption that the sooner we passed through the rubber plantation the better. However, seconds later just as we neared a top speed of 50 mph, we were all jolted by an explosion under the right rear portion of the jeep.

Desperately struggling with an out-of-control steering wheel while slamming on the brakes with both feet only made the situation worse, as the vehicle careened toward the soft shoulder on the opposite side of the road. For whatever reasoning prevailed at that moment, I released my feet from the brakes and shifted into 3rd gear. To my amazement, the violent behavior of the steering wheel quickly subsided allowing me to regain control. As the jeep decelerated to a complete stop on the shoulder, Tiny jumped out and with a quick examination of the right rear tire said, "Bog, we got a blow out."

We ruled out that a sniper was the cause because what we heard just before "*Mr. Toads Wild Ride*" was clearly not a gunshot. Tiny was right. It was a blow out. Had it been a booby trap or a road mine we would have been obliterated from the blast.

While bantering back and forth as to how and why we

managed to find ourselves here, in the middle of this god-forsaken rubber tree plantation, Ed and Tiny decided to get the tire jack and lug wrench, both of which were generally stowed under the back seat of every US Army Jeep, while I decided to fire up the rear-mounted radio and call the Tactical Operations Center to determine why the highway to Vung Tau was empty of people and traffic.

51

"But before we do anything break out a bottle of that Jack Daniels"

Youth and complacency fueled with alcohol are recipes for disaster and we had it in spades that day. To my astonishment, the radio didn't work. And that wasn't all. There was no portable jack or lug wrench. Our meticulous planning included everything but common sense. In our haste to hit the road it never occurred to us that we might succumb to such a plebeian fate as a flat tire. Too late to think about what we should have done.

After a collective series of blasphemous screams by all, we energetically scoured through every square inch of the jeep in hopes of finding anything that could be made to improvise for a jack and wrench. Luckily, Ed found a pair of ordinary pliers under the front passenger seat, which might work in removing the four lug nuts of the flattened tire. Maybe. We still needed a jack to lift the rear end of the jeep high enough and long enough to remove and replace the flat with the spare.

We were in discussion when Ed said, "You know what, Bogie. You take the pliers and try to get the lug nuts loose. Tiny and I will lift the damn thing while you change the tire. But before we do anything, break out a bottle of that Jack Daniels. If I'm going to be a human car jack or — for that matter, end up MIA or get our asses blown up out here — I want a drink!"

His well-chosen words broke the tension. We broke

into laughter and did just that, having traveled the emotional rollercoaster starting with fear, then anger and ultimately to "Who cares?" all within the span of minutes. We guzzled the entire bottle of Jack and went to work. Removing lug nuts from the wheel of a flat tire with a pair of pliers is no easy task, but I managed to do it. Using the strength of two water buffaloes they managed to lift the jeep high enough and long enough for me to remove the flat and replace it with the spare in record time.

Problem solved.

We made it the rest of the way to Vung Tau without incident and never did see a living thing on or off that highway. I drove right past the military police checkpoint on the outskirts of Vung Tau without stopping, an act of total disregard of military protocol I attribute to my rendezvous with Jack Daniels. Certainly, had I tried to pull that stunt during the nighttime curfew the MPs posted there would have been justified in blasting all of us out of our jeep.

Prior to our departure to Vung Tau L-R: SP/4 Ed Lewin,
SGT Hank 'Tiny' Fraley, Author.

52

"You gotta be three of the luckiest sons of bitches this side of the DMZ."

arking in front of the R&R Center, I turned to Tiny and said, "You know, you and I being NCOs, one of us has to check in with the Officer-In-Charge. You up for it?" "I don't know, Bog. I'm pretty fucked up. Besides you're better at talking shit than I am."

Entering the R&R Center and feeling absolutely no pain, I was approached by a captain, the OD (Officer of the Day) and I sensed from the scorn on his face that he was not going to be any part of a welcoming party. I immediately snapped to the position of attention and delivered what I considered a snappy salute. Returning my salute, then resting both hands on his hips, he leaned forward while sniffing the air around me, glanced at my name tag sewn above my right breast pocket and at the 18th Military Police Brigade shoulder patch affixed to my left shirtsleeve and barked, "Ah, Specialist Bogison. You with the 720th?" I replied in the affirmative.

"You drove right through my checkpoint didn't you?" he shouted. "Yes sir, I did." I responded. "You realize that you could have caused a friendly fire incident! Not only did you endanger your own life but the lives of the two passengers with you! You're damned fortunate that my MPs out there didn't blow your asses away. Now, just exactly who authorized you idiots to travel on a highway that was closed to all traffic?"

"Our In-Country R&R orders authorizing us to spend the next three days and nights here in Vung Tau. We received no information about any road closure." I retorted, while handing him a copy of the orders. Scrutinizing our orders he said, "What's the matter with you people up there? What kind of people do you have running your Tactical Operations Center? We notified everybody from Long Binh to Saigon early yesterday evening that the highway was closed to all traffic; military and civilian. That whole area is crawling with NVA and VC!"

"Well, that explains it." I murmured under my breath. "Explains what?" he barked. It was at this point in the conversation I really didn't care what this captain thought or what he proposed to do. Without being told, I transitioned from the position of attention to the more relaxed posture of standing at ease by separating my legs while placing my hands behind my back. I then casually related the sequence of events relative to our journey. I told him the reason we drove past his checkpoint was simple.

After our experience on that deserted highway we had no intention of stopping for anybody or anything until we reached the R&R Center. Sarcastically, I added, "Had we known that the highway was closed I wouldn't be here having to explain anything."

"You've been drinking Specialist. That's not acceptable behavior for any NCO operating a government vehicle! " Then appearing somewhat moved by my explanation, he simply shook his head and said, "You gotta be three of the luckiest sons of bitches this side of the DMZ. (Demilitarized Zone, separating North Vietnam from South Vietnam) Get out of here and report to my desk sergeant. He will escort you and the two fools you came in with to your hotel."

He glared at me, and added:

"Don't even think about getting back into that jeep or I'll

have my MPs throw all three of you in our other hole, an air-conditioned conex box. Is that clear Specialist?" "Yes sir!" I barked out, then snapped a sharp salute, performed a flawless about face and managed a fairly steady gait towards the desk sergeant some fifty feet away.

So much for my feeble attempt at concealing intoxication. That captain could easily have had me spend my three day vacation in one of those conex boxes.

The hotel was located a short block away from the R&R Center and about a stone's-throw from the beach. It had all the outer appearances of a typical 3-star hotel in the States. Our 2nd floor room had wall to wall carpeting, three single beds with real mattresses, a small refrigerator, a real flushing toilet with a sink and adjoining shower hot and cold running water.

Air conditioning was a large electric ceiling fan coupled with the sea breeze entering the open unscreened picture window that provided a panoramic view of the beach below and the South China Sea. We were rolling in all this luxury and after explaining to Tiny and Lew that we were in the captain's words, "the luckiest sons of bitches this side of the DMZ," Lew said, "Well, it's time to drink to all those dumb fuckin' VC that knew better than to fuck with a couple of Bushwhackers!"

We spent the entire afternoon, the evening and early the morning of the next day downing Jack Daniels Whiskey and Carling Black Label Beer, celebrating.

Late the following morning as I struggled to focus my eyes through the haze of a sizeable hangover, I noticed several small thin gray-colored objects moving slowly on the ceiling. Dismissing it as a figment of my still intoxicated state, I turned onto my left side to find myself staring directly into the eyes of a small gray lizard sitting motionless on my pillow, just a few inches away.

The entire hotel was home to dozens of these harmless

creatures climbing on the walls, floors and ceiling. Clearly not an acceptable condition expected in any typical hotel or motel in the States, out here these guys served as natural selection in the control of flies, insects and other indigenous pests. There was just no getting away from nature, even in a hotel.

Most of my memory of our three days and nights in Vung Tao are shrouded in an alcohol induced blur. Virtually all of our time was spent trying to out-drink four Australian Army artillery guys we met on the beach on our second day there. It was a draw. Nobody passed out. Our conversations with them confirmed where I had already decided to spend my 7-day out-of- country R&R destination: Sydney, Australia.

These guys even provided written directions and addresses of the best hotels and bars in the city. We thoroughly enjoyed their company as well as their dry sense of humor which was a match for the three of us.

On our third and last full day in Vung Tau, I managed to get my hands on a surfboard. These warm waters were home to a host of poisonous creatures including that same small black sea snake I was introduced to while wading in the Đồng Nai River four months earlier. I easily spotted three of them bobbing about while riding the ridiculously small waves in the crystal clear, green-blue waters of the South China Sea. Several hundred yards away along the shallow waters of the shoreline helicopter gunships were spraying machine gun fire directly into a large school of sharks.

We were told that such aggressively determined activity was not only a deterrent against human-shark encounters for idiots like me, but also served as live-fire exercises for helicopter door gunners. The activity created a continuous feeding frenzy for the never-ending influx of sharks that congregated there.

Machine gun fire is not an acceptable means of preventing shark encounters in today's world, nonetheless it was very effective in keeping the meat-hungry monsters away from me. Regardless of conditions, I was not going to be deprived of an opportunity to enjoy the activity I truly missed.

Besides, I had already accepted the strong possibility that I was living on borrowed time.

Three days and nights pass very quickly and any hope of extending our vacation were dashed when the road to Long Binh reopened to traffic, just hours before our scheduled departure. The trip back was uneventful. This time the highway hummed with military convoys, vehicles, bicycles, mopeds and pedestrians traveling in both directions. An astounding difference from what we experienced just three days earlier.

As to why we weren't warned about the road closure before our departure, we never fully understood.

People assigned to our Tactical Operations Command Center were adamant in their explanation that none of the personnel assigned there had ever received any notification that the highway had been closed. We had no reason to question them as most of the people assigned there were former grunts like us, and would have notified us of the situation immediately. Unfortunately, miscommunications were all too common. The right hand didn't tell the left hand what it needed to know. Somebody dropped the ball. That R&R captain was right. We were lucky. Again.

53

Back on the water

During my second and third weeks on the water I got on-the-job training with the 458 guys relative to all aspects associated with PBR operation, which included many hours behind the wheel on each of the six boats learning to negotiate evasive maneuvers. The VC were adept at concealing explosives (mines, especially) mingled in floating debris such as drifting plants, trash or small branches of fallen trees.

Unlike the operation of a motor vehicle when an attempt to avoid striking an object in the road is made by negotiating a sharp turn to the right or left, on the water it is entirely the opposite. Avoiding objects afloat required that the operator aim the bow directly at the obstacle, then negotiate a sharp turn at the last second to avoid wrecking broadside. Common sense to those familiar with such things.

It made no sense until I'd seen the maneuver actually demonstrated. Avoiding deadly mines cleverly camouflaged as small, harmless floating islands of debris was a constant concern of the entire crew. In addition to the various forms this hazard could take, coxswain and crew remained watchful to avoid the navigational hazards on and below the surface of the rivers. Everyone memorized trouble spots that were exposed during low tide cycles.

The PBR was an extremely maneuverable and forgiving machine. The boat stopped practically on a dime by executing the "quick-stop" maneuver traveling at full speed. Automatic transmission allowed the operator to switch back and forth from forward to reverse by pushing right and left throttles up or down. Any object not secured or any person not prepared for the action could easily be tossed into the air and overboard. Communication between the coxswain and crew was crucial.

Chuckie Bowen introduced me to the quick-stop maneuver during our getting-to-know-you phase of my training. Early one morning and without warning, seated comfortably on the deck between the barrels of the forward twin .50s, both knees bent and feet firmly pressed against the raised rail at the tip of the bow, I felt this sudden violent jolt that was both exhilarating and terrifying.

In an instant I was completely enveloped in a dark hollow tube of green water. The experience was similar to riding a surfboard within the curl of a large wave, while desperately maneuvering through it to get back out into the open air before the liquid mass could crash on top of me. On the boat, maneuvering was not an option.

However, for every violent and sudden action there is an equally abrupt and robust reaction. The momentum stopped dead and my ass was promptly catapulted skyward. The bow slamming violently back into the water and my ass slammed back onto the deck. Somewhere in the process, I instinctively grasped the barrels of the .50s in a death-grip that prevented me from being flung into the water. A good laugh was had by all, including me.

The stunt was standard operating procedure developed by the 458 guys as an initiation of sorts to introduce new guys to life on the water.

The "180'" was an evasive tactic used when it was necessary

to reverse direction while cruising on-step at full speed.

Everybody and everything floating on these waterways was suspect, ranging from the single fisherman in his small sampan powered with a single paddle or an old Briggs & Stratton gas engine, to the larger family operated, multi-tiered sampans. Torn pieces of fish netting, clumps of leaves intermingled with twigs and assorted debris were all carefully scrutinized and typically blown up by tossing a concussion grenade.

The small cylindrical containers came armed with a six-second delayed blasting cap that detonated when the ringed pin (followed by release of the gray metal lever spoon) was removed. Classified as offensive weapons, they had a smaller casualty radius than our fragmentation grenades. Lethal shockwaves created by the detonation were employed as an anti-personnel depth charge specifically designed to incapacitate suspected underwater enemy divers.

We also employed the weapon for less militaristic reasons: to reap an abundance of stunned fish that floated to the surface seconds later.

54
Assuming a new responsibility

E ach day and night during those first few weeks afloat were mentally and physically taxing. Twelve hours on a PBR or on the barge took some getting used to. Initially, I recognized that working on deck affected my balance slightly. I needed to find my sea legs. My body was always in motion, swaying slightly, and the sensation remained with me long after I stepped ashore. But just as I had in the bush, I was able to adapt quickly.

Steinberg and Canada showed up daily on the barge, but neither of them ever spent any significant time with the PBR crews. And I rarely had contact with Henry. None of these guys even entertained the thought of coming out after dark. As for Sergeant York, mild-mannered surfer from Hawaii, his concern was the welfare of a local Vietnamese family, not anything to do with military protocol.

All of this suggested that I would have more influence on these PBR crews than I was initially led to believe. Within days, I started eliminating some of the asinine restrictions the crews had been living under before my arrival.

The men were relieved that they no longer had to wear steel pots all the time. Instead, I left it up to them to decide when they should wear the thing. As for the bright orange life jackets that made them stand out as nice easy targets for a VC sniper, I told them to toss the jackets aside and wear them only when the situation made it obvious. Sitting out on that river in daytime 110 degree temperatures was not fun. Demanding that these guys wear steel pots, flak jackets or bulky life vests during the entire twelve hour watch was unreasonable. It was dumb.

These guys had enough experience and common sense to know when and under what conditions they should have to don safety items. I emphasized that each crew apply common sense to any situation they encountered and when Steinberg, Canada or Henry were spotted act accordingly and communicate the sighting to the rest of us, especially me. Lastly, I assured them that I would back them and assume responsibility for any action they took. My transition into this assignment would be much easier than my initial experience in the bush.

L-R SP/4 Ed 'Shakey' Marley, Author, SP/4 Swensen, 458 Trans. Co, SP/4 Glenn Barmann, LT. Steinberg, SP/4 Denny Taylor, SP/4 Robert Lynn, SP/4 Ed 'Klinger' Kelleher, SGT Ed York 458 Trans. Co. foreground.

L-R: SP/4 Ronald Mason, SP/4 Joseph Keene, 'Young Jack' (458), SP/4 Swenson (458), SP/4 Ed 'Klinger' Kelleher.

SP/4 Denny Taylor on board a PBR behind the Aft 50 caliber machine gun.

Boat Barge

L-R: Unk Vietnamese Interpreter & close friend of SGT York, York, SP4 Rasmussen.

L-R: SP/4 Swensen (458), SP/4 Denny Taylor eating take-out food on the deck of their PBR docked on the Dong Nai River adjacent to a Vietnamese Restaurant in Bien Hoa.

L-R: Author, SP/4 Ed "Shakey" Marley, SP/4 Harry Marineau -- Master Machine Guinner and Photographer.

SP/4 Jim 'Sandy' Sanders — Master Machine Gunner.

SP/4 Chris Lowe — Masterfully enabled our PBRs to fly on the water well beyond the manufactured specification.

55
Friday, April 17, 1970, 18:25 hours

It should have been like any other uneventful and thankless watch but this one was anything but. Hour upon hour, day after day and sometimes weeks at a time were filled with unadulterated boredom interrupted by fleeting moments of pure terror. As in all horrific events, this one came out of nowhere like a bad storm and at 18:25 on Friday, April 17, 1970 it would be among my personal worst.

The ensuing thirty-six hours tested the limits of my sanity, along with the sanity of those who bore witness with me. At 18:00 my crews relieved the day watch at the French Pier. Whalers left the pier loaded with personnel from the 1st Ambush Platoon enroute to its designated ambush site. The 2nd Ambush Platoon had already been delivered. Each PBR was assigned a call sign that began with the NATO phonetic alphabet, followed with the watch identifier and assigned patrol sector.

For instance, call sign "Mike Papa 1 November" translates to "Military Police PBR, Day Watch, North Patrol unit." Number 2 in Mike Papa signified the night watch. "Charlie" indicated the Center Patrol unit and "Sierra" designated the South Patrol.

As NCO in charge of the watch I was assigned a separate call sign. For the evening in discussion I assigned myself to the *458 TC* crew operated by Chuckie Bowen with Taylor, Marineau and Kelleher and assigned to the Central Patrol unit, i.e. Mike Papa 2

Charlie. However, as events unfolded I found myself on board all three PBRs at various times.

Standard operating procedure at the start of each shift called for the MPs to conduct a thorough inspection of all weaponry, along with the assorted ammunition associated with each weapon. Simultaneously, 458 guys conducted a thorough inspection of the boat, topping off fuel tanks while checking fluid levels. In all, the procedure was usually finished within 30 minutes.

Having completed inspections early, each PBR proceeded to its respective operating area. Conforming to our routine, my crew proceeded south, nearing the Harbor Master Tower several hundred yards ahead. Cruising at 1600 rpms (approximately 15 mph) the loud drone of our engines sometimes superseded familiar sounds like aircraft passing overhead. Now, nearly fifty years later, I recognize that my ruminations on the engine drone coupled with the sound of water against the hull often lulled me into brief moments filled with absolute peace and serenity.

This evening was no exception.

My idyll was interrupted by a frantic call over our radio from the harbor master bellowing, "To the Mike-Papa unit approaching Hotel Mike (Harbor Master Tower) you have an out-of-control chopper about to splash down 200 meters north and west of your location!" Followed immediately with, "Correction it has splashed down. Stand-by!"

Hyper vigilance set in as all eyes turned north and west. However, there was nothing to suggest that a helicopter was anywhere in sight. As Chuckie jammed the engine throttles forward maneuvering a wide sweeping right turn into a northwesterly direction we spotted debris comprised of bits and pieces of type-written documents floating on the water. But where was the crew?

Where exactly and how far into the depths of the river below us was the chopper? Was this a hostile or non-hostile event? There were no immediate answers. We had to assume that the chopper was hit with small arms fire and that the drone of our engines prevented any of us from hearing.

Anxiously, as all guns and eyes scanned in every direction for anything threatening or suspicious, dozens of documents adorned with the 25th Infantry logo began emerging from the depths below us. Hundreds of white sheets surfaced on the dirty dark green waters in all directions.

Just as I was coming to grips with the situation, the radio operator advised me to direct all my PBRs to retrieve the documents. What the hell did that mean? The papers were more important than lives? Before I could respond, the radio operator advised us that a South Vietnamese patrol boat and a harbor tug boat several hundred yards west of the French Pier were attempting to rescue two possible survivors.

He added that the helicopter was a courier assigned to the 25th Infantry and logged at least ten passengers and crew. Disregarding my save-the-paper instructions I directed the crew of the north patrol PBR — Zirk, Lynn, Rasmussen and York — to assist in the rescue. It was while trying to locate casualties that a South Vietnamese patrol boat some 300 yards away drew my attention to a series of high tension power lines that crossed a bend in the river on the western shore.

One of four large electrical power lines had been severed and lay on the western shore suggesting the obvious that this was the causal factor in the crash. All the wires were intact when we passed by them just minutes earlier. Assumptions were confirmed when the radio operator advised us that this was a non-hostile event. I had witnessed various fixed wing and rotary aircraft perform unorthodox maneuvers at treetop levels to avoid being hit by hostile small arms fire before. Perhaps this was one of those situations, interrupted by of all things, a man-made object.

Assuming that everybody on board the craft should be in the vicinity where the two survivors were discovered, some 300 yards north and west of our location, I directed the crew of the south patrol PBR (Mason, Keene and Swensen) to meet us at that location.

The retrieval of the documents would have to wait. While on route, Zirk radioed that they were transporting the two badly injured victims to the French Pier so that the pair could be dusted-off to the 24th Medevac Hospital on Long Binh Post. Initial observations and reports from responding medevac personnel indicated that both victims, a captain and a staff sergeant, were not expected to survive.

As our PBR cut through water soaked documents, I scanned the entire surface of the Đồng Nai and estimated that the debris field littered with these documents was well over 200 yards in diameter. It would be impossible for any of us to determine precisely where the chopper entered the river. Currents ran strong and it was virtually impossible to predict where the current might sweep an injured or lifeless body. Documents swirling on the water offered no answers as they moved in any direction that provided the least resistance.

For the next hour or so, at my direction all three PBRs methodically traversed the width of the Đồng Nai 400 yards north and south of the location where the captain and sergeant were rescued. Time was crucial and we were running out of it. Each passing minute with no trace of life coupled with dusk now turning to night, the grim reality of what lay before us started to set in.

Our rescue had evolved into a recovery mission.

❧❦

56
Dusk turning to night

Throughout these proceedings the harbor master radio operator intermittently reminded me to secure the documents. I knew precisely how difficult I was making his situation by ignoring his pleas. No doubt, he was being badgered by a superior to salvage the documents. Figuring that I had managed to buy at least an hour searching for men instead of papers regardless of their importance, I relented and directed the north and south PBRs to expand the search area and secure documents. My crew turned south.

Fresh in everybody's memory was the drowning of Johnson, McArthur and Hemke, back in January. The bodies were recovered several miles south and west of French Fort along the western banks of the Đồng Nai. It seemed logical to all of us that if we were to find anybody it would be south rather than north, and closer to the western, not eastern, shoreline. Dead or alive it was imperative that we find them. Thoughts of their capture, mutilation or execution bore heavily on my mind. When I was in the bush I knew that if I, a lowly grunt, was captured alive by the VC or the NVA there would be no bargaining. Immediate torture, execution and mutilation. In that order.

Having accepted the reality, I always ensured that one live M-16 bullet was stored alongside the cleaning kit within the confines of the stock of my rifle, and one live .45 bullet for my pistol stored in my left pants pocket. For me. If the crash didn't kill these guys a terrible fate might surely befall them if we didn't get to them first.

Several minutes into our journey south, keeping about 100 yards between us and the western shoreline, cruising between 15-20 mph, more documents started popping up alongside us. Slowing down to a crawl Marineau and I leaned over the side and started gathering handfuls while Taylor manning the front twin .50 and Kelleher had the aft .50. The situation was deteriorating quickly as the moonless nighttime skies set in, severely restricting our visibility.

PBRs were equipped with a powerful headlamp affixed to the right side of the front .50 machine gun turret and could easily illuminate objects or targets over 200 feet away. An effective tool for the task at hand, but clearly not a safe choice under the circumstances. Cruising along the shoreline wasn't safe, either. Operating the headlamp would light us up like a Christmas tree and skimming close to the shoreline against a backdrop of dense foliage in the daytime was risky business, doing so at night was simply foolhardy. I weighed these options as we plodded our way south retrieving the trail of documents ahead of us.

A glance at the documents revealed the names, ranks, serial numbers and listed the military occupation status of hundreds of officers and enlisted men affiliated with the various divisions and battalions operating in III Corps. Now, after a little over an hour into this incident, it all started to make some kind of sense. It should have dawned on me when the radio operator kept repeating that this chopper was assigned as a "courier" along with his continual pleas to retrieve the paper that this was a serious priority. But it didn't.

He tried to tell us these were secret documents without having to broadcast the information. It was common knowledge that every English-speaking North Vietnamese interpreter from Saigon to Hanoi monitored our radio frequencies. In the hands of the VC, the information gleaned from these pages would be a goldmine of intelligence revealing not just names of assigned personnel assigned to the various units, but would undoubtedly have exposed the strengths and weaknesses within III Corps.

The importance and the urgency in salvaging these documents became abundantly clear. In retrospect, it wouldn't have changed a thing. The helicopter boys were always there when we needed them the most. They were the guardian angels who brought death from above to all those determined to kill us. The respect and admiration we all held for these guys could never be overstated. It was now our turn to be there for them. We just had to find them.

We were well into the second hour of our search, following the paper trail which took us south towards the northwestern shoreline of the southernmost of the two islands in the middle of the Đồng Nai. It was that same mysterious island leper colony - Cù Lao Ba Xê - we were forced to make landfall when our whaler broke down months earlier.

As we approached the shallows adjacent to the shoreline, it was Taylor who directed our attention to the unmistakable figure of a lifeless body, face down and floating among a thicket of reeds several yards from the shore. Now, as the gravity of situation took hold of me, I had to make some hard decisions. Fast.

We were in a remote and unfamiliar area devoid of any light, with the western shoreline of the Đồng Nai just a few hundred yards to our rear. Our presence so close to the island posed a serious threat if we made any kind of enemy contact. We all knew the local population was keenly aware of our daily routines and movements. So were the VC, and it made sense to assume that all the activity associated with the crash of the helicopter got the attention of prying eyes. The typical crew of a PBR comprised of a coxswain, plus the forward .50 caliber gunner and a gunner on the aft .50 caliber.

As NCOIC with a crew of four provided more options, I reasoned that Marineau and Kelleher could jump into the water, retrieve the body and lift it up and onto the rear deck. Chuckie remained at the helm for a quick departure, with the Taylor on the .50s providing security to the front and me manning the aft weapon. Jumping into waist-high water Kelleher and Marineau eased their way towards the shore some 30 feet away. I watched the pair painstakingly push and pull the body alongside the starboard side of the boat and noticed was how uncharacteristically large the body was.

The man, stiff as a board, appeared to be 5'10" and well over three hundred pounds. As they positioned the corpse closer I leaned down to grasp a lifeless arm. The distance from the deck of the boat to the water was three or four feet. I felt layers of skin separating from the arm causing me to lose my grasp, much like sliding the sleeves of a shirt up or down. Simultaneous to this horror, I felt the entire arm separating from the shoulder accompanied with the sounds of bone, tendons and muscle being twisted and torn.

I recognized that our method was not going to succeed in plucking the body out of the water and onto our deck. None of the appendages could be pulled or pushed to any significant degree without the real possibility of them separating from the torso. Throwing caution to the wind, I jumped into the water assuming that the three of us could surely lift the body from the water and then propel it up and over the rail.

A reasonable proposition at the time, but not even close to achieving the desired result. All the while came the realization that if we didn't develop a solution quickly we could easily be gunned down like sitting ducks by an unforeseen foe. Faced with that possibility, I called out to Chuckie to direct him to assist us as the engines idled at a low hum.

Grasping whatever part of the body he could to maneuver it on deck, the three of us in unison pushed it up to the rail of the PBR to end the fiasco. Chuckie immediately extended his hand out to mine and pulled me back onboard and returned to the controls. As he slowly reversed from the shoreline I pulled Marineau and Kelleher back on the rear deck.

Once all of us were onboard, Chuckie slammed the throttles forward full speed towards the western shore then negotiated a wide sweeping right turn toward safer waters north of the island.

Looking NW-The first body was recovered adjacent to the northwestern shoreline of the larger island. The second body was recovered directly west of the large island and along the western shoreline of the Dong Nai.

French Pier.

Midway into the turn Taylor yelled, "I think we got another one over there!" pointing towards the western shore. As Chuckie eased the throttles back and pointed the craft southwesterly, the unmistaken profile of a lifeless body, floating face down came into view just a few yards away.

The entire western shore of the Đồng Nai was unfamiliar territory. Land west of it lay within the 1st Infantry Division's tactical area of responsibility. I had even more reservations about our safety in these waters than the area adjacent to either of the two islands. A heightened sense of awareness rapidly set in and those old familiar symptoms I experienced in the bush started to churn in my gut.

As Chuckie carefully edged the PBR into the shallow waters near the shoreline, Kelleher and Marineau hopped over the starboard rail and made their way towards the body, about fifty feet away. As they laboriously pulled and pushed the dead man towards our craft I grew impatient with every passing second, anticipating the worst. As they sloshed alongside the craft I immediately saw that the body of this victim was equally as heavy and just as cumbersome as the one we had just retrieved.

Utilizing the same procedure as before, only much quicker, we managed to secure the second body onto the rear deck as Chuckie steamed away to safer waters.

This had been no easy task and in spite of our youth, exhaustion started to set in. There was no time to dwell on our state. Communicating with the harbor master, I requested that he contact the 557th MP Company and direct them to send a motorized patrol to the French Pier to assist us in setting up a command post to help a Graves Registration Unit (Army coroners) conduct a preliminary identification.

Two hours into this scenario and not one senior ranking NCO or officer had made their presence known or offered any assistance. I received no contact from Henry after my repeated requests to TOC authorizing permission to have the day watch crews return to the French Pier.

My mind was in overdrive and decisions had to be made. I was beginning to believe that the success or failure of this rescue/retrieval operation rested with me and me alone.

57
Decisions

As we made our way to the French Pier, Marineau, Kelleher, Taylor and I carefully rolled both bodies over, face-up, to collect the dog tags dangling from chains around their necks. In the process, we discovered that the arms of both victims were barely attached to the torso. Staring at the bodies I couldn't believe what I saw. The incredible bloating stretched the usually baggy-fitting jungle fatigues so tight that small tears were forming near the thighs, waist, stomach, calf and buttock areas.

Boot laces strung through the metal loops of their jungle boots were stretched to the limits, the feet inside them about to break through the canvas and rubber soles. Their dark faces were bloated and contorted, with both eyes bulging out of their sockets. Upper and lower lips had swollen at least three times their normal size and the tongues were grotesquely distended, protruding several inches and completely concealing upper and lower teeth.

Nothing about their condition suggested anything human, save the four appendages and the clothing. There was absolutely no way to determine whether they were black, white, Latin or Asian. It was a ghastly sight that Hollywood with all its magic could not have duplicated.

Easing the boat gently towards the French Pier I saw that our deck was over four feet below the pier. To get the bodies on the cement pier required the collective strength of all five of us to lift it over our heads then somehow propel it upwards with sufficient force to avoid the real possibility of having the corpse fall back on us, or lose it to the shallow waters and shore below.

Less than thirty seconds of thought convinced me we were not going to even make the attempt. Instead, I directed Chuckie to position our boat toward the shore next to the pier, reasoning that shifting the remains from the deck to the shore would be simpler, quicker and far less hazardous. After putting both bodies back into shallow water we picked them up and placed them on dry ground several yards away.

There they laid, face up, side by side with rubber ponchos draped over them. Dog tags were placed on top of the ponchos for processing. It was during this process I was informed that we would get no assistance from any motorized military police company to provide security for our make-shift Command Post. Apparently, all of the motorized patrol units assigned to the 557th MP Company, and the nearby 615th MP Company were engaged in more pressing events. As for the Graves Registration unit, they wouldn't be responding anytime soon, either. I was told to expect them to arrive sometime the following morning.

There was still no response to my request to bring back the day watch PBR crews. Clearly, we were alone and there was also no doubt I was responsible for whatever happened. As often seems the case, we would have much to do with a whole lot less.

Whalers Doug Newman, Jared Kelley, Shakey Marley and Glenn Barmann had monitored the radio all along as events unfolded, and volunteered to assist after completing their mission. Stepping up without having to be asked was a common theme shared by all these misfits, these snuffies, these Bushwhackers of B Company. And as for the day watch PBR crews, had they known of our plight they too, would have returned to their boats and assisted us without me or anybody else having to ask.

As luck would have it, strategists in Battalion determined

that primary ambush sites designated for the 1st and 2nd Ambush Platoons had to be aborted. Caught in that all-to-common situation wherein the left hand fails to communicate with the right, only added to our plight. Planning and coordinating 1st and 2nd Ambush Platoon movement to an alternative ambush site took several hours.

More importantly, the four whaler crews would transport personnel throughout our TAOR without the benefit of a PBR nearby to provide any fire support should they encounter hostilities. Leaving the bodies unattended was not an option. I directed two men from my crew to remain at the French Pier leaving Zirk, Lynn, York and Rasmussen to continue retrieving documents. The passage of time blunts memory, but leaving only two guys at the French Pier didn't sit well with me. I reasoned that a nearby PBR would provide some kind of back up for the pair, should the need arise.

58

There is nothing heroic about anything here

Meanwhile, my crew (minus two crewmembers) along with Keene, Mason and Swensen in their PBR continued patrolling southbound on opposite sides of the Đồng Nai retrieving documents and carefully scanning the waters for more bodies.

Several hours passed when I spotted what looked to be a body drifting along the western shore, almost a mile further south from where we had recovered the first two victims. As Chuckie cautiously maneuvered closer to shore, I jumped in the waist-high water and slowly made my way to the unmistakable figure of a third body. Like the others, this one floated face down. As I grasped a shirt collar I felt stitching that signified he was an officer.

Trying to put all thoughts of being ambushed out of mind, I grasped an exposed cold and swollen right forearm, and followed up with a robust tug in an effort to quickly pull the mass towards me. To my horror, layers of skin immediately started slipping away from the bone as an accumulation of torn skin caused the firm grip of my hand to slide unnaturally to the palm and thumb area. Instinctively, I released my hold, causing the head and shoulders of the body to slam directly into my thighs while I thrashed about in the shallows trying to regain my footing.

Quickly recovering from that blunder, I grasped the throat area with my left hand and left leg with my right and with a healthy push propelled the body face down towards the PBR thirty feet away. I repeated the process three times more while fighting the unyielding current of the Đồng Nai.

Thoroughly exhausted at this point and knowing that Chuckie, Taylor and I were not going to be successful in getting this body onto our PBR, Chuckie suggested proceeding very slowly to the safer waters near the middle of the river, while I maintained a firm grip on the corpse with one hand and grasped a rope tied to the top rear rail of the PBR with the other hand. Then, with the help of Swensen, Keene and Mason on the opposite bank meeting us, we could transfer the body onto the deck of either of the PBRs.

I didn't hesitate. It made sense. And the sooner we reached safer waters, the better. Watching me struggle to rotate the body face up, Chuckie jumped in to help. Taylor remained on deck manning the aft .50. Within seconds, Chuckie was back at the controls and heading toward safer waters at a snail's pace. All the while, I held the neck and throat of the body tight between my upper and lower arm and within the bend of my left elbow, desperately holding the rope with my right hand. It was a physically demanding ordeal that required the strength and stamina of someone far more capable than my 160 pound frame.

Plodding along at less than two miles per hour to a destination only several hundred yards away, the journey was repeatedly interrupted because I kept either losing my grip on the rope, or the stranglehold around the corpse's neck, loosened by the force of rushing water. My face was buried in the back of the body's head, and any movement by me along with the forward movement of the PBR caused strands of his hair and skin to be detached from the skull, much of which was deposited all over my face and throat.

With no free hand to rid myself of the stuff, the intermittent turbulence of water created by the wake of the PBR mercifully freed me of some of it. This abhorrent situation plagued me for the entire crossing.

Because of his extensive experience navigating the Đồng Nai, Chuckie found a nearby sandbar and promptly shut down the engines. This provided me a brief, much-needed respite standing in water up to my chest impatiently awaiting the arrival of Swensen, Keene and Mason. All the while amazed at the overwhelmingly large number of assorted thoughts I managed to process at the most inopportune moments.

Standing there in complete silence, I carefully scanned the indistinct landscape of the western shore, while trying to ignore the pounding of my heart along with the sounds of water gently lapping at the sides of the PBR and the body I held by the collar. I wasn't expecting to see anything, just hoping that I wouldn't hear anything. It dawned on me during the disconnect between senses that my .45 pistol was still fastened in the holster of the gun belt I had strapped around my waist and now under water.

My thoughts switched to questioning whether the damn thing would even work, accompanied with a series of theories on why it should. Seconds later, I thought of my father's last words to me at the airport, "Just get your ass home. No hero shit." I looked at the contorted features of the face of what was only yesterday a live human being and concluded that there is nothing heroic about anything out here.

A sweeping realization of death and a peek into the future of what may be my own destiny ricocheted in my thoughts at the time.

Swensen and crew of *Karen Ann* wasted no time meeting us. Their hasty arrival definitely reduced the chances of our getting ambushed. It took the collective efforts of Mason, Keene, Swensen, Taylor and me to transfer this body to the deck of *458 TC*. The five of us rolled the body over exposing features of what once was human as I struggled to remove the dog tag chain which was embedded deep in the folds of the swollen neck and throat.

I felt the remnants of skin tissue on my hands, under my fingernails along with sticky clumps of scalp hair and tissue cling to my clothing. There was no way to avoid it but I wasn't going to dwell over the misery I felt building inside me.

Besides, this wasn't the time or place for such feelings. As we headed to the French Pier, I determined that in spite of the difficulties shared by both crews in retrieving this, our third victim, deploying two PBRs at a recovery site would be far more prudent than having just one crew attempting corpse retrieval.

In the approaches to the French Pier, several crew members and I jumped into the shallows and carried the body ashore, alongside the other two remains. With me now on board with the crew of *Da Fuzz* along with *458 TC* close behind us we proceeded south in the search of more bodies, while the crew of the *Karen Ann* remained in the vicinity of the French Pier.

I would like to think that I had the presence of mind to consider that alternating crews in the handling of bodies would allow some break from an ugly task. Over 40 years later, I cannot say that with any certainty. The crews of all three PBRs shared equally in the grotesque chore. It would be several hours later and well into the early morning hours of the next day before *458 TC* spotted body number four in the middle of the Đồng Nai, several hundred yards south of the southernmost island.

Just like the others, he was bloated, stiff, floating face down, both arms extended outward and bent downward at the elbows with hands and forearms under water. The upper torso was slightly bent at the waist, both legs were spread and bent at the knees. At first glance the sight reminded me of the head and torso of a bobbing mannequin, devoid of lower appendages.

Now, in deep waters with no shallows nearby for us to stand in, getting the body on deck proved to be even more problematic and, regrettably, more gruesome. With Zirk and Marineau, we lowered ourselves into the water and put a rope around the beltline. Rasmussen, Lynn, Taylor and Kelleher struggled to pull it up, still face down, and onto the deck of the PBR. To assist in the process, the three of us grasped the rope tied to the deck rails and jointly heaved up the weight. Sounds of constricting wet rope tightening around the bloated waistline, the crackling of stretched skin tissue along with the noise of bones crunching with each tug filled the air, interspersed by the thud of the body slamming against the hull.

A physically exhausting ordeal for all. More importantly, in spite of the extra manpower along with the fire power of two PBRs, not a single gun was manned. We were sitting ducks out there and if Charlie wanted to slaughter us, we certainly gave him ample opportunity. There had to be a better way to do this.

Heading to the French Pier we turned the corpse face up. He was a crew member of the craft, possibly the crew chief/door gunner validated by the unique jungle garb he was wearing, typical of those worn by helicopter crewmembers. His body was just as grotesque as the others but from what little light that there was it appeared that the advanced stages of decomposition were having a more pronounced effect on disfiguring his facial features.

The skin was shedding off in layers. Hands and fingers were asymmetrical, as though they had been mauled. He was right-handed which was indicated by the right-handed holster attached to the barely visible pistol belt. Violence associated with the crash had twisted the pistol belt and repositioned the empty holster from the right side of the hip to the center of the distended stomach. The sheer ferocity of impact force caused the .45 to be ejected from the holster and into the depths of the river.

☙❧

59
More Decisions More Help

A t the French Pier, Jared Kelley made contact on the radio and indicated that all of the Boston Whalers had completed their mission in relocating the 1st and 2nd ambush platoons. Along with Doug Newman, Shakey and Glenn Barmann he would meet us at the French Pier. My watch read 03:00. The addition of four whalers to assist us was welcome news. More men and more guns meant more security. York eased our PBR into shallow waters adjacent to the pier, and the six of us struggled to transfer body number four from the deck to the shore next to the others, just a few yards away.

Grasping any of the appendages to gain leverage easily resulted in one or more of the appendages to detach. I now came to the realization that with each passing hour, retrieval of any remaining bodies out there would only become more difficult, mentally and physically, for all of us.

While this was going on, the whaler crews arrived. Laboring to remove the dog tags, I turned and looked up to see the forlorn expression on Jared's face standing over me muttering, "Jesus Christ, Bog." I have no recollection as to what I may have said in response.

With added resources, I directed two whalers to stay in the vicinity of the French Pier and continue the search for documents or bodies. The other two whalers were to search south. All three PBRs patrolled eastern and western shores. Near the site of the fourth body we discovered body number five, like the others face down. This one was lodged between two sampans docked in shallow waters in the mud flats.

With the added firepower of two whalers and all three PBRs, we felt comfortable illuminating the area with our powerful headlamps to help in the recovery effort.

Again, we jumped in the water. Our remaining PBR and the two whalers positioned a short distance behind us, concealed in the darkness were prepared to deliver deadly machinegun fire to cover our movements.

Under the glaring lights this one struck us with horror. Bloating of tissue along with the familiar stench was magnified by the grotesque condition of the face, which was strikingly more gruesome than the others. Bulging eyes, tongue, and lips, various parts of the head and face were gone. There were bite marks, torn flesh and scads of hair ripped from the head. Carnivorous creatures that lurked in the depths of the Đồng Nai had engaged in a feeding frenzy.

Examination of hands and arms revealed flesh torn and ripped in the same manner. As we pushed and pulled the floating body the short distance to the transport PBR, I looked at the people around me. All eyes were transfixed on the remains of the face. No words were spoken. Eyes and facial expressions spoke for themselves. Thoughts of anger and resentment turned to apathy among some, others showed empathy.

I was not immune to such thoughts. I fought my own inner battle with the same conflicting emotions. When we reached the PBR sitting in roughly two feet of water, we strained to lift the body level with our armpits. We continued to struggle to push the body above our shoulders on the deck but the sheer weight and mass of the corpse was too much to bear. The exhausting process culminated in all of us falling in the water with the body on top of us.

We floundered in a frantic effort to extricate ourselves from both the weight of the body and the soft sandy river bottom below us.

The instant we were clear of the body, we all stood up together. Silence was not golden on this occasion. Loud exclamations containing a litany of profanities filled the air. Fears of being ambushed by an unseen foe were gone. Rage, frustration and exhaustion took their toll on everyone. While the shouts grew louder, my world grew more silent. Water sloshing, coupled with voices hurled about, were barely discernable above a hissing drone that played in my head.

I was filled with rage and resentful that I was here having to deal with this nightmare. I was weary trying to make sense of it all. It would be at this precise moment and at this juncture in my 21 years that my life changed.

Apathy, detachment and a developing hardened shell became my close companions heralding the creation of a new comfort zone. In the midst of the chaos reasoning became rather simple. I had no time for sympathy. These things happen in war. I would withdraw from all of it.

As for compassion, if there was any left to be found in this place, it would remain with those in possession of a stronger faith and a far nobler soul than mine. For now, I reasoned, the quality of my soul was irrelevant.

60

"Bog, why don't we just attach a rope around his chest and drag him behind the boat."

My introspective drone world was broken by the sound of my rank and name being called. "Sarge! Sarge! Sergeant Bogison!" Bruce Zirk leaned over the rail of the PBR no more than three feet to my rear, screaming. I turned, shook my head as if to clear water from my ear and said, "Yea, what do you need?" There was no water in either ear. I was not deaf. It was a ruse conjured up to conceal a moment of weakness and judgment in me, their supervisor. Seems I was progressing in my ability to embody something I already knew. I was not their fearless leader.

My mind, now clear of the philosophical conflicts I wrestled with moments earlier, turned to Zirk who said, "Bog, why don't we just attach a rope around his chest and drag him behind the boat." "Yea, except what good is that if his arms come apart while dragging him?" somebody interjected. "We won't know unless we try. Fuck it! Get some rope." I responded and then asked, "Who's the cowboy here? To which Zirk added, "We need a lasso-kind of knot." Chuckie, with a rope slung over his shoulder, jumped from the boat into the river and said, "Here. I got it."

We all watched Chuckie Bowman, city boy from Chicago, expertly attach a sophisticated lasso over the head and arms of the body.

He cinched the rope firmly beneath both armpits and suggested we all rotate the body face down. "I think this is how they recovered your recon guys back in January. I should have thought of it earlier." He was referring to the loss of McArthur, Johnson and Hemke. It made sense.

The body was about ten feet from the rear of *458 TC* when Lynn firmly attached the rope's end to the rail. Chuckie slowly eased the throttles forward spewing a powerful wake over the tow. This was in addition to the continuous flow of water under and over the body as we headed out. Clearly, continuing in this manner the body would suffer even more disfigurement, including loss of limbs. The tactic was halted. I told Zirk to allow another ten feet of rope in order to extend the distance between our tow and the transom, reasoning it would eliminate our jet-pump wake effect from slamming against the body. It did.

A slow, painstaking journey to the French Pier several miles away took the better part of an hour and required periodic stops to monitor the body's condition. On arrival at dawn I was relieved to see four Graves Registration specialists had already launched their preliminary investigation. Day watch crews were there, too. Their arrival gave us a compliment of three more PBR crews.

Zirk, Lynn, Marineau, Kelleher and I jumped off the boat as Chuckie eased the PBR toward the mud bank. All of us hauled in the rope. Forever locked in memory is the sound of our wet rope constricting the water-logged corpse to produce non-stop crackling noises, like those made by a tree trunk swaying in the wind moments before it is about to snap.

A crusty old master sergeant, the NCOIC of the Graves Registration unit, assisted us in placing the body on an open olive drab plastic body bag. The old timer assumed that I was in charge and directed me to give a brief statement relative to the who, what, when, where, how and why of our search and involvement to begin his investigation into the   deaths. Standard US Army Serious Incident Report procedure. He and his crew collected all personal effects of the victims, including the documents we recovered.

Shortly after giving my statement, Zirk reported that the whalers and *Karen Ann* crew had located a sixth casualty. Swift currents had moved this body to the deep waters in the middle of the Đồng Nai. He added that they needed our help in securing the area as soon as possible. It was 07:00 now and the curfew imposed on the indigenous population between 7pm and 7am was lifted. Soon, the Đồng Nai would swarm with hordes of Vietnamese fisherman and their water craft, along with military supply ships, naval and Army gunboats and tugboats with barges in tow.

More importantly, our rope was needed. All of us understood the urgency in their request.

We dodged and weaved through the — now — congested waterways. My mind was filled with questions wanting answers. I was relatively certain that we had collected all, if not most of the documents onboard the chopper. The biggest mystery by far was not knowing exactly how many bodies were on that chopper? I assumed that we would soon have an answer from the 25th Infantry Division. Morning roll call would raise concerns when the men could not be accounted for. And where was Sergeant Henry, or any commanding officer for that matter? The battalion brass in charge of the 720th had to be aware of the incident. Where were they? Questions with no answers.

We spotted *Karen Ann* and several whaler crews surrounded by two dozen or more Vietnamese fishermen in their sampans. We heard the screams of crewmembers ordering the Vietnamese in broken English and Vietnamese slang to vacate the area. Our added presence intimidated the locals. All the while, our guys were yelling in pigeon Vietnamese, "Didi mao! Di-mao! Didi fucking mao!" (Pronounced Dee-dee mow — as in cow — means go away.) And, "I cockadow VC!" (I kill Viet Cong!) And lots of, "Get the fuck out of here!"

The exchange lasted only a few minutes before we all realized the futility of accomplishing anything with slang, commonly used by all military personnel in the field. Many of these fishermen were nothing more than decoys attempting to distract the crews while their confederates removed whatever they found on the body. A common theme in many instances like this, unfortunately. There is no doubt some of the fishermen were affiliated with the Viet Cong.

We learned very early on that most of the native population could not be trusted. Our ability to survive demanded a thorough understanding of cultural and political differences. Life was cheap here. My initial impulse was to grab the nearest M-16, let loose and kill all of them. I was not alone. Rage was evident in the eyes and faces of others there with me. Fortunately, collective restraint prevailed. But my patience had grown thinner by the minute and, regrettably, so had my judgment.

61
The Unexpected

If there was ever a single lifetime event I had the power to make vanish forever, it was the recovery process of the sixth corpse. Turning to the task of securing the body, the rope was handed off to several whaler operators steadying their boats on opposite sides of the body. Employing whaler operators facilitated the operation in that they could attach the rope without any of us having to jump into the water.

Reach from PBR rail to waterline was between three and four feet. Distance from whaler rail cap to waterline was inches or less. All the operator had to do was reach out and tether the body. This particular victim was another officer, a captain. We all focused attention on the whaler operator's growing frustration attempting to secure the rope. Having got that bit done, he yanked on the leash end with a force far beyond what was necessary.

The body slammed violently against the hull. Inexplicably, he then reached out with both hands, grasped the watch on the left wrist and wrenched it free and said, "Fuck this! Fuck him, he's not gonna need this anymore!" stood up and put the watch in his pants pocket.

Next, he threw the leash over the rail, sat down, slammed the engine throttle of his whaler forward exclaiming, "Fuck this shit!" and sped away.

Standing on the rear deck for several seconds, I quickly turned my back, momentarily trying to pretend that what I had seen never happened. I said absolutely nothing and did absolutely nothing. I should have. His act shook me to the core and that all too familiar hissing drone-like sound found its place in my head again. I directed the crew to secure the rope and proceed to the French Pier, body dragging behind.

Then, I separated myself from the crew and sat on the foredeck between the .50s and wrestled with what I should have done, could have done and, now, what actions I knew I was obligated to take as a Non-Commissioned Officer. All those who bore witness to this thing were equally conflicted about what happened and I had no doubt that they wondered why their fearless leader did nothing. The man responsible for this action (I will not identify him even now, decades later), was by all accounts someone we had relied on in the past, both in the field and on the water. He wouldn't stand a snowball's chance in a burning inferno to avoid the full penalty weight of the Uniform Code of Military Justice, and he had no clue of what the Code was capable of doing to him.

I was the witness who had an intimate understanding of what the wrath of our military justice system could do. Too many men with a moral compass still intact had witnessed this incident and it would only take one of them to make a report. The man would be convicted and sent to Leavenworth Prison to serve out a minimum sentence of hard labor for a term of no less than six years. All this, for something he probably wouldn't have even considered just hours earlier.

Clearly, rationality had abandoned him. I would have to deal with this later, when the hissing sounds subsided.

❧❧

62

"Bogison! Bogison! What the hell are you doing? Don't do it! Bogison Don't do it!"

Approaching the French Pier we were astounded by the size of the waiting crowd. A multitude of villagers loitered on the nearby shore. Graves Registration had moved their command post from the open area to a more secure site under cover of the pier. As we drew closer, I spotted a half a dozen parked military police jeeps along with a dozen or more US military officers standing around, some of whom were having their pictures taken with a backdrop of the bodies we recovered stacked neatly in a row. The circus- like atmosphere was disgraceful.

Slowly slipping into shallow waters next to the pier, a loud voice bellowed from inside the crowd of officers, "Hey, that's an officer you are dragging there! What the hell is the matter with you people?" This inanity provoked an immediate shout back by Chuckie, while carefully maneuvering closer to shore, "Yea, he's dead! And officers die just like we do!" That was followed up with me yelling, "And where the fuck were you people when we needed you last night?"

I knew the instant I yelled it that I had stepped in it. Enlisted men don't talk to officers in that tone coupled with that kind of jargon. It didn't matter now as I fully expected to be stripped of my rank. Knowing I would be confronted with the issue, I directed the crew to remain on board. I untied the rope from the rear rail and jumped into the shallow waters to pull the body to shore, some twenty yards away.

Ignoring any commotion that may have stirred up from the pier, I found myself in approximately three feet of water laboriously pulling and tugging the rope. I was exhausted and I should have had help doing this as my feet were having a difficult time maintaining a steady gait in the rise and fall of the rock-covered riverbed. Stopping to gain a firm foothold, I pulled the rope with as much strength my body could muster in an effort to float it closer to me.

It was during this process, that I inadvertently lost my footing and fell backwards, face up and under the water.

Embarrassed by this clumsy maneuver, I immediately thrust myself upward with both hands now firmly planted on the rocky bottom to rid myself of this predicament. In doing so, and to my horror, my face was now pressed against the face of the dead captain directly above me. Gasping for air where there was none, I inhaled a mouthful of water and began to frantically thrash about desperately trying to break free. By the time my head and upper body emerged from water, I was on my knees, struggling to standup and unsuccessfully trying to minimize the gagging that followed.

Forcing myself into a swift recovery, I noticed a young Vietnamese man and what appeared to be a teenaged Vietnamese girl sloshing from the shoreline towards me. Initially, I thought that they were offering to help me but the girl started laughing and pointing at the dead captain while repeatedly shouting, "Number one GI! Number one GI! Cockadow! Cockadow! Number one GI!"

She and others in her growing crowd cheered that this dead

captain was a Number one GI because he was dead. She was a Viet Cong sympathizer or, more than likely, a Viet Cong soldier incognito.

So much for restraint. The hissing sounds had returned as an appalling wave of wrath and vengeance consumed my entire being. Instinctively, I reached for my .45 automatic pistol in my holster on my right. I was losing it. I had every intention of striking her across the face with it. In sync with my movement, from the muffled din of my world came an explosive shout, "Bogison!"

Ignoring the distraction, I unfastened the leather flap of my holster by lifting it up, allowing my right hand to grasp the butt of the pistol just as another scream bellowed again, "Bogison!"

The hissing sounds in my head subsided as I cleared the weapon from its holster. I heard the same voice again, "What the hell are you doing?" It was a voice I knew and it stunned me momentarily. Then, as I swung my right arm towards my chest preparing to strike her head with my pistol in a backhanded motion, her male companion backed off, her facial expressions of laughter change instantly to terror.

That familiar voice hollered, "Don't do it! Don't do it, Bogison!" Now, just yards away in the crowd to my left, it brought an immediate halt to my intentions. I recognized the voice and as he emerged from the crowd the identity was confirmed. The voice belonged to none other than my commanding officer back at Fort Riley, Captain Z. Only he wasn't a captain anymore, he had been promoted to major and assigned to the Battalion Headquarters staff.

I holstered the gun, took one large step toward the girl while stooping down so that my face was within inches of hers, and growled very slowly, "I cock-a-dow VC! Didi fucking mao! Get the fuck out of here. Now!" As she turned to run away I noticed that her crotch area and the entire inner leg portions of the black silk pants she wore were wet with urine. Had the major not intervened when he did, I am certain that she and her male companion would have suffered great bodily harm at my hands.

I started to gather the rope as the Graves Registration people rushed to my side. They removed the lasso, rolled the body over and carried it off towards the pier. I could tell that the crusty master sergeant was just as disgusted as I was about the fun park atmosphere he found himself working in. None of these officers had any official business for being here.

As I collected the rope, Major Z motioned me over to him and as I was closing the distance between us, blurted out, "Are you in charge of these people?" to which I responded without saluting, "Yes, sir I am."

"You were going to kill that girl weren't you?

"The bitch and the little bastard with her are VC!" I yelled back, knowing that by responding with a self-incriminating statement would be a huge mistake.

"You don't know that and just what do you think you are doing out here?" he asked.

To which I responded by asking, "Just what the fuck do you think we've been doing out here since 1800 hours last night, sir?" as I wiped away debris and a dead man's skin clinging to all parts of my face, using a shirt collar.

My demeanor and lack of respect clearly demonstrated that I was not the same kid he lectured a year earlier. What more did I have to lose? I expected to be stripped of my rank for the insubordination displayed minutes earlier by insulting the dozen or more junior officers standing around making asses of themselves taking photographs of each other posing with bodies of dead men. Besides, I was already up to my ass in a quagmire of criminality involving the theft of a dead officer's watch.

The conversation continued like an interrogation. He

questioned every decision I made the previous fourteen hours, and he wasn't shy about it. I was being lectured and publicly humiliated in the presence of my crew and everyone within earshot of the outbursts that spewed from his mouth, and his condescending behavior.

The gist of the conversation focused on the major's condemnation of my judgment as the NCOIC authorizing military police to retrieve the body of a United States Army officer in the "despicable manner" — as he put it — that he witnessed.

He added, "You are going to answer for this and your reckless behavior with Vietnamese people. Make no mistake about it!"

Clearly accepting that this was not my finest hour, I provided only direct responses to his questions and otherwise remained mostly silent - while fiercely resisting the desire to deliver a wild fist to his face.

Justifying or providing any sort of detailed explanation was pointless. The man was incapable of thought.

When his rants waned he asked, "How many more bodies are missing?" to which I responded, "I don't know, I was hoping you could tell me. We were told that the chopper was a courier and logged at least ten passengers plus crew. Two were rescued when it went down. We have retrieved six bodies so far, one of which we believe is the crew's door gunner. We haven't found the pilots yet, so we have no idea how many more may be out there"

❧❧

63

"Say the word, Bog"

Assuming the conversation was over, I turned to walk back to the boat. Three or four steps away I heard, "Where do you think you are going? We're not finished here." When I turned to face the major he said, "I want to go on that PBR for the next recovery."

"Is that an order, sir?" I asked.

"Yes, it is Specialist. You need some supervision."

Great. Precisely what we all needed now, a rear echelon idiot to demonstrate the prim and proper way to collect dead bodies instead of the shameful and "despicable manner" he had witnessed. Nobody was pleased. For reasons that are made obvious later, names of my crew and the PBR we boarded will remain anonymous.

The crew's silence and the acrimonious expressions on their faces should have been an obvious indicator of the potential powder keg that could explode at any moment. Our major was oblivious. All of us were physically and mentally exhausted, appalled at what we had witnessed, sickened by the stench of death and now repulsed with the mindset of the only man on board that had nothing to contribute but discord.

An hour or so into our search, we spotted the seventh body in the same manner as the others, bobbing up and down in a remote waterway among the reeds adjacent to the western shore of the Đồng Nai where it meets the Buông. As we inched into the shallows, I was interrupted midsentence by the major while making a radio request for an additional PBR to assist us.

"Disregard that request. We can handle this."

After throwing the microphone onto dashboard of the boat, I turned to question his decision. Before I could utter a word, the major jumped off the boat and began sloshing his way in waist-high water toward the body forty feet away. Despite warnings by several crewmembers respectfully advising him to avoid grabbing the body by its limbs, he did exactly that. While tugging the left arm at the elbow, he experienced what we all had experienced six bodies earlier.

To the major's dismay and our disgust, layers of skin filled his hand as some of it fell from the bone and back in the water. Undaunted by his display of carelessness, he continued pulling the body by the same arm towards the PBR, only to discover that the arm was tearing away from the torso. Some shook their heads in revulsion, others turned their heads while I silently wrestled with the rage building up inside me over his callous arrogance.

Closing the distance between us, he insisted that we all jump in and assist him in raising the body up and putting it on the rear deck.

When I calmly explained that the procedure would disfigure the remains even further, he shook his head and said, "That's an order! Get in here, all of you. We are putting this man onboard." Reluctantly, four of us complied leaving the coxswain on board to assist in securing the body to the rear deck. None of the machine guns were manned. No one controlled the PBR. We were sitting ducks.

Our illustrious major showed no concern for the safety of the crew, even refusing to allow a man to remain as the aft machine gunner.

Major Z had absolutely no understanding of tactical

operations.

It was after several bungled attempts to lift the body up to the rear deck that finally brought an end to the misery. The debacle resulted in the left arm being virtually detached. Assisting one another we pulled ourselves back aboard. I glanced at the three crewmembers silently making their way towards the bow, their faces flushed in anger. Two of the crew who stood above the body had the same rage in their faces, their eyes now focused on the corpse.

I caught my breath bent over the dead man, both hands firmly placed on my knees. And then it all started. After a few deep breaths, the major moved past the body towards the coxswain's flat and exclaimed, "That is how you people should have recovered these bodies instead of dragging these men with ropes tied to them like cattle! Who the hell do you people think you are?"

I knew the instant these words poured out of his mouth, the fuse to that powder keg welling up within all of us throughout this living nightmare had been lit. As I raised my head, my eyes locked on the aft machine gunner, his right hand on the holster of his .45 automatic pistol muttering, "Say the word, Bog."

The major either heard the ambiguous utterance or perceived a threat because the instant he started to respond, a flurry of angry shouts by most of the crewmembers instantly filled the air. I teetered on the edge of sanity. As the broad-based insubordinate screams directed at all forms of authority continued, my mind spun with the unpleasant circumstances I knew we would all confront in the days to come.

Hell, I even considered shooting the bastard myself, and in the milliseconds that followed a half-dozen different scenarios challenged what little calm I had left. Veiled threats conveyed by the men at military authority were obviously directed at the major. Sensing the menace he had provoked he made a feeble attempt at regaining control of the situation he found himself drowning in by shouting, "That's enough. You're not military policemen, you're pirates! All of you are looking at a General Court Martial, here!"

Instantly and without any forethought, I snapped back, "Nobody is going to a court martial major, because nobody is gonna remember a fucking thing that was said or done out here. Go ahead take your complaint to battalion. Who's gonna believe you? You don't have any witnesses. None of us knows what the fuck you are talking about, major!"

A momentary silence followed. Then, "You're in a world of shit, Bogison," he calmly retorted. Knowing that I had really stepped in it, I said, "That may very well be, but right now and with all due respect, I really don't give a shit, sir." No further words were spoken, just the mesmerizing drone of diesels and the splatter of water against the hull as we proceeded full speed back to the French Pier. I was all in, way over my head and drowning in that world of shit.

Our attention was drawn to the military personnel and heavy equipment scattered about the pier. A tugboat pulled a large floating barge with a heavy duty crane, and some dredging machinery was moored next to the pier, along with several 2 1/2 ton military trucks and some earth moving equipment parked nearby. A Huey was setting down on an adjacent clearing. We tied the PBR against the cement wall and Graves Registration removed the body.

It was a simpler operation for them now, then it would have been for us fifteen hours earlier. Rise and fall of the Đồng Nai had changed considerably from the previous evening. Now, approaching noon, the tidal level had risen over four feet putting our deck just inches below the pier. I watched the major disembark. Without uttering a word he disappeared into the crowd of villagers loitering behind the barricades that the recently arrived 557th Military Police Company set up.

Amazing to see the volume of resources that finally managed

to arrive at this place. We couldn't get anything during the hours of darkness when it was really needed. Relative to the sights and sounds of all the activity my memory is clear, but I cannot recall whether the dozen or more military personnel affiliated with all this equipment were Army engineers, Navy Sea Bees or a combination of both.

There was no time to mull over all the Catch-22s that had befallen me. I was directed over the radio to continue the search for bodies and recover papers and debris associated with the crash. All this in addition to providing security for military personnel dredging the Đồng Nai attempting to recover the helicopter. Further, my crews were to coordinate tasks with day watch personnel in accordance with directives received from the harbor master.

I caught a glimpse of Lieutenant Steinberg onboard one of the day watch PBRs as we passed by later that afternoon. Sergeant Henry was nowhere to be seen, which was no surprise. Several hours into this operation we were finally advised that all passengers and crewmembers on the ill-fated 25th Infantry helicopter had been identified. The only personnel missing, the pilot and the co-pilot, were probably still strapped to their respective seats somewhere in the depths of the Đồng Nai.

If there was any high note in this horrific incident, my crews could take some kind of pride in knowing that we left no man behind. As for recovering any debris of the downed chopper or additional papers floating on or near the river, none were seen. It appeared that we had been successful in that aspect of the recovery operation.

∞

64
"What kind of a circle jerk is this?"

Throughout the afternoon and into the early evening hours, the tugboat stayed moored alongside the large barge midway between the eastern and western shore, not far from the power lines that caused the accident. Later, sights and sounds of the huge crane and dredging equipment and the helicopter hovering above suggested that the downed chopper had been located. As their combined efforts continued, we watched the shattered remains of the chopper break the surface as the crane operator slowly swung it onto the barge.

What remained of the cockpit came into view, the bodies of pilot and co-pilot could be seen in their seats. Their deteriorated condition was much worse than the others. Left was nothing more than contorted remnants of flesh, some hair and exposed bone devoid of any facial features. It took several additional hours to move the barge and equipment to the opposite side of the river.

On reaching the other side of the Đồng Nai, a large crowd of villagers was lined up all along the shoreline like ants. Mingled in that crowd were a dozen or more military personnel, which initially I thought were South Vietnamese soldiers. However, as we drew nearer, I realized that these were all American officers wearing the 18th Military Police Brigade patch on the upper arm sleeve of their jungle uniform shirts. Within minutes they boarded the barge and swarmed around the remnants of the chopper. Easing our PBR next to the tugboat to get a better view of the commotion, we were appalled for the second time as we watched these officers pose for photographs next to the horrific remains of the two warrant officers trapped in the cockpit.

Over the din of our idling engines, I looked at a graves registration sergeant, and shouted, "What kind of a circle jerk is this? Don't you guys have a fucking officer that can stop this shit?" All I received was the nod of his head, the annoying look on his face, followed by his murmur, "No. We do not." Clearly, he was as disgusted as we all were but helpless to do anything as he was outnumbered and outranked.

My shout above the drone of engines was heard by all, as most of these officers and gentlemen as defined by their commissioned ranks began to surreptitiously leave the area. However, there was a captain in the company of a lieutenant who approached us from the deck of the tugboat and asked, "Who said that?" Silence, as we all looked at each other. "Who said that?" he added in a stronger tone. "That would be me!" I retorted, as he examined my name tag and asked, "Specialist Bogison! You do understand what insubordination is don't you?" "Yes, sir, I do!" I replied. "Change your attitude Bogison, you're an NCO." "Yes sir, I'll get right to work on that!"

I snapped back, while turning my back to him, signaling to the coxswain to wind up the engines. The rear jet valves violently churned up the waters, spewing it all around the pair as we sped away. What the hell? Why not add more gas to the mess I wallowed in?

It was nearing our 26th straight hour on the water when somebody finally recognized that some of us might need to be relieved. My crews and I were directed to return to Long Binh Post for a brief respite which would allow just enough time for all of us to shower, shave and perhaps even get a hot meal.

The first thing we did was remove our clothing which reeked of decay, then chucked the assorted attire over the sandbags outside our hooch and dashed to the showers.

Scrubbing down with the soap and cold water brought assurance that all remnants from those dead bodies had been cast off. Nevertheless, the stench of death remained and lingered with us even days later. When we entered the mess hall which had finished serving meals for the battalion hours earlier, the cooks were kind enough to fire up their ovens and prepare a hot meal.

Sitting at a table waiting, I immediately started reflecting on all the serious issues I would have to answer for. My instincts, along with my personal history with the major, convinced me that he would issue a formal complaint to the commanding officer of the battalion relative to my acts of insubordination, my interactions with the Vietnamese girl, coupled with those veiled threats that were directed at him.

This, I accepted as a given, however, my primary concern was focused on the theft of that watch and what now to do about it. Deep in thought, I determined that upon our return to the water, I would take the man aside and direct him to present the watch to the Graves Registration unit. Explaining that he had inadvertently placed the watch on his person during the recovery process and absentmindedly forgot to put it back on the body at the French Pier. There was no justification for his action. This act of errant behavior was inconsistent with his character.

At the time, I reasoned that he had become the victim of his own demons. Undoubtedly, this place and all interactions within it had a profoundly negative influence on one's ability to rationalize right from wrong. Deep in thought wrestling with these issues, I was suddenly distracted by the persistent tapping of a finger on my left shoulder. I was being greeted by a staff sergeant I had never seen before, directing me to follow him to the Battalion Headquarters immediately. Any hunger pangs I may have had, were no more.

April 19, 1970 French Pier, L-R: Author,
Chuckie Bowman.

April 19, 1970 French Pier-debriefing of chopper crash. L-R: SP/4 Jared Kelley, SGT Ed York, Author, SP/4 Denny Taylor, SP/4 Gary Rasmussen, SP/4 Glenn Barmann, SP/4 Swensen SP/4 Ed "Shakey" Marley.

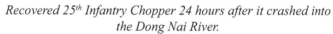

Recovered 25th Infantry Chopper 24 hours after it crashed into the Dong Nai River.

65

"And you son, are looking at 99 plus 1!"

During the short walk from the mess hall to battalion headquarters, the staff sergeant, asked, "What the fuck happened out there besides that crash?" All I said in reply was, "You wouldn't believe it." The instant I entered the battalion headquarters building, my body was hit with a cold blast of air from the ceiling fan above me. Air conditioning, I asked myself? Yes, this place actually had refrigerated air. Initially, it felt exhilarating compared to the 110 degree atmosphere I had grown uncomfortably accustomed to for the past nine months.

The exhilaration quickly faded as I followed the staff sergeant, passing through a series of hallways and offices with the sounds of typewriters tapping and a soft vintage orchestra playing music, interrupted by the occasional sounds of radio transmissions barking out information. All the while, my hearing was becoming muffled followed with those feint hissing sounds again along with something else that was new to me. My peripheral vision was inexplicably fading.

As we approached the closed door of the battalion commander's office, the staff sergeant knocked on the door, opened it and said, "Sir, Specialist Bogison is here."

"Get him in here, Sergeant. That'll be all," bellowed a voice from within. Entering, I turned and walked briskly towards the man standing behind a desk cluttered with papers. Affixed to the front of the desk was an OD placard with white colored letters inscribed, "BATTALION COMMANDER 720th Military Police Battalion." Standing to his immediate left was the major. The expressions on both their faces made it abundantly clear to me that my perilous journey into the unchartered territory of facing serious charges before a General Court Martial had begun.

Snapping to attention while holding my salute, I barked out "Sir, Specialist Bogison reporting as ordered, sir!" waiting for the return of his salute which was the proper protocol. There I stood, frozen in that position for what seemed like 30 seconds or more as he slowly and with great deliberation eyed me up and down, both his hands on his hips. The Battalion Commander, Lieutenant Colonel Robert E. Stromfors, was a towering figure at least five inches taller than my lanky six foot frame.

Finally, snapping his heels together returning my salute, he said as he sat in his chair, "That'll be all, Major. You, (nodding at me) sit down." For whatever foolish reasoning I possessed at the time, I blurted out, "I'd rather stand, sir!" Big mistake. As he rose from his chair, placing both hands on his desk while leaning over it closing the distance between us, he shouted, "You will sit down! Now! Specialist!" Like the dead weight of a bag of lead I immediately dropped into a chair.

He remained leaning over his desk and yelled back, "If any of this shit that has been reported to me is true, there will be a Court Martial. And you son, are looking at 99 plus 1! In Leavenworth! Do I have your attention, Specialist?" Ninety-nine plus one meant I faced a ninety-nine year sentence, plus one day.

He had my attention all right, my undivided attention.

His first question caught me completely by surprise when he asked, "Did you authorize any of your people to misappropriate personal property from the bodies of these dead men? Specifically, a watch that was taken from one of the dead officer's wrist?" As dozens of thoughts raced at lightning speed I felt my world closing in around me. How the hell did he learn of this so quickly I asked myself, then responded, "No, sir! I did not authorize anybody to take personal items from any dead bodies, including those of any officers."

My response was the truth. Not reporting the incident at once was an omission, an intentional oversight. When the Colonel asked, "Did you witness anybody take personal items from these bodies?" I responded with a bold-faced lie and said, "No, sir, I did not." All the while knowing that if I was convicted of providing false information during a criminal investigation and lying under oath during a court martial, I would face a minimum of five years imprisonment.

"Did your crewmembers threaten the life of my staff officer? Yes or no, God damn it!" he bellowed, to which I immediately replied with, "What? No sir!" "What's that?" he shouted, "No sir, nobody threatened anybody. I saw no such thing, sir!" I bellowed back, all the while being nervously hopeful that my body language wasn't exposing the lie that had just rattled out of my mouth.

"Why should I believe you Bogison?" he asked, slowly backing away from his desk and into his seat. "Sir?" I asked. He just stared at me while I teetered on that now familiar edge between notions of right and wrong, feeling certain that he could see right through my facade.

As those feelings welled up, he shouted, "And what about the Vietnamese girl at the pier? What were your intentions with her?" My mind vacillated, as he added, "There were no less than ten officers that witnessed your actions!" My voice along with the composure I was desperately trying to discover deep inside me finally started to emerge.

"I wanted to cave her head in! She was a VC and so was the little bastard that was with her. I know a VC when I see one. What are we supposed to do with these people? Hold their hands in the daytime and then ask for permission from Battalion to kill them when they move against us at night?" I exclaimed.

He immediately fired back, "You're out of line Bogison! Way out of line! Better think before you open that mouth of yours. It could cost you a lot," and then added, "The only reason I am accepting your explanation on this matter is because Sergeant Major Wilkinson tells me you are a good soldier; and I have great respect for my Sergeant Major Wilkinson!"

A long period of silence followed with the colonel glaring at me and me staring at the "BATTALION COMMANDER 720th Military Police Battalion" desk plate in front of me.

The incessant hissing sounds in my ears were silenced when the colonel said in a softer tone, "Son, you know, sometimes things can get pretty confusing out there. The next time, you are directed to report to me, if there is a next time, I might not be able to help you. Now, get out of here. You and your crews are finished for now. Go back to your people and all of you, get some rest. Report for duty tomorrow night."

Rising from the chair, I saluted and as I approached the door he asked, "Is it true some of my officers were taking pictures of themselves next to the bodies?" As I turned to face him, I said, "Yes sir, that is true."

And then as I reached for the doorknob he asked, "Did you insult a group of officers by implying they were engaged in a circle jerk out there?" "Yes sir, that is also true." "One last question. Son, was it necessary to drag the bodies behind your boat? Was there no other way?" "Sir, we tried everything. Every time we tried to get them on the decks of our boats, limbs would start to break apart. Dragging them slowly behind us was the only way we were able to keep their arms and legs attached. For both, officers and enlisted men."

The colonel solemnly shook his head and said, "That's all."

As I walked down the hallway and towards the front door I realized that this place and everything associated with it was far removed from the world I had grown accustomed to. I didn't fit in it and the instant I closed the front door behind me I was glad to be out. I expected to be confronted by the major waiting for me outside, but I was pleasantly surprised to see that he was nowhere in sight. For now anyway, I could breathe a little easier. I headed directly to the NCO Club, drowned what sorrows I may have had with several shots of whiskey, stumbled to my hooch and collapsed face down on my bunk.

L-R: Lieutenant Colonel Robert E. Stromfors,
CSM Peter D. Pauli.

Early the following afternoon, I was rudely awakened by the incessant pounding on the door of my hooch and the familiar voices of Shakey and Barmann barking out, "Bog! Bogie! Hey, you in there?" Discovering that I was in the same position I left myself in the night prior, I pushed my face from the pillow in an effort to sit up, but not before slamming my head into the metal framework of the top bunk. Trying to comfort my aching head with both hands, the pair burst into my hooch as Shakey asked, "Bog you alright? Man, that was some shit last night, but it ain't nothing compared to what we just heard!"

"Wait. What are you talking about? What happened last night?" I asked.

"Where the hell were you, Bog? Charlie threw a couple of 122s at us last night. They came pretty close. They flew right over us and blew up somewhere next to the Medical Dispensary." Barmann explained. "Yea, I thought for sure the first one was gonna hit us. I don't think anybody got hit." Added Shakey. "I'll be damned. Never even heard it." I muttered.

Fully awake now, I listened intently to what Barmann and Shakey had to say regarding rumors circulating about somebody tossing a grenade in a battalion officer's hooch. As they continued relating this information my mind raced. I immediately assumed that if the story was true, the battalion officer was none other than the major and the person or persons responsible for the act had to be one of my own crewmembers. The more I thought the more I was convinced. The timing of this incident was just too much of a coincidence.

As Barmann started suggesting that our people may have been involved, I interrupted him mid-sentence and demanded, "That's it. I don't want to hear any more of this shit. Get this and get it right. Don't say a fucking thing about this to anybody. If this is true, heads will roll. I don't even want to hear anybody asking about it. If anybody even whispers about this or anything related to it, tell him to shut the fuck up. The less everybody knows the better. Now get the word out, now."

The expression on their faces told me that I had made my point. It seemed my days with the 3rd Platoon found me in the right place at the right time. My days on the water had just begun and already I was in the wrong place at the wrong time. What a difference twenty-four hours could impact on one's life. There was no time to dwell on things I had absolutely no control over. The war didn't stop and I still had responsibilities in spite of the fact that those nagging unresolved issues associated with the crash of the helicopter stayed with me.

Right or wrong, I chose not to report the man responsible for stealing the watch.

Was it right not to? I could say that at the time that by doing so could have revealed a link to the more serious issue - tossing of a grenade at the major. If that story was true, would we hang separately or together? Was it wrong not to report the incident? The answer is yes, in every moral sense it was. Surviving family members of that dead officer were deprived of a very personal possession. I found myself sitting on the fulcrum between the rights and wrongs of this dilemma in the days and years to come.

Recovery operations took a heavy toll on the entire PBR/ Boston Whaler Platoon. It is safe to say that all of us lost a part of ourselves in the process. Recognizing some of the doom and gloom around me, I decided that we needed to find some kind cathartic release. After studying the heavy wake created by our PBRs at various speeds, I imagined the possibility of catching and riding them with a surfboard.

Convinced that it could be done, I scrounged up heavy duty cloth fiberglass, some resin and the foam padding used to pack 8-inch naval artillery shells, along with wood and rebar from some

Navy guys stationed on the Saigon docks. Within two nights on the barge and away from the prying eyes of Steinberg, Henry, Canada I managed to assemble a functional albeit unsightly and extremely heavy ten foot surfboard.

Getting caught in any of this activity would result in serious disciplinary action. We never got caught and nobody really cared.

66

April 17/18, 1970 Recovery Operation
Downed Helicopter
Official Report (Edited)

D ecades after the corpse recovery mission I happened on the Army's official findings in the investigation of the catastrophe. Its dry, matter-of-fact tone is in glaring contrast to the terror of the event and the horror of our recovery experience.

The primary mission of this aircraft was to fly the division courier while interjecting passenger pick up and drop offs during the courier run.

While on its final mission of the day, the aircraft was flown to II Field Force (red carpet helipad) arriving at 17:12 hours (local) to pick up the division INO officer at 1800 hours. During the hour ground time at II Field Force, WO Harig, Simeonoff, and CW2 Cross, departed the aircraft and went to the II Field Force Officer's Club, located approximately one block from the helipad, for supper. All three returned to the aircraft at approximately 18:00 hours.

The crew and passengers departed red carpet helipad at 18:12 hours to return to Cu Chi base camp. The wind was out of the south at 7 knots, visibility was approximately 15 miles, sky condition was 4,000 scattered with a temperature and dew point spread of approximately 32/24.

At approximately 18:25 hours while flying at an altitude of approximately 70 feet AGL, the aircraft struck two stranded steel cables.

The first striking the center of the nose of the aircraft cutting the radio compartment cover in half, then sliding up over the roof of the aircraft cutting the UHF antenna and air vents, then into the controls of the aircraft cutting the fore and aft, and lateral cyclic servos.

This tension on the mast of the aircraft gave it an excessive nose high attitude at which time the main rotor blade struck the wire, shattering the blade and breaking the wire, while the second wire, which was just growing taut, pulled the aircraft into a nose low attitude, broke due to stress from the weight and velocity of the aircraft and the aircraft went into the river vertically, nose first.

It is suspected that as the aircraft was sinking, three bodies floated to the surface of the river. One was SSG Quellette who was rescued by the Vietnamese, another was SP/4 Hunter, the only Negro on board, and the third person unknown. Fifteen minutes after the accident occurred a US Harbor Craft tug boat arrived at the scene and picked up SSG Quellette, and transported him to the old the French Pier located next to the Cogido Barge Site. SSG Quellette was then taken to the 24th Evacuation Hospital by ambulance and admitted at 19:00 hours.

All crew and passengers were recovered.

Crew members:

WO1 Dean Allen Harig, age 22, Aircraft Commander, A/25 AVN 25 Inf., Superior, NE.

WO1 Frederick M. Simeonoff age 22, Pilot A/25 AVN 25 Inf., Spenard, AK.

SP/4 William Kenneth Hunter, age 23, Crew Chief, A/25 AVN 25 Inf., Lynchburg, VA.

SGT Frederick Curtis Marsh, age 30, Gunner, A/25 AVN 25 Inf., Egg Harbor, NJ.

Passengers

CPT Howard Rivers Andrews, Jr., age 27, 25 Inf., Huntsville, AL.

CPT Robert John Zonne, Jr., age 27, 25th Inf. Midland, TX.

CW2 Alvin Euclid Cross, age 35, Pilot Passenger, A/25 AVN 25 Inf., Greensboro, NC.

SSG D. P. Ouellette, age unknown, 25th Inf. (survivor).

SGT Jack DeWayne Tuggle, Jr. age 20, 25 Inf., Valparaiso, FL (posthumously promoted).

SP/4 Michael Joseph Weik age 20, 25 Inf., Ft. Worth, TX. PFC Howard Dennis Landry age 20, 25 Inf., Baton Rouge, LA."

67

Not so friendly fire

Early one evening a week or so later, Boston Whaler Operators, SP/4 Doug Newman and SP/4 Ed Santry had just dropped off an ambush platoon when Santry's whaler developed engine trouble.

As Newman pulled alongside to assist in towing the disabled craft back to the barge, the pair came under small arms fire from a passing South Vietnamese Patrol Boat. My crew along with another PBR crew responded to what turned out to be another friendly fire incident. An all-too common tale. Newman's statement, slightly edited, concerning the incident follows:

Jumping into the water didn't seem to be viable so we just hugged the bottom of the boat.

The intensity of the fire kept us from getting to the radio or even our flares. After a considerable amount of time there was a break in the barrage. I tried to get to my flares when the firing started again. It was at this time I caught shrapnel from the round that went through the steering column and into the engine. After a second assault, an illumination flare was fired and the attack ended. What we didn't know was that the troops we had dropped off were down range of the Vietnamese PBR fire.

Someone was able to fire a green flare which apparently was instrumental in stopping the attack. The PBR drifted over and we could see it was a Vietnamese crew with an American Advisor. I discovered a large chunk of metal embedded just below my right elbow. It had fused to the skin so bleeding was minimal.

I tried to drive off but the round that hit my steering prevented me from navigating in a straight line. After a period of time I was taken to shore and transported to the hospital for treatment.

Signed: SP/4 Douglas D. Newman.

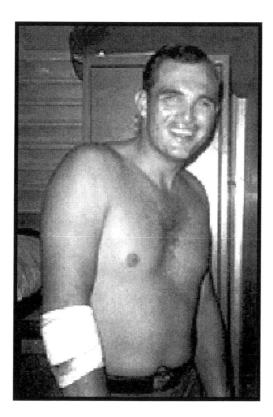

68

"Where are we taking you, Lieutenant?"

Two weeks passed since the recovery operation and I hadn't heard anything, not even a rumor. It was like nothing happened. Highly irregular, in my experience, considering that the military justice system was typically swift by the standards of the time. I fully expected all of us to have been interviewed by Army investigators and standing before a general court martial by this time.

It was the first week in May and I had newly completed the 10th month of my 14 month tour of duty. Just days before the chopper crash, I extended my tour to September 10th, instead of my obligated tour which would end on July 6th.

After considerable deliberation, I decided to take a chance on extending my time in hopes of leaving Vietnam and the Army five months early, and in one piece. Arriving home in early September would ensure that I could enroll and attend college within a few days of my homecoming. It was gambling with my life but I was confident of my ability to perform my responsibilities. More than all of that, I was growing increasingly concerned about the welfare of the people I had to answer for, both on the water and in the bush.

I needed them and they needed me. I was not ready to leave

them. Most of these guys had been drafted for the obligatory two years and entered the Army six months to a year after me. My additional time and grade in the Army made it easier for them to approach me when they looked for answers to their questions, in spite of the fact that I was nothing more than just one of them with one more stripe on my sleeve.

It was on an evening early in that first week of May when I received a radio call from the 1st Platoon leader. Words had it that this lieutenant, name long forgotten, commanded a lot of respect among the men of 1st and 2nd Ambush Platoons. A rare distinction for Bushwhackers in 1970 Vietnam. He requested that I meet him at the old spooky brick factory, on the Đồng Nai shore.

I knew precisely what he needed.

Our whalers were down for repairs and strategists plotting artillery missions in our tactical operations center were redirecting the 1st Platoon to an alternative ambush site on the opposite side of the TAOR. No doubt about it, they would have to make the perilous journey on foot, through jungle and swamps under the umbrella of a full moon. The lieutenant, obviously concerned about the welfare of his men, would plead with me to transport the platoon with my PBRs. I knew all too well how foolhardy and suicidal it could be for them to move on foot.

My decision was simple. We would transport the men to their destination.

However, the consequences of the decision could be dire. I had been repeatedly told that under the new rules of engagement transportation of ambush personnel on PBRs without prior authorization was strictly prohibited. In accordance with that edict, the likelihood of getting authorization was remote, and even if we had approval it would never have come in a timely manner.

My challenge was multidimensional. Violating the standing orders created a loyalty divide between B Company and the

458th boat guys and their Lieutenant Steinberg. All of us from B Company - regardless of how much or any time already served in the bush - knew that being sent out there to serve as an infantry grunt, for any reason and at any time, was inescapable. Taking care of our own was a given, which is not to suggest that the 458th didn't have their own credo. They did.

Their foremost responsibility was care, custody and control of their PBRs. 458 Transportation Company and B Company crews were akin to the harmony of well-functioning parts in a fine-tuned machine. My decision was like throwing a handful of dirt on that machinery. Telling them to transport ambush personnel to their destination violated orders. It was prohibited. Moreover, I would be asking them to move men from the western shore of the Đồng Nai to the opposite side, deep into the eastern and northernmost reaches of our tactical area of operation all while navigating in shallow and hazardous waters of the Buông.

I needed every man I could get, including the collective skills of whaler operators Shakey, Kelley, and Barmann as they were intimately familiar with the Buông.

After assembling crews and whaler operators on the deck of our barge, my instructions were direct and nonpartisan. I emphasized that nobody had to volunteer for this assignment, but I strongly urged my fellow Bushwhackers, all of whom were capable of operating a PBR, to assist me in moving 1st Platoon, and I assured everyone that I would assume full responsibility for this decision.

None of the Bushwhackers hesitated. A few grumbles among the 458 guys. All of them stepped forward and agreed to pilot the four PBRs. Everybody knew that this was a dangerous undertaking. The unmistakable sounds of four big diesels travelling at a slow pace and under a full moon could easily be detected for several miles in any direction, particularly while navigating the Buông.

Shakey, Kelley, and Barmann were assigned separate PBRs to serve as pathfinders and monitor the radio, and transmit cautious maneuvers for the coxswains. The fourth PBR trailing behind us was designated as our rear guard.

My boat was piloted by Chuckie Bowen with Denny Taylor on the forward twin .50s, Ed Kelleher was on the aft .50, and Shakey Marley was our pathfinder. In our approaches to the brick yard we were signaled by 1st Platoon's flashing red lens light. As was the custom, all boats silenced their engines, timed at just the right distance and speed to gently float to shore 50 feet away where I was met by the lieutenant. As I lowered a hand to help lift him up on the rear deck, he said, "You knew huh?" to which I said, "Yea, I knew. Get everybody on board but just on the first three boats. The fourth boat is strictly for killing, not transporting. Where are we taking you, Lieutenant?"

"About half a click north of the Rabbit Ears. I owe you Bog. Big time!" he said as he shook my hand and directed his platoon sergeant to get the men on board. Within seconds the formerly clean decks were loaded with men and mud, as we headed south towards the bend east at the bottom of the boot to begin our journey. Our boat took the lead.

⑥⑨

"Bog, you remember that night when somebody put that kabar to your throat?"

Traveling at less than ten miles per hour, those familiar gut wrenching feelings I experienced on the whalers while being transported to an ambush site just weeks earlier had returned. However, dodging and weaving around sandbars, fallen timber and floating debris masterfully guided by the collective skills of Shakey, Kelley and Barmann eased some of that tension.

It was about midway into our journey, when Shakey tapped me on the shoulder and muttered, "This is fucking crazy. You know it, Bog?" "Yea, I know it. Right now, I don't know if I'm more concerned about getting wasted out here, or what I'm gonna face tomorrow explaining why I authorized this shit to the lieutenant if he finds out. Well, it don't mean shit anyway. We both know why we're doing this."

Shakey added, "Yea, and so does Kelley, Barmann and anybody else that knows what it's like to hump out there on a night like this. If Charlie's out here tonight, we are all sitting ducks on these slow moving monsters. I never thought I would feel so damned jumpy riding on one of these things especially with all these people and all this firepower. I'd feel a lot safer out here on my own whaler, with my own machine gun, with

Barmann and Kelley trailing behind me. This is fucking insane, Bog. A guy could get killed out here."

And then out of nowhere Shakey said, "I guess now is as good a time as any. Bog, you remember that night when somebody put that kabar to your throat?" "Yea, I do? Who the fuck was that?" I asked. "Well, that somebody was me. I'm sorry Bog, but some of us really thought you were CID and that you were planted here to bust us." "Bust you! For what?" I asked.

"Well, it's pretty common knowledge that some of us "heads" smoke dope while "juicers" like yourself and the rest of the NCOs drink. None of us 'heads' could even imagine having to deal with humping in the bush every day and night, get busted for smoking a joint, and then get sent to Long Binh Jail. I'm sorry Bog, and so are the rest of us for ever doubting you. I figured I better let you know now. Hell, I might get my ass snuffed out here tonight."

"God damn it Shakey, I know who the 'heads' are and I know who smokes shit and who don't. I also know that most of you boys have the presence of mind not to smoke that shit when we're out in the field. What the fuck you boys do on your own time back at Long Binh is on all of you, not on me." I answered.

"You gonna bust me Bog?" he asked. Shaking my head I asked him, "For what?"

"You know, for threatening you and putting that kabar to your throat?" he continued. "No, God damn it. I have too much respect for you and every son-of-a-bitch out here with me. Two things I want to know though, was that a .45 you had jabbed against my back and would you have cut my throat if I really was CID?" Shakey responded, "No and yes. I had the butt end of my bayonet against your back, not a .45. I couldn't fire a gun out there or else the place would be crawling with dinks (GI slang for VC). If you were a CID agent to bust us, yes, I would have cut your throat or tossed a grenade next to you. Everybody would have assumed a

342 / UP-CLOSE & PERSONAL

dink did it, not one of us."

"Well, thanks for letting me keep my throat. You know you really wouldn't have done me any favors by doing so, you know. Basically, I'm a pussy, but don't let the rest of the boys in on that. Let's keep that between you and me. Any other crimes you want to confess to Father Bog?" I asked sarcastically. "No, but being the part-time Catholic that I am, thanks Bog."

An answer to the mystery that eluded me for past three months was now solved. Shakey confessed. It got him some healthy respect from me. We were lucky that night, as the impending doom we all felt certain would descend on us never came. The ambush platoon was dropped off without enemy contact and the perilous journey back to the barge with all four boats and crews was accomplished without incident.

Now, all that mattered was to scrub down the decks to remove traces of mud and debris and get back to our primary mission of patrolling the Đồng Nai.

The remainder of that evening and throughout the early morning hours of the following day were uneventful. Within minutes of his arrival onto the barge later that morning, Lieutenant Steinberg approached me and said, "I need to talk to you now, over here." He led the way and boarded an unoccupied PBR moored a considerable distance away from the rest of the men. He said, "Okay. I already know that you transported an ambush platoon last night. So, you can spare me the bullshit you were about to tell me. You wanna tell me why?" To which I replied, "No, not really sir."

"Well, let's try now!" he barked.

"It was my decision and my decision alone. All of your 458 people were adamantly opposed to it."

"Well that's all very noble of you Specialist Bogison, but that doesn't answer my question. Why did you authorize the use of PBRs to transport an ambush platoon when you clearly don't have the authorization to do so?" he asked.

To which I responded, "With all due respect sir, I don't think you would understand my reasoning for doing it."

"Oh, really. Do explain!" he snapped.

I then spelled out in great detail that I did so based entirely on my own experience as a squad leader responsible for the safety and welfare of the men assigned to me. I added, "The lieutenant of that ambush platoon was charged not with just the lives of one squad but he was responsible for the lives of an entire platoon. Our PBRs gave him the means to do just that."

I concluded, "I stand by that decision and I would do it again. I'll request a transfer back to my ambush platoon with First Sergeant Collins at the end of watch today, sir." To my astonishment he said, "Next time, have the courtesy to advise me rather than me having to confront you. There will be no need for a transfer. You are not going anywhere. You have an Australia R & R coming up next week. You need it. I'll see you when you get back."

And as he turned to walk away, he pointed to a dried mud encrusted boot print on the rear deck of the PBR, and said, "My boys know how to keep the decks clean and mud free of Bushwhacker boot prints. Might I suggest that you ensure that your Bushwhacker PBR crews do the same?"

Life's lessons can have a profound effect on the way we judge people. Such was the case with Lieutenant Steinberg. I had misjudged him completely.

70
Seven days, seven nights, Sydney, Australia

It was Glenn Ward who offered to drive me to Tân Sõn Nhất Airport for my flight to Sydney, Australia. Ward was intimately familiar with all roads that led to and from every the gin mill, clip joint, and places that housed ladies of the evening from Biên Hòa to Saigon, and parts in between. Clip joints exist in any city throughout the world and in the US wherever military personnel are stationed or travel to. They are bars and/or brothels established for the express purpose of cheating or robbing servicemen. The man was a natural ambassador of good cheer to the local population, along with the rank and file of B Company.

Arriving on the tarmac, Ward said, "Bog, I got you here in one piece and I'll be here to pick your ass up seven days from now. Now, ya'll have a good time in Sydney now y' hear?" I didn't know it at the time but just days later, Ward, along with others from B Company would be involuntarily attached to units selected to spearhead a massive secret invasion of Cambodia. Formulated by the Nixon Administration, thousands of US military personnel were taken from their respective units to boost efforts by the South Vietnamese Army to capture and destroy NVA sanctuaries deep in Cambodia.

Prior to boarding our commercial jetliner, all military personnel were directed to change out of jungle garb and into civilian attire. It was a bit of a shock slipping into these clothes, shock shared by most of the strangers with me who hadn't worn civilian clothing in months. To my surprise, pants that used to fit me ten months earlier were now several sizes too large. The 175-pound frame I carried had diminished to less than 160, and my 31-inch waist had dwindled down at least two inches.

I wasn't alone. Others were in the same predicament. It didn't really matter to any of us. Just the thought of getting out of this place was good enough. When I entered the cabin my eyes swiveled to a pair of round-eyed women seated next to each other, clad in short skirts. I asked myself, "What are they doing here?" This was my first sighting of an American woman since I arrived in-country. I knew we had Army nurses on Long Binh Post, but I never saw one, not even when I was transported to the dispensary after my bout with drinking water from the Buông.

No less than five guys blocked my way down the cabin aisle, all of them unsuccessfully trying to engage the women in conversation. I couldn't blame them for trying but it was plain to see that these girls were interested in a classier example of the male species. During this observance of futility-in-action, came the all too familiar command presence of what everyone suspected was an Army officer behind me who bellowed, "All right gentlemen, leave the ladies alone so the rest of us can grab a seat. Now!"

Bottleneck resolved.

The first leg of our trip took us to Darwin where the airport looked like something you might find in a 1930s Central Africa jungle movie.

The terminal, surrounded by several dirt pathways, was a simple but rather large wood-framed, screened-in structure with a series of timeworn ceiling fans providing some relief from the stifling heat. Devoid of any significant vegetation it was nothing but barren sun-baked dirt and scrub for as far as the eye could see in any direction. It was every bit of what I would have expected it to look like, in what Australians referred to as the "Outback."

An hour later we were back in the air. Approaching Sydney, the skies were overcast. A male voice on the intercom told us we could expect light rain and cool temperatures. Not the 110-degrees I was accustomed to. When I selected Sydney as my choice for an R & R destination, it never occurred to me that the seasons are reversed in the southern hemisphere. I quickly dismissed my misjudgment, as I was determined to put Vietnam and all of those nagging unresolved issues associated with the chopper crash behind me.

All that mattered was that I didn't have to answer to anybody about anything for the next seven days and nights.

Or so I thought.

Sydney is beautiful and my recollection of the city after all these years is relatively clear. It reminded me of San Francisco. Waiting for a taxi I soaked up the sights and noise around me and for the first time in months I felt safe, secure and very comfortable. The sounds of sporadic small arms fire, incoming/outgoing artillery and the constant drone of low flying aircraft were replaced with ordinary traffic, horns and people speaking English albeit, marginally different from the parlance I was accustomed to. My cab driver was a talkative middle-aged man who revealed after just a few minutes of conversation that he was very familiar with the routine of befriending newly arrived American servicemen.

Implying that he could "reasonably render" whatever services he could provide during my entire visit. He suggested that I consider allowing him to conduct a tour of his city for me. A hustler to say the least, but he was precisely what a GI needed to steer clear of some of the unsavory people and clip joints, most of which were reputed to be located in the Kings Cross section of town. We had repeatedly been warned that Kings Cross was "Strictly Off Limits" and any serviceman seen there would immediately be placed under arrest by the combined efforts of the US Military Police and the New South Wales Police.

Just passing through the area by misadventure or stupidity with no specific intent could get you arrested for Disorderly Conduct. Next thing, you would be promptly whisked away to a jail cell occupied with other hapless GIs who were lured there for whatever reason. And there you would remain until your scheduled return flight to Vietnam. Hence, no R & R and the real possibility of facing a court martial, fine and/or thirty day sentence in LBJ awaited your return. Kings Cross was at that time, a notorious crime-ridden sanctuary for all the deserters and black marketeers wanted by the US Government.

Arriving in front of the Carlton Rex Hotel, and reasonably comfortable with my new found friend, I instructed him to meet me in the lobby the following morning for that tour of the city. The Carlton Rex was listed by the US military as an approved lodging resort hotel for servicemen and their families. The standard was equivalent to any five-star hotel at home. On that first night I indulged in the luxury of a long hot shower, tore open the covers to the bed and literally crashed face first on the mattress. I have absolutely no memory of anything or anybody from the time my head hit the bed early that evening until I stumbled back on my feet and into the bathroom nearly twenty-four hours later.

It was the longest period of time I had ever spent asleep in bed, the likes of which I have never experienced since. After another long, hot shower and a shave I noticed that a small light affixed to my telephone was constantly flashing. Having never experienced the luxury of staying in a high-end hotel before, and completely unfamiliar with the services these establishments offered, I ignored it.

Besides, I had absolutely no use for a telephone. Who would call me and for that matter, who would I call? The cost to make a long distance phone call to Lorraine or my family in those days was beyond prohibitive, it was ridiculous.

Mulling the issue, my silence was interrupted by the annoying ring of the telephone just inches away, which nearly jolted me out of my chair. Answering the call produced a man from the front desk telling me that two messages were left by my taxi cab driver expressing concern about my whereabouts and welfare. A third message was left from a member of the Hotel Security Staff advising me that they had entered my room twice to conduct a welfare check on me at the behest my taxi driver.

As it would turn out, my decision to take advantage of the man's taxi services throughout my entire stay in Sydney was a wise one. In spite of his flimflam mannerisms the man was sharp-witted, attentive, and large on loyalty. As the relationship developed he would refer to me as "Yank" and I called him "Pop." I regret that I cannot remember his real name.

The following morning in the hotel lobby I saw my new-found friend leaning against a wall reading a newspaper. As I approached, he immediately folded the paper and said something to the effect, "You had me worried, Yank. I had the chaps here at the hotel check to see if you were still alive. Must have been a pretty tough night."

After apologizing for not appearing for our prearranged meeting on the previous morning, I assured him that it had nothing to do with alcohol or any amorous escapades. I spent the rest of the morning and the entire afternoon seated in the back seat of his cab while he gave a grand tour of the city, all of which I have little or no memory of. I do however recall him taking me to Bondi Beach on at least two separate occasions. There, with the ambient temperature between the low and mid-60s and in the cold waters,

I froze riding waves on a rented surfboard, setting me apart as the only fool out there not wearing a wet suit.

This act, of course, did not allow for me to just remain anonymous, ride the waves and blend in. No. My presence drew nearly a dozen or more of the locals paddling over towards me like a pack of jackals to a lone zebra.

Understanding the tribal mindset of the surf culture in the US, which comprised what I perceived to be a sort of collective consciousness of its own kind, together with its own proclaimed territorial space. I immediately recognized that the same kind of mentality prevailed here.

I had invaded their territorial space and they were on their way to tell me as much. In California you settled the issue by either ceding wave after wave to the locals, or you bullied your way in and around them riding the wave with or without their permission. Either way, it could get physical fast and I simply wasn't up to it. Instead, I rattled off a brief apology for invading their space then told them about my recent acquaintance with some of their own countrymen serving in Vietnam and what one of them told me to expect from most of the people of Australia which was, "Because we were brought together here in Vietnam to share in a common misery, you would be welcomed by most of the people of Australia."

With that said, all tribal issues dissolved. All of them took me in as though I had known them for years and treated me like I was some kind of royalty. It culminated in a demand that I spend an evening with four of them in a local surfer-themed bar. Little did I know that a typical evening of drinking in Australia traditionally begins at or near 8 pm and does not end until well after dawn on the following morning.

They refused my money and paid for everything. Regrettably, I don't remember any of their names. All of the older men and women were extremely polite to us. The instant they heard you speak, they were quick to engage you in a conversation especially about their interactions with Americans arriving on their shores during World War II. My father was among the tens of thousands of servicemen stationed there just before they shipped out to engage the Japanese during the Philippine Islands Campaign, in 1945.

Here I was walking past some of the same places he might have passed some 25 years earlier. All of us servicemen were easy to spot, day or night, alone or in a crowd. We were all clean shaven, and had short hair. Australia may be an isolated continent in a wholly different hemisphere but the youth there were no different in appearance than most of their contemporaries back in the US.

Most young men I saw there flaunted long hair with beards, wore bell-bottom pants and sandals and were accompanied by young girls wearing mini-skirts, "swede" hats adorned with peace symbols attached to love bead necklaces. I sensed that their opposition to the war in Vietnam was far more restrained than it was at home. Regardless which side of the fence one sat on during the war in Vietnam, the conflict was the Number One topic of debate back in America. In Sydney, I didn't sense any of that.

71

"So put the hard-ass attitude back where it came from. Back in your ass!"

Early in the evening on about my fourth night in Sydney, I found myself among a packed crowd of American servicemen at a popular pub, one among those listed and approved by the Army. Australians refer to their bars as pubs. While seated at the main bar and well into my third whiskey, a booming albeit familiar voice rang out behind me and above all the noise, "Bogie! Bog, there you are, God damn it!" Immediately recognizing the voice to be none other than my First Sergeant Hardin Collins, I turned to look behind me and stepped off the stool, scanned the smoke-filled area and there he was, emerging from the throng.

I was instantly greeted with a handshake and an introduction to the attractive American female guest he had with him. Temporarily flabbergasted, I mainly listened as he rattled on about the great time he was having in Australia with his female guest. I thought it somewhat strange that here I was socializing with my First Sergeant, both of us out of uniform in civilian clothes in yet another foreign country.

In spite of his insistence that I call him by his first name, it was out of respect that I continued to call him Top. The whole situation seemed so surreal. Moving from the bar and to a nearby table, the three of us consumed drinks and engaged in a lengthy conversation relative to the similarities and differences in the customs of Australia and the US.

As the conversation dwindled, Top turned to his female escort and suggested that he would meet her later that evening at his hotel. Taking the cue, the lady left and as she walked into the crowd he said, as his facial features transitioned from congenial to solemn, "All right Bog, we need to talk because I gotta make a lot of decisions. Some of 'em involve you and your snuffies. I spent a lot of time yesterday trying to find you. This might take a while so I'm gonna go get us a bottle of that scratchy Australian Whiskey you got there. We're both gonna need it. This time it's on me."

It was the instant he rose from the table and turned to walk towards the bar that the reoccurring nightmare I hoped had passed into obscurity came back in view. The downed chopper. And just like that, I wasn't in Australia any more. I was back in Vietnam. My mind went into overdrive scrambling with a load of "What ifs?"

What happens if I say this? What happens if I say that? What happens if I just get drunk here and say nothing?

As quickly as the questions channeled through, came the thought of walking right out of there and making the trek down to Kings Cross to join other deserters. The thought faded just as quickly and was rejected by conceding that doing so would only defer the inevitable. Besides, every story I heard about deserters never ended well. There I remained, tormented. What follows here is the best recollection I have of the colorful conversation and the heartfelt advice First Sergeant Hardin Collins had to offer me.

Minutes later, Top returned to the table with a bottle and

two empty glasses. Nothing I found in Australia was small. The volume of whiskey in that bottle I estimated had to be well over half a gallon. Standing there, he slammed two glasses on the table, opened the bottle and began pouring into my glass, all the while staring directly at me without saying a word. He gave himself a full glass of the stuff, put the bottle on the table and eased into his seat all the while not uttering a word.

He then raised his glass and said, "Bogison, to your future, and mine!"

Youth fueled with alcohol can sometimes provoke some pretty foolish assumptions which in turn can produce some equally impudent words at the most inopportune time. I was no exception. Staring back at him, with my glass in hand but still on the table I blurted out, "Maybe I don't wanna drink to that future. What the fuck is this? My First Sergeant tracks me down . . . here in Australia? And who is the bitch with you? You two working with CID now? Nice act! You know, I wasn't camped outside of your office begging with excuses to get me out of the bush like some sergeants you and I both know did."

That ought to have been enough said. But not for the Bogster.

"Four months humping in that swamp my life was pretty simple. I was even getting used to laying out there in all that duck shit smothered in leeches. You're the one that put me out there on the water telling me that you were doing me a favor. In less than one month into this clean, dry and leech-free duty, I'm swimming in a world of shit. I didn't ask for any of this."

And as my rant continued without regard for any form of decorum, he just glared at me as he slowly downed two full glasses.

Growing impatient with my ramblings, he slowly rose from his seat and while leaning towards me he calmly and firmly muttered, "Are you done, junior? Just who in the hell do you think you are? Listen, fuzz-nuts, you think you're the only shitbird in this green machine that was forced to eat shit sandwiches without the luxury of having it served on bread?'

Slight pause, then:

Get your fucking head screwed on right now before I forget why I'm here, because I'm about ready to rip it off and shit down your neck. . . I am not the fucking CID and that lady is a very good friend of mine. So keep her out of this. . . I am your First Sergeant and believe it or not, I am here to help your dumb ass! So put the hard-ass attitude back where it came from. Back in your ass! Save that shit for your snuffies! Try listening. You might learn something."

Another brief interlude, followed by:

Now, have I made myself clear here, Sergeant Bogison?"

Still somewhat skeptical, I leaned back in my seat and with some restraint sarcastically replied, "Okay, Top. What the hell do I have to lose? The Colonel already told me I was looking at 99 and one. Can you top that? Top!" to which he angrily retorted, "Apparently, I have failed to make myself very clear in this matter. Jesus H. Christ, you are about the thickest son of a bitch. . . One more smart-assed word out of your mouth and I'm walking right out of here and then, you sir, can sink or swim in your very own world of shit all by your lonesome!

This ain't my problem son, and I damn sure don't need to wallow in it with you! I got twenty years in. Five more and maybe another tour in this fucking war and it's adios motherfucker for me. What's it gonna be for you? You want me to walk out of here?"

Acknowledging that his was the voice of reason, I removed the chip on my shoulder, and said, "All right First Sergeant, you got my attention. Where do I go from here?"

Sliding his chair closer towards me and lowering the volume of his speech he explained that the 720th Military Police Battalion would be among those selected to be deactivated within 90 days in compliance with the Vietnamization Program. The men assigned to A and C Companies would be cannibalized and reassigned to various military police companies north and south to the Mekong Delta.

As for B Company, those currently assigned to the three ambush and recon platoons would be reassigned to the 188th Military Police and redeployed far to the north, near Đà Nẵng. From there they would replace US Marines Armed Forces police units from the 1st Marine Division which was being systematically deactivated and transferred back to the US. People like me assigned to the PBR Platoon, were likely to be sent to other PBR river convoy units to the south at a place called Cat Lai.

Responsibility for reassigning all of us from B Company fell squarely on his shoulders. Throughout this part of the conversation he emphasized that all of this information was known to only a handful of people outside of the Battalion, while repeatedly saying, "Keep your mouth shut about all of this." Any reservations I may have had about him minutes earlier, were now long gone.

"Look," he continued, "I don't know what kind of grab-ass-stick assholery you and your snuffies may have pulled out there when that chopper went down and frankly, I don't give a shit. My only concern was, and it always is, that we don't lose anybody. That sir, you accomplished and you have my sincere thanks."

What came next brought it all back to me.

"But if what I heard is true, that some of our candy-assed battalion officers were taking pictures of themselves next to the dead and a certain sergeant had the balls to tell them they were a part of a big circle jerk, then for those actions and those alone, that son of a bitch has to be saved. Now listen to me. The break-up of this company is about to begin and everything is gonna turn into one big cluster-fuck for the whole battalion with everybody in it, from the commander on down."

Confirming what I had learned about the Army on my own long ago, he continued.

"Ain't nobody gonna know what's up from down. People are gonna be shuffled from one end of the fuckin' place to the other. New snuffies will be arriving in-country at the same time a whole bunch of our snuffies will be goin' back to the States. Perfect timing for some of us to get lost in this big pot of shit while all the brass back at Battalion is busy stirring it up. Are you following me on this or have you still got that head of yours up your ass?"

"Yes sir, I do. And no sir, my head is free and clear." I replied.

"Good." He continued, "Now, because some of our people have PBR experience, naturally, they will be transferred as replacements to the PBR units at Cat Lai. I don't have to send you there, I can have you transferred with most of the company up north to Đà Nẵng. The choice is yours. If it were me, I would consider the move to Đà Nẵng. The cluster-fuck started down here will not end here. The shit-storm it created down here will only get bigger up there. Trust me on this."

His twenty-plus years of hard-earned wisdom came to the fore.

"When the Army breaks up one unit then reshapes it into another one, it takes months for the shit-infested cloud it created and all the dust with it to settle. By that time you'll be long gone and out of this shit-storm you are now floating in. For what it's worth, had I known what your situation was out there that night, I would have given you whatever you needed to get the job done. I didn't find out about it until the following morning."

That bit of information answered some nagging doubt. Then,

he summed up.

"Let me know what your decision is when you get back. The sooner the better, and keep your mouth shut. This shit will pass." It was during this exchange that a deeper understanding of the man's true character emerged. One he had concealed very well within the confines of that hardboiled façade of his. After acknowledging his concern for my welfare he jokingly stated, and then requested:

"Now that the father and son talk is over, I will not swap spit with you. But I am ordering that upon your return to that land of shit we both love and miss, you will appropriate two cases of Jack Daniels for me so I can make good on a couple of promises." To which I sarcastically replied, "All right daddy, I can arrange that. But as long as we are asking for favors here, I got one. How about some kind of recognition for what my crews accomplished out there? They recovered everybody onboard that chopper and they secured all those important documents under some very difficult circumstances."

The conversation concluded with him responding, "Don't push your luck, sonny. I don't make a habit of handing out medals for people doing their job, but because you asked, I'll think on it." He gulped the remaining half glass full in his hand, rose from his seat, slammed the glass on the table, and as he turned to walk away said, "See ya back in paradise, Bog."

I watched him as he made his way out of the crowded bar then glanced at the nearly empty bottle of whiskey in front of me. To my amazement I realized that it was he not me, who had consumed just about three quarters of the stuff. He never once demonstrated anything in his speech or movements to suggest he was impaired.

There I remained deep in thought while sipping away at what was left in the bottle. Thinking of the conversation I just had, it was peculiar that no mention of the stolen watch nor anything relative to threats made to an officer was brought up. More importantly, no mention was made of any fragging incident. So was that just a rumor? Was it possible that even in his position and close proximity to the upper echelon in the chain of command that he was not aware of these things?

Or, could it be that he was very much aware of everything and felt obligated to intercede in some way on my behalf? Dwelling on it raised more questions than answers. Nevertheless, this father-son talk was more reassuring than disheartening.

Assuming as Top put it, "This shit will pass" I still had a very important decision to make. Do I take the road south to Cat Lai in unfamiliar waters with boats and crews I don't know? Or the road north to patrol the unfamiliar streets of Đà Nẵng in the company of the very same people who had my back out there in the bush? Being at the right place at the right time can be a good thing, and as Top put it, "Perfect timing for some of us to get lost in this big pot of shit while the brass back at Battalion is busy stirring up more."

However, being in the wrong place at the wrong time is a different matter altogether. Instinctively, I knew the road north was the only logical choice before me. Nonetheless, the entire situation weighed heavily on my mind for the remainder of my R&R in Australia. For those few remaining days in Sydney, I took in two American movies. "Easy Rider" starring Peter Fonda and Dennis Hopper at which I promptly fell into a deep sleep after struggling through the first five minutes, and "Butch Cassidy and the Sundance Kid" starring Paul Newman and Robert Redford.

Evenings were spent bar hopping. Time flew.

As my return flight to Vietnam began its steep descent toward Biên Hòa Airbase, I scanned the landscape surrounding it. Staring at the sparsely covered lush green patches of jungle surrounded by those familiar muddy swamps, dirty rivers, tributaries, and streams I questioned my judgment as to why I hadn't scheduled my R&R until the very end of my tour. After seven days and nights awash in clean sheets, flushing toilets, hot water, and all things large and small that I had once taken for granted were gone.

Just about everyone I knew scheduled their R&R destinations as soon as they were eligible, which was within days after serving six months. Ostensibly, I reasoned that by taking my R&R after having served over 10 months, I could endure the remaining 4 months of my tour handily. Now, with little more than a 100 days left to serve in this god-forsaken place I would have to recalibrate my mind and body anew, back to all those unnatural things that wars create.

It wouldn't take long. The instant a slight breeze of hot humid air accompanied by the putrid stench of dead bodies brushed over me as I stepped onto the tarmac, all thoughts of Australia and all those wonderful little luxuries were gone. About a 100 yards away glancing to my left, I saw over a dozen olive green plastic body bags neatly stacked on the flatbed of a 2 1/2 ton truck waiting to be transported to the nearest Graves Registration Facility for processing.

Would it really have mattered when I took my R&R? My final analysis of the question suggested that it was like everything I associated with my war in Vietnam, it was the state of my mind at the time that cued many decisions.

Jim Gufford, not Glenn Ward, met me at the airport to take me back to B Company. During our drive, Jim said that Ward along with a dozen or more other guys from our unit had been temporarily assigned to various US and South Vietnamese infantry units participating in a surprise invasion of Cambodia. On learning of this development I think we all speculated in some form or another that the war was either widening into a longer or more deadlier kind of meat grinder, or it was possibly the beginning of the end of this nonsense.

Thirty days or so later all of our guys would return alive and in one piece, with nothing spectacular to report. Ward, assigned to direct military personnel and armored vehicular traffic near a checkpoint at the Vietnam-Cambodian border, told us, "Cambodia is just a little bit cleaner than Vietnam, but not much."

We were never told what the campaign may or may not have accomplished. Only many years later and like everyone else, the answer is, "Not much." In my absence and according to Gufford, "Sarge, all you missed were some bar fights and, oh, yea Charlie slammed a few rockets into Long Binh a couple of nights ago, which I personally did not appreciate!"

On my arrival in the Company area I immediately removed a bottle of Jack Daniels, slipped the entire bottle into a standard issue OD sock and tied the open end into a knot. Inside the sock I placed a small folded piece of paper with words, "Welcome back to paradise, Top. I'll do better up in D instead of in C. Thanks, Bog." I then walked over to First Sergeant Collins' office and placed the mystery sock into one of his desk drawers.

In doing so I sealed my fate. I wouldn't be going south to Cat Lai, I would be going north to Đà Nẵng.

72

Ambush on the Đồng Nai River

Just 24 hours earlier I was eating breakfast in Australia waiting for my return flight, and here I was back on the water cruising aboard the *Stoned Geni* alongside Sergeant York and the crew of the *Da Fuzz*.

It was nearing 11:00 approaching the area where we recovered the last body of that chopper crash, and all the ensuing insanity associated with it. As I counted up the 31 days that had passed and still no investigation, it dawned on me that this day May 18, marked the birthday of my grandmother, my Uncle Charlie, and that of my sister.

Mere moments of thought into this revelation were interrupted by the unmistakable sound of rocket propelled grenades detonating, immediately followed by heavy small arms fire and intense .50 caliber machinegun fire less than a mile away to the south. The thunderous and continuous drone of powerful .50s caliber machine guns suggested there were some very angry Army/Navy gunboat crews settling a score with hostiles on or along the shores of the Đồng Nai.

Instantly and without any exchange of words, our boats proceeded full speed ahead. Seconds later, we monitored the radio traffic between the crew of a PBR gunboat reporting to the Cat Lai Tactical Operations Center that the convoy of assorted military watercraft they were escorting was under small arms fire from the eastern shore of the Đồng Nai's approaches to the Buông

River.

I grabbed the microphone of our radio and advised the Operations Center that our two Cogido PBR gunboats were responding to assist with an estimated time of arrival of less than a minute.

Gradual implementation of the Vietnamization Policy, along with all the restrictions it placed on the combat operations of American ground personnel, imposed some serious challenges to the new rules of engagement. B Company was no exception as virtually our entire Tactical Area of Operation was considered a Restricted Fire Zone. Without getting into great detail, this now meant that *"generally"* before taking any aggressive action against the enemy, we needed the approval from the bureaucratic chain of command.

Those of us assigned to river operations came under the same asinine restrictions, along with the doctrine that restricted us to patrolling waters within the confines of our Tactical Area of Operation. And under no circumstances were we allowed to cross over those boundaries. My notification to the Cat Lai Operations Center of our intentions, without first contacting our Tactical Operations Center, was a blatant violation of those standing orders.

I had no authority to allow our PBRs to respond outside the boundaries of our TAOR. The location of this ambush in progress as reported by the Cat Lai PBR crew was directly south of the Buông and clearly within the 9th Infantry TAOR.

Approaching the confluence of the Đồng Nai and Buông, I saw two Cat Lai PBRs spray .50 caliber fire into the Đồng Nai's eastern shoreline, about a 100 yards south of the Buông. Crew members of two tug boats abreast of each other, towing a large barge carrying ammunition had stopped northbound in the middle of the river and were also pouring .50 caliber rounds into the riverbank. I looked up at the wheelhouse at one of the tug boats and saw it had received a direct hit from what appeared to be an RPG.

At the same moment, I watched another Cat Lai PBR with a casualty on deck slowly proceed to the north side of the Buông, headed to an incoming medevac helicopter attempting to land. I instructed our crew to provide a field of fire and security in a northerly direction for both the helicopter and the PBR, now engaged in transferring the wounded, while Sergeant York's crew gave security and assistance to the PBRs, concentrating their fire on the eastern bank of the Đồng Nai.

In the process, Ed Kelleher and I jumped off our boat and assisted four badly wounded soldiers/sailors board the medevac. A brief look at the injuries to these guys during the transfer to the chopper suggested to me that none of them would survive their wounds. Shortly after our arrival all firing ceased.

As the smoke cleared the destructive force of our .50s had decimated the once lush and dense vegetation, which by my estimation cleared an area some 30 yards wide and 50 yards deep. With the arrival of a hunter-killer team of two Huey helicopter gunships overhead, we continued transporting the less severely wounded from the deck of the targeted tug boat and onto the medevacs.

The distorted remains of the Vietnamese Wheelhouse Operator who was killed instantly in the attack lay in pieces on the deck beneath his helm. Blasts from the RPGs had shattered several windows and sent flying shards of glass and pieces of metal in every direction, most of which found their mark on crew members in the immediate vicinity of the wheelhouse. Several crew reported receiving bullet wounds, as well.

Having completed evacuation of the wounded along with the body of the dead Vietnamese, we assisted the Cat Lai PBRs in escorting the battered convoy the rest of the way to its destination, the Biên Hòa Ammunition Supply Depot.

During that uneventful journey I hoped not to be standing tall in front of somebody demanding to know under whose authority I allowed my PBRs to leave our tactical area of responsibility. Fortunately, it never happened. The only inquiry came from Lieutenant Steinberg who asked immediately upon my return to the boat barge, "How'd it go? All our people okay?" After briefing the sequence of events to him, he responded, "No need to make any report on it. The Heavy Boat Transportation people will be writing the Serious Incident Report. Good job."

Obviously, the lieutenant had monitored radio traffic between us and the Cat Lai PBR guys. He was genuinely concerned about the welfare of all of us. I am reasonably certain that under the directives of these new rules of engagement he was bound by, he would have been obligated to report the incident to his superiors, but as far as I know, it never happened. For that I am grateful.

It should be stated that the decision to offer assistance by willfully disobeying a strict standing order was not mine alone. Instinctively, every crew member onboard was of the same mindset. Rules of engagement be damned. Let's get there now. For me to have suggested otherwise would have provoked chaos, distrust and a plague of other maladies among the men in the days following. After all, it could just as easily have been us out there waiting for help that was less than a minute away.

I ended that day believing that the four critically wounded we put on the chopper were Navy personnel manning Navy tug boats. Thirty-nine years later I learned the full story of the incident.

May 18, 1970 Aftermath of the tugboat ambush on the Dong Nai River.

Cat Lai PBR crew transporting tug boat casualty to the medevac chopper.

L-R: SP/4 Robert Lynn, bottom, SGT Ed York, Author,
SP/4 Ed "Klinger" Kelleher, top Unk.

L-R: Vietnamese Interpreter, SGT Ed York, Unk, SP/4 Ed "Klinger"
Kelleher, Unk, Author, SP/4 Robert Lynn.

In the days after the ambush I noticed that there were more Vietnamese army and navy personnel than Americans aboard US watercraft as crew members. It would appear that the Vietnamization thing was beginning to take shape and with it stir up mixed emotions in me on several levels.

On the one hand it was somewhat comforting to know that the Vietnamese people were going to start shouldering more of the dirty work in this, their war. On the other hand, it didn't appear to me that the Vietnamese army or navy was anywhere close to being prepared to assume the responsibility. The entire government structure along with upper echelons of the South Vietnamese military officer corps was rife with corruption.

I witnessed no *esprit de corps* in the rank and file of their army, and my observations of the local population was just as discouraging. Overwhelmingly an agrarian society, the typical Vietnamese family was more concerned about how much rice they could produce for their immediate needs, than they were about having anything to do with democracy, nationalism or communism. As for those living in cities and hamlets, there was no telling which side of the war they chose to support. Lastly, and more importantly, I wrestled with the question, who do you trust? In my mind, it was not the Vietnamese people.

Martial Law imposed on the citizenry established a curfew between the hours of 19:00 and 07:00. Anyone observed moving about between those hours was considered hostile and subject to the deadly consequences authorized under the rules of engagement.

With each passing day it appeared that the Vietnamization process emboldened the local fishermen to begin their day ten to fifteen minutes before the curfew was lifted. As the numbers grew and curfew violations became more blatant — despite repeated warnings by our crews — it became apparent that chaos was in the making, facilitating VC penetration of our TAOR. This would bolster resistance to our Bushwhackers.

Those of us who played hide and seek with the VC in the interior reaches of our operational area had an intimate understanding of the dangers. Not so with our *458 TC* partners. As night dissolved into dawn, a full hour before the curfew was lifted and while standing on the deck of a PBR operated by Sergeant York, I spotted over a dozen occupied sampans merge into the Đồng Nai from an obscure estuary north of French Fort. As we cautiously approached them from a distance of about a hundred yards I directed our South Vietnamese Army interpreter — utilizing the onboard public address system — to order all of them to disembark from their sampans and onto the adjacent shoreline. In absolute defiance of that order the entire group continued their journey without even an acknowledgment of our presence.

Instinctively, I grabbed the nearest M-16 rifle, removed the magazine along with the first ten live rounds then quickly replaced them with live tracer rounds. Tracer rounds produce a continuous bright red arc as they travel down range. Often, a fully loaded 20-round magazine will contain a tracer round after every fourth shot. The purpose is to assist the shooter in adjusting his aim at the intended target in the hours of darkness. My silence throughout the performance of these maneuvers, followed by the insertion of the live magazine into the rifle, the loading of the weapon and then immediately pointing the weapon directly at the group caused consternation among those on board.

I directed our interpreter to bark out a final warning to the group, again directing them to disembark. They refused.

As I raised the rifle, Chuckie Bowen shouted, "You're not going to shoot. . . !" just as I squeezed out four or five rounds in rapid succession well above the heads of the group, immediately followed by spraying the remainder of the rounds directly into the water several yards in front of the sampans leading the flotilla.

I got the desired result. The majority of the group immediately dispersed in a half-dozen different directions and disembarked at various spots along the shoreline. However, several made a hasty escape back into the estuary from which they had come. I had no doubt they were Viet Cong infiltrators. My actions that morning were not appreciated by Chuckie Bowen, Sergeant York, and Young Jack of the *458 TC* as they held to a more compassionate concern for the Vietnamese people. It was their belief that these were impoverished fishermen and shooting at them was unnecessary. A contrasting point of view.

73

Pink Elephants?

Not everything was doom and gloom. One afternoon, during our surfing session, a Huey chopper zoomed past at treetop level then powered straight up to maybe 500 feet. The pilot negotiated a very sharp U-turn and began a direct pass at us. Not a real comfortable feeling as this maneuver suggested he was about to make a strafing run at something very close to our position.

The door gunner waved and pointed to the eastern shore of the Dong Nai several hundred yards north and east of us. Jumping on the PBR I saw the chopper set down on an elevated clearing on the eastern shore. Relieved that this encounter was not going to develop into a hostile one, we proceeded directly toward the aircraft. During the short trip it occurred to me that this might not be a friendly meeting of the minds. This could very well be a serious discussion with a superior officer concerning who and why are we surfing behind a US Army PBR. A court martial offense.

The door gunner walked towards us waving his hand and laughing. A good sign. As we pulled alongside, I greeted him with a handshake. These were 9th Division helicopter guys. The door gunner said that the pilot wanted to speak with the guy on the surfboard, and we walked the short distance to the chopper. I entered through the open cargo door, the din of the blades now reduced to a tolerable hum. The pilot and copilot introduced themselves. The pilot asked, "How long have you guys been getting away with this? We heard there were some crazy Navy guys doing this in these parts but you guys aren't Navy."

After an exchange of how the board was built and me extending my gratitude on learning that the rumors about surfing behind PBRs was believed to be a Navy thing, I suggested they continue the rumor.

I don't remember how it started, but the discussion turned to "one-upmanship as to who had witnessed the most bizarre sight or sound in Vietnam. The copilot, a real smart ass, said, "Well, we have seen pink elephants on more than one occasion." Studying his face briefly, I asked, "You are shitting me, aren't you?"

"Not one bit. I'll bet you a hundred bucks MPC," he responded. Being the fool that I was at the time, I answered with, "Make it two hundred, MPC." (Military Payment Certificate was issued to all military personnel in lieu of real "greenback" US currency.) The bet now accepted, arrangements were made for them to pick me up the following day at the 93rd Medevac area on Long Binh Post.

Bright and early the next morning the boys picked me up and gave me a birds-eye tour of the Mekong Delta area. Two hours in the air and no elephants. The door gunner let me unleash his M-60 machine gun on suspected targets he identified as VC bunkers, which gave me a healthy appreciation for what these guys can do from the sky.

On a more sinister note, I could see how habit-forming it could get. Conceding that no elephants were observed, the copilot insisted that I make a date same time, same place the following day. He assured me that I would be parting with my two hundred dollars. To his credit, the door gunner warned me, "He's not shitting you. We got pink elephants down here." After setting down, I made my way to the NCO Club.

One hour in the flight the following morning, there they were. Four of them, all pink. Any fool could have figured it out. The soil in the Delta is much the same as it is in many other parts of Vietnam, red. When these beasts sweat or languish in puddles of water, they roll themselves thoroughly in the soil. Sweat on their hides turns the red dust into a pink hue. Hence, pink elephants. Being the good sport that he was, the copilot turned down my two hundred dollars and said, "It was worth more to see the look on your face when you saw your first pink elephant."

I gave the door gunner forty dollars and directions to a quartermaster sergeant I knew in Bien Hoa. I told the gunner to use my name, plus the forty dollars, and the sergeant would hand off two cases of Jack Daniels and two cases of Johnny Walker Red Whiskey. The lesson here. Have an open mind.

Crew of the 'Stoned Geni L-R: SGT Ed York, SP/4 Robert Lynn, SP/4 Bruce Zirk, Author. Reasoning at the time - introduction of this activity might alleviate some of the doom and gloom we sometimes faced. Nonetheless, it was a reckless decision on my part, as it would have resulted in serious disciplinary action for all, had we been caught.

Author. Discovering the best way to ride the wake of a PBR was to trail behind the wakes of 2 PBRs travelling at approximately 1600 RPMs (10 mph) alongside each other. This would create a 'V' shaped, 3-4 foot wave.

74
Boredom among other things

Crews assigned to patrol the northern edge of Bien Hoa were essentially on their own due to the size of the patrol area and the considerable distance separating them from the nearest PBR.

I generally assigned myself to the central patrol. Boredom fuels emotions. We were all subject to it. Throw in a little anger and perhaps a little loneliness and out pops a distraction, some of which could be very amusing. It wasn't uncommon for me to receive a stern inquiry from the tactical operations center radio operator relative to some earth-shattering explosions from within our area being reported from other tactical operation centers, in and around Bien Hoa.

Letting loose a concussion grenade, holding it for three seconds after the spoon is released and then tossing the thing as far as possible created a deafening explosion before it could hit the water.

And on the occasions when South Vietnamese Army units reported .50 caliber anti-aircraft tracer rounds flying wildly through the evening skies over their area, our crews were the cause, by responding to the Vietnamese who did the same to us. Of course, I knew precisely who the responsible parties were along with the methodology associated with the cause of the disturbance. Just as these spontaneous acts of mischief took hold of us out in the bush, the same behavior existed on the water.

The most noteworthy incident occurred early one evening on our barge with a device that had been created with the ingenuity of a 458 guy. An event that was incredibly insane. We had all grown a little weary of the constant complaints made by civilian contract workers employed by the South Vietnamese Government to dredge portions of the Dong Nai. Specifically, complaints about our lack of courtesy in reducing the wake we created as our PBRs passed one of their shuttle craft. Most of the complaints were unwarranted, and I had grown increasingly irritated with the arrogance of these overpaid jerks. I was not prepared for what followed.

A 458 guy asked if he could have the honor of shaking up our unfriendly civilian neighbors. Without much thought I agreed to his request. Several minutes later he appeared with a handheld illumination parachute flare and said, "Well. This will shake the shit out of 'em." Then he slapped the bottom of the flare sending it up hundreds of feet in the direction of occupied barges moored several hundred yards away.

We patiently waited to hear the pop and see the parachute flare float gently down to the deck of the barge. Instead, the entire area as far as the eye could see was greeted with such an incredibly loud explosion that it caused some of us to freeze in place, or in my case instinctively drop to the deck. So overwhelming was the explosion that within seconds the radio was abuzz with units from Bearcat to Bien Hoa and all places in between trying to determine the cause. The roar of laughter was so contagious and long lasting that I could not immediately respond to the flow of inquiries bellowing from the speaker.

When I asked our young Einstein about the nomenclature of

his creation, he confirmed what I already suspected, it contained C-4.

I had him demonstrate how he managed to have the damn thing detonate, and the explanation was even more revealing and frightening. He showed me how he carefully removed the parachute along with the attached illumination disks, then meticulously inserted approximately one quarter of a stick of C-4 into the empty tube. He then removed the top portion of a fragmentation grenade (the blasting cap, spoon and safety pin all attached) and inserted the blasting pin directly into the C-4.

Just before slapping the bottom of the flare to ignite the propellant within the contents of the tube to initiate flight, he said he pulled the safety pin from the grenade and let the spoon fly. Six seconds later, the blasting cap from the grenade would ignite, setting off the C-4 in mid-flight.

This is a peek into a mind occupied with boredom.

75
Boats and Grenades

Generally, I balanced my time between the three PBRs and completed paperwork while monitoring the radio. About midway into a night watch I experienced difficulty making radio contact with the crew of *Stoned Geni,* manned by SP/4 Zirk and his partner SP/4 Lynn. Radio traffic between us was interrupted by an annoying, intermittent squelching noise. Initially dismissing the unusual phenomenon, I went about my duties. Later in the watch that following morning I attempted to contact the pair by radio. No response.

Minutes later I received a feint transmission from Zirk indicating that the crew was docked at the Ammo Dump outside Bien Hoa (a regular stop in that patrol area), adding they would continue patrolling within the hour. An hour or so later my next communication with Zirk took another turn. When I suggested that his crew meet me in the central patrol area, I got a feeble response suggesting that we meet a little later in the morning. My suspicions grew. It takes a rogue to understand one. It was readily apparent that these boys were engaged in some nefarious activity and were desperately trying to buy time.

But for what?

After a series of miscommunications that continued for the remainder of the morning, and just minutes before we made a change of watch, I stood on the barge awaiting arrival of *Stoned Geni* and watched as the crew approached the barge. The instant they began securing the craft to the anchor posts, Zirk hopped aboard to engage me in a conversation riddled with excuses for what he referred to as "mix ups" in communications.   Glancing at the rest of the crew during Zirk's impromptu monologue I could see that these guys were too wired to have had just another boring night on the water, like the rest of us. They were scurrying around like agitated mice hastily completing the protocol in securing their vessel.

Interrupting Zirk I asked, "Have I got anything to worry about here?" with him answering, "No. No Bog." "All right then. Call it a night." That said, they scrambled onto a morning watch PBR, wound up the engines and made a quick departure to the French Pier for the customary change over.

I chuckled to myself as I boarded *Stoned Geni* to make a cursory inspection. Everything appeared in order until I took a closer look at the deck and railing area in front of and adjacent to the twin front .50 turret. Familiar as I was with the workings of fiberglass and resin, I noted that a feeble attempt in the use of the stuff was made to disguise what appeared to be some minor but recent damage.

Half of the mystery solved. I could only imagine what could have caused it. Don't know if I got the entire explanation in the days that followed or if I confused the entire event with an explanation by Zirk at one of our reunions some 45 years later. Regardless of when, he told me it was a mishandling of one of those concussion grenades slipping out of Lynn's hand, landing between the .50 turret and the outboard railing, that caused all hands to abandon ship as the explosion tore into the deck. Luckily, the grenade did not fall into the gun turret and detonate all the stored ammunition, blowing up the PBR and everything with it.

It had to have been quite a sight, watching everyone jump for their lives off a dry boat and into the Dong Nai.

In spite of our differences, the 458 guys were second to none when it came to maintaining the fine working order of all the PBRs and Boston whalers in our inventory. The same can be said of our guys regarding the maintenance of weaponry attached to these vessels. That would include the entire compliment of 458 and B Company personnel assigned to the PBR Platoon.

Although split into two separate groups comprised of 12-hour shifts, no major issues regarding the performance of all moving parts come to mind. The crews of both watches were in fact just men and boats crossing paths every day and every night. Remarkable actually, considering the continuous and constant grind of night crews handing off the mission to the day crew and back again every day, every night.

Because of this routine, concern over any acts of sabotage to our equipment was of little or no interest. That is, until word came down that some crew members with the Cat Lai PBR detachment sustained serious injuries from some tampered concussion grenades. It was discovered that a significant number of grenades had been manually altered to detonate within one or two seconds of removing the safety pin and releasing the spoon. Not the six second time delay set at the factory. Because our crews had received a recent shipment of these grenades the entire inventory was removed from our arsenal and handed off to Army Engineers for disposal.

Standard-issue fragmentation grenades were substituted. Fortunately for us, there were no casualties.

About this same time we suspected that sabotage played a role in the tampering of fuel gages on one of our boats. Early one morning on a day watch sometime in June, SP/4 Ed Kelleher and I were aboard one of our PBRs patrolling Dong Nai waters north of Bien Hoa. Traveling southbound at 35 miles per hour, both of our Detroit diesel engines inexplicably shut down.

L-R: Vietnamese Interpreter, Author, SP/4 Ed 'Klinger' Kelleher, receiving a welcomed tow from another crew after running out of fuel drifting helplessly miles north of Bien Hoa.

As our vessel came to rest, Swensen - our 458 guy - frantically opened the engine compartment doors located amidships, directly behind the coxswain's flat. He began looking for a quick fix. Repeated efforts to restart the engines were unsuccessful and he concluded that we were out of fuel. Meanwhile, I grabbed the wheel in an effort to keep the bow of the boat in the center of the river in a strong northbound current.

During this process, the current caused us to swing a full 180 degrees, pointing us northbound and moving at a pretty good clip. Losing the current was not an option nor was beaching the boat. We were now free-floating in totally unfamiliar waters and territory among some of the thickest vegetation I had ever seen.

Convinced that there was no fix, Swensen took the wheel as I went to relieve Kelleher manning the aft .50, giving him access to the front gun turret. We still had electrical power.

With me struggling at the wheel and Swensen examining the engine compartment, Ed had the presence of mind to grab the radio and report our situation and approximate location. It would take the better part of an hour for the central patrol PBR to reach us. Here we remained, at the mercy of a fast current taking us further north and deep into the tactical area of the 25th Infantry Division.

During this uneasy period, Swensen said that it was highly unusual that the fuel gages registered full with no diesel in the tanks. Less than an hour later Denny Taylor and Rasmussen arrived alongside and towed us back to the barge. A thorough inspection conducted by the 458 guys revealed that the fuel tanks were empty. Fuel gages were determined to have been defective or tampered with. Six weeks later, the 720th Military Police Battalion was dismantled.

76

"I wanted to kill all of them, Bog."

Almost two months passed since the chopper crash and still no word from Battalion. Nothing. No news was still good news. Rumors were swirling about a drastic change coming, hints that B Company was to be dissolved and that we would be transferred to military police line units. It was hard for me to keep my mouth shut, but I did what I was told and remained silent. We were seeing more and more ARVNs congregating in our company area, indicating that a closer working relationship with them was in the making. I for one, did not look forward to it.

The French Pier was used as our staging area during changes of watch and refueling. Typically, the 458 ensured that several high-capacity portable fuel tanks were replenished daily. Maintaining security for US military equipment was necessary and it was incumbent upon the ARVN to provide it.

But what should be isn't always what is. More often than not, for whatever reasons, the task fell on us. This meant I had to provide one of our guys to remain several hours, alone, without a radio on the pier, armed with an M-16. I resented it and so did everybody else. Especially the poor bastard having to do it. The job required at least two men in a gun jeep (M-60 machine gun), with a working radio. We were shorthanded as it was getting a little tiresome being told to do more with less.

When I spoke to Sergeant Henry all he ever said was, "I'll look into it." The best I could do was send a PBR to make a periodic check on the welfare of the guy.

I assigned Zirk to the task late one afternoon to replace the 458 security team which had been directed to leave their post. Thinking nothing more of it, we continued our duties. Less than an hour later the PBR checking on Zirk requested that I meet them at the French Pier. When I arrived, it was one of the 458 guys who approached me and said, "You better go see Zirk. He caught a ration of shit from a bunch of ARVNs that took all our diesel. He's really pissed."

Zirk was pissed alright. The blonde-haired, usually mild mannered Wisconsin native. "Bog, don't ever give me this fuckin' detail again. I wanted to kill all of 'em, Bog. There were thirty of the fuckers. They threatened to kill me and told me they were taking our diesel. The assholes were serious. What the fuck! And these are our allies! Fuck the gooks. They were gonna kill me. And if I ever see any of them again, I'll kill 'em!" As he spoke he trembled slightly, as did his voice. His face glowed red, and both eyes flooded with anger. I never put Zirk in that situation again. He would have killed them and I wouldn't blame him.

So much for our Allies.

77

Just another casualty of war

Two weeks later, after completing twelve scorching hours on the river, my entire crew was seated underneath the French Pier on dusty concrete in the shade. We were waiting for the arrival of the night watch crew to relieve us, hop onto the deuce-and-a-half to take us back to Long Binh. I anticipated another soulless night of whiskey in the smoke-filled NCO Club, and several hours listening to some Asian band perform the latest American hits.

I was interrupted by the sound of a high explosive M-79 grenade somewhere in a hamlet just north of the pier. Instinctively, everyone jumped up, scrambled to get their weapons and formed a semicircle with backs to the Dong Nai.

Seconds later, screams came from several sources as two Vietnamese villagers came into view about a hundred yards away, running towards us carrying a child. Some of the 458 guys ran toward the villagers as I directed the rest of our crew to widen our perimeter, suspecting a possible diversion.

As the men approached, we could see that the child they were carrying — no more than four years of age — was bleeding profusely about the head and upper torso. With blood-curdling screams from the child ringing in our ears, Shakey shouted in my ear, "You gotta call in a chopper. That kid is gonna die if we don't call it in!" All I remember is saying, "Find somebody that speaks some Vietnamese and find out what happened first." Adding, "For all I know this is a trap."

Just then Jared Kelley said, "Bog, the older guy is the father, the other guy is an uncle. The father said, the boy found a piece of metal and the thing just blew up. He swears that's what happened. He is begging to get his kid to a hospital." "Yea, right. How do we know that kid wasn't going to plant that thing next to one of us?" I screamed back. The faces around me spoke volumes. Clearly, I was alone on this one. Reluctantly I yelled back, "All right, God damn it. Call in a dust off. You and Shakey guide the chopper in, load up the kid and his family and get the fuck back over here. I'll hold your 60."

The chopper arrived quickly to pick up the injured child along with his father and uncle. Several minutes later the medic on board radioed back advising that the child had died.

French Pier, 4-year old boy being transported to medevac chopper L-R: SP/4 Denny Taylor, Boy's Uncle, Boy's Father, Unk, SP/4 Jared "Loco" Kelley, SP/4 Ed "Shakey Marley.

There was no trap, no diversion. Our government encouraged the indigenous population to turn over any live ordnance they encountered to local authorities, in exchange for a financial reward. This appeared to be precisely what happened. While playing, the child uncovered a live M-79 grenade and during the handling it exploded. Just another innocent victim of this war. My initial assessment was based on the totality of my experiences and interactions with the Vietnamese people during the previous eleven months. A complete and absolute lack of trust.

The foundation of the wall I subconsciously constructed was rock solid. I was evolving into a brute who cared nothing for the child or the Vietnamese people. I had become what an Army at war trains its soldiers to do. Win. Damn these people.

78
The shakeup

About the first week of July, 1970, the word was out. The 720th Military Police Battalion would be no more by the end of the month. All of A, B and C Companies would be disbanded and those of us still serving our tours would be sent to various military police companies throughout South Vietnam. It was exactly how Top called it back in that Australian gin mill when he said, "When the break-up begins everything is gonna turn into one big cluster-fuck." What a call.

Three day in-country R&R passes were cancelled, including those poor saps who had scheduled their seven day out-of-country R&R months earlier. Morale plummeted, attitudes changed, discipline slumped. Everyone thirsted for information. Contributing to the confusion was the unending influx of new NCOs, along with assorted enlisted ranks plucked from assorted military police units who now took up residence with us. I walked into my hooch and found a pair of bunk beds and several wall lockers had been added. Who were these guys?

It was the beginning of the end of B Company Bushwhackers.

Our company area became a reception center with new faces appearing daily. Nobody knew why, including our new neighbors. Rumors swirled, adding to the uncertainty. We were told our orders for reassignment would be issued soon. Meanwhile, the three ambush and recon platoons and those of us assigned to PBRs continued with our respective missions. Unnecessary risks? I never addressed the question. It was understood.

Each day became a stomach turning grind.

July, 1970 - Author, SP/4 Glenn Barmann, SP/4 Swensen (barely visible, peeking out of the cockpit).

79

"Bog, Shakey's got a knife to some Sergeant's throat!"

Early one evening I was alone on my bunk reading a magazine when Jared Kelley and Glenn Barmann burst into my room. Jared blurted, "Bog you better come quick. Bog, Shakey's got a knife to some sergeant's throat!" Tossing the magazine aside, I leaped out of bed and ran behind Kelley and Barmann to a couple of hooches away where a sizeable crowd mobbed the entrance. I made my way through the crowd and saw Shakey facing the crowd, standing on top of a bunk bed directly behind a staff sergeant almost twice his size, with his kabar knife in his right hand firmly pressed against the guy's throat.

Shakey's left hand clutched the sergeant's scalp pushing the back of the guy's head deep into Shakey's gut. Shakey was screaming, "I don't give a fuck. I'll kill you, you motherfucker!" Whatever the guy had said or did to unleash Shakey's rage, the look suggested he was genuinely sorry. He garbled in a whisper, "I am sorry man! I am sorry! Don't do this!" A pathetic sight, to be sure.

Breaking into the suspense I said, "Shakey, I know you're pissed. But whatever is going on here has to end." "Bog, this piece of shit has been telling everybody we are a bunch of pussies. And he has been telling all his asshole sergeants that we never spent any time in the bush. Fuck him! We're not taking any more shit from these punks!"

Don't know exactly what I added to the conversation but Shakey released the sergeant without further incident.

I escorted the man to my hooch, accompanied by the sound of insults hurled at him. "Keep him away from us Bog. Next time might be different!" The man was shaking and could barely speak. A livid red mark deeply imbedded across his throat was clearly visible. After I spent the better part of ten minutes explaining the mission of B Company and how stupid his actions were, he concurred and again apologized profusely.

I suggested he grab all his gear and find a bunk over at A or C Company, adding that I could not guarantee his safety. I was also candid with him about the futility of him pursuing a criminal complaint. There would be no witnesses to corroborate his story, including me.

I never saw him again.

Do I believe that Shakey would have done it? Yes, most assuredly I do. Little did I know at the time, the same frustration and anger that consumed Shakey when anybody questioned his role as a combat infantry military policeman would later become an issue for the rest of us in the years to come.

80

"The choice is yours. Take the shots or risk becoming mad dogs yourselves"

It was July 25, 1970 my 22nd birthday when we got the news we all waited for. The entire company, along with all the new faces among us, was assembled on the parade ground directly behind our company area. Here we were told that most of us would be transported up to Da Nang and reassigned to the 188th Military Police Company, 504th Military Police Battalion. We would replace First Marine Division personnel assigned to the Armed Forces Police responsible for patrolling the city's streets.

Some of our guys were sent to the 716th Military Police Company in Saigon, others as replacements to the units north and south of Saigon. Some PBR guys were assigned to the Cat Lai PBR Platoon. As for our Tactical Area of Responsibility, the 25th Infantry Division would absorb it, joined at the hip to various ARVN units.

The Vietnamization Program in full swing.

After orders were distributed, a battalion officer spoke a few words of praise — six bags of shit actually — then announced, "You are all dismissed with the exception of the 3rd Ambush & Recon Platoon and the PBR Platoon who will remain in formation."

Emerging from the crowd as it dispersed was a Medical Corps captain accompanied by two or three enlisted personnel, all adorned with 93rd Medical Evacuation patches sewn on their jungle garb. The captain wasted no words. "You men are quarantined. The dog you called Chocolate has been destroyed. The animal tested positive for rabies. Those of you that had any contact with the animal in the past 60 days is subject to the risk of acquiring this lethal and painful disease. You are especially susceptible if you had any exposed minor cuts or scratches while handling the animal. There are a series of fourteen immunizations you must receive as a precautionary measure to ensure against the disease and its deadly effects."

A chorus of groans accompanied with an occasional blasphemous utterance filled the air, followed by somebody in the group asking, "What happens if we didn't touch the dog or only petted it?" The captain responded, "The choice is yours. Take the shots or risk becoming mad dogs yourselves. I can't sugarcoat this thing. I need to set up your immunizations immediately."

Well, that was simple enough. Nobody wanted to go home as a mad dog so we all agreed to submit to the daily torture for the next 14 days. In essence, it required all of us to meet at the 93rd Medical Detachment at precisely the same time each day. Not five minutes before or five minutes after, but precisely at the same time every day. There, we were directed to lie on a table face up.

The medic or doctor then pinched between his thumb and forefinger a significant portion of skin on either side of the lower stomach area. Next he applied some alcohol then injected a very thick serum sideways directly into the skin between his thumb and forefinger. It was a slow and painful process which took the better part of 30 seconds. Show up late for an appointment, we were warned, invalidated the treatment and meant starting the entire process over again. Some, like John Main, were allergic to the serum and remained hospitalized for weeks.

81
The Transition

O ur company area teemed with activity. All our equipment, including the armory, the inventory of motor vehicles assigned to us, along with personnel records, stockpiles of quartermaster supplies and all things associated with B Company had to be packed up and shipped north to Da Nang. Among some of the motor vehicles were two jeeps and a deuce-and-a-half I had been responsible for misappropriating from other units.

Any IG (Inspector General) inspection during the inventory phase of this move would raise questions. In an effort to forestall any questions I gathered a group of confederates to assist me in removing the B Company vehicle identifiers and re-stencil them with A and C Company identifiers. We then removed them from our motor pool and abandoned them on the streets adjacent to A and C Company.

Along with all the confusion we had to inform families, friends and lovers that our mail will need to be forwarded to a new Armed Forces Post Office number. The change would definitely affect the timeliness of receiving mail from home. Another moral buster. By the end of July, a couple of our guys were assigned to drive vehicles in a convoy headed to Da Nang. Among them was Crazy Marich who later reported that the convoy was ambushed, killing a lieutenant and several others mid-way in the journey. He claimed that senior NCOs volunteered him for the assignment just to get rid of him. He could be right on that.

Crazy did stir up a lot of angst among virtually all of the lifers in B Company. Glenn Ward and Jim Gufford were among a few in a river convoy hauling the remainder of our motor vehicles on a barge. A 24-hour trip wound its way through the heart of South Vietnam. On the last day in July, the rest of us, with all the gear we could carry, assembled in the company area awaiting transport by truck to Bien Hoa Airbase. It was here that I caught a glimpse of Top as he made his way into the empty shack that had been his office. He passed me with a wink and a nod and said, "See ya, Bogie." It would be the last time I ever saw or heard from First Sergeant Hardin Collins. No news continued to be good news.

Thanks Top.

82
Next Stop Da Nang Airbase

Familiar sounds of diesel trucks backing into our company area. We piled aboard and minutes later waved goodbye to what was left of B Company Bushwhackers. And that was Carlos Lozano scheduled to leave for home within a few days of our departure. It was a pathetic sight. Here stood one of the original good guys who took care of me when I first arrived. I could imagine what was going on in his head as our departing dust cleared, leaving him in what was now just an abandoned collection of buildings.

At Bien Hoa Airbase we were told to grab a seat on the tarmac and wait. Looking around I noticed a large group of brand new guys in the distance and felt sorry for them. I also started to feel a little sorry for myself. Just over a year ago I was one of them. I could have been home by now if I hadn't extended my tour. I had absolutely no idea what lay ahead. All we were told was that our new residence was a Marine firebase outside the city of Da Nang. My home for the next forty days and nights. Within the hour we were shuffled onto transport planes and airborne on a short, uneventful flight.

I was in awe at the size of the place. Later, I was told Da Nang had the longest runway in the world. The place was easily twice the size of Bien Hoa Airbase. It also had a powerful stench of death. Not surprisingly so, because one of the larger metal buildings housed the Graves Registration Unit. We assembled off the tarmac and spotted our trucks parked and idling a short distance away, with bumper markings of the 188th MP Company. We were greeted by senior NCOs none of whom I had ever seen before, ordering us to mount up.

I had an uneasy feeling.

83

Camp David Land Freedom Hill

Pulling up to the gate of this obscure outpost, two Marine corporals wearing Armed Forces Police brassards and "AFP" in black letters painted on their white helmets, waved us in. These were the guys we were to replace. A short distance later we jumped off the trucks in what was our billeting area. Everything here, the signs and buildings, was painted in official Marine Corps colors of scarlet and gold. Nothing even remotely looked Army. Accommodations, few as they were, looked like the ones we were accustomed to. Tin roofs were weighed down with dozens of sandbags. Snake-shaped trenches and fox holes topped off with sandbags. My best estimate is that the whole area encompassed about a ½ mile square. Well-built perimeter bunkers occupied by several Marines armed with .30 and .50 caliber machine guns dotted the landscape.

I was herded into one of two buildings designated as sleeping quarters. No special housing for me or the NCOs I arrived with. NCO rooms were taken. Not that it mattered. I threw my gear on the nearest bunk. Then it hit me. I was two hours overdue for my daily rabies injection.

Great. After taking care to arrange my daily injections at Long Binh — five thus far — here I imagined the worst. When I scheduled my injections I chose the afternoon. It fit my schedule. Everyone else arranged morning visits and received treatment before we left. I had to find the nearest medical dispensary, not far away, where I met a Navy Corpsman who took me to the doctor, a Marine Corps captain.

After explaining my situation to him he just stared for a moment and said, "Well, I was told to expect several dozen of you guys requiring treatment. It was my understanding that the uninterrupted continuation of this treatment was to begin tomorrow morning. I wasn't expecting this. You realize, of course, that you will have to start your series of injections all over again." Precisely what I didn't want to hear, as I stepped up and onto the table between us and asked, "Shall we begin, sir?"

Thus began my sixth in a series of twenty rabies shots. I completed the series with ill grace.

From my perspective none of these geographic and unit changes were welcome. Those of us from B Company didn't fit the majority mold of the newly formed MP company. Outnumbered and surrounded by regular line military police people, our guys were singled out by senior NCOs and assigned crummy details. Also, our bunch was admonished for the condition of our uniforms. Rear echelon people wore tailored uniforms. Our unit had answered to a different tune in a different habitat.

Proud of having performed as infantrymen and river rats, all of us wore the unofficial "Bushwhacker" rocker above the 18th Military Police Brigade patch on the upper left shirt sleeve of our jungle fatigues. In addition, our PBR boys sported unauthorized patches depicting the profile of a PBR, sewn to the right breast of their jungle shirt.

And why not?

None of our B Company brass, or any of the lifers for that matter, said anything to prevent it. Here, virtually every lifer and officer was unimpressed — and often clearly disturbed — by our custom insignia and demanded that it be removed. Open resistance set the tone. Because I was among the very few B Company NCOs connected to these men, I was confronted with the issue and encouraged to enforce removal. In spite of the fact that I wore an illicit tab myself, their request was acknowledged and I said, "I'll see what I can do."

Marines stationed here were clearly sizing us up. Our first few evenings were unpredictable. When our people decided to hit the Marine watering hole, the only place on the outpost where liquor was served, things got a little tense. B Company personnel were school-trained Military Policemen despite the fact that virtually none of us had any practical experience in the enforcement of military law.

Basically, we were grunts. We dressed like them and, clearly, we acted like them. Here, Marines were impeccably dressed, spit-shined boots and brightly polished brass, and enforced military law without having been formally trained to do so. Everything these Marines learned about policing was on the job. The only recognized US Military Police-trained people in all the services at this time were members of the US Army. Navy SPs (Shore Patrol), Marine Corps MPs, and even US Air Force APs were not school- trained. Personnel were assigned as "details."

That is, involuntarily selected to perform a necessary function.

Clearly outnumbered and viewed as interlopers by our Marine counterparts, we remained steadfast in our actions and our demeanor projected that we were not to be messed with. Tensions eased and service rivalries ended quickly when we partnered up as teams. Most of our people were assigned to gun jeeps with a Marine Armed Forces Policeman and a Vietnamese Policeman performing street patrol in Da Nang.

Others, like myself, were assigned to various physical security posts and perimeter bunkers in defense of our fire base. The working relationship with our Marine colleagues quickly materialized into a very good one.

84

"I wouldn't mess with these guys. They get messed with enough."

The badgering continued from some lifers, insisting that our guys remove their Bushwhacker patches, along with some of the disrespect they claimed they were experiencing from B Company personnel in general, all ended one evening about the second week we arrived. Sergeant Torres was among the small band of NCOs that made the trek up to the outpost with me. During the journey and the days that followed, I received an earful from him on how undisciplined much of B Company was. Dismissing much of it, I suggested that he consider what they had accomplished rather than what they lacked in military protocol. I also added, "I wouldn't mess with these guys. They get messed with enough."

To his and my regret, he could not or would not accept my advice.

Days after our arrival, NCOs residing in the main hooch with the men were overly concerned about obtaining materials to build separate quarters for themselves. My reputation for securing things made me their go-to guy. In spite of a lack of resources in our new environment, I managed to produce several pallets of plywood and some building materials. I had no desire to build a room for myself, "short-timer" that I was. I was going home soon.

All NCO hooches were built and occupied within days.

A few short hours after their completion somebody tossed a concussion grenade, along with a tear gas grenade, directly into Sergeant Torres' hooch. He had been asleep and emerged shaken but unharmed. For the next several days he was occupied with installing chicken wire on the open ceiling of his room, and installed padlocks on his door - inside and outside.

No suspects were ever identified, and there were no more complaints from any lifer about Bushwhacker patches or discipline issues.

It was during an afternoon trip to pick up building supplies at a Navy Supply Depot when I heard sporadic small arms fire on the highway a short distance ahead. My truck was trailing behind an Armed Forces Police gun jeep following a convoy of ARVN 2 ½ ton trucks loaded with South Vietnamese soldiers. The convoy stopped to let the gun jeep speed ahead toward the gunfire.

As gunfire intensity grew, I jumped out of the cab with my M-16 and bandoleer of five magazines, and took up a position behind the left front fender, expecting to receive incoming fire from the right side of the roadway. In moments, I was among dozens of South Vietnamese soldiers who took up positions around me, expecting the same thing. Nothing. As the din of gunfire subsided, I heard the sirens of Armed Forces Police and National Police (Vietnamese) gun jeeps racing in our direction. As they passed us, gunfire stopped.

After waiting in silence for several minutes, I walked on a slight incline toward the responding gun jeeps that had stopped on the opposite side of the highway, a hundred yards away. About thirty feet from the hill I had to skip around several streams of blood slowly trickling on the asphalt, like water gradually being released from a garden hose.

There, on the road and in the open bed of a bullet- ridden ARVN 2½ ton truck still idling were half a dozen or more dead

South Vietnamese soldiers, along with another dozen or so dead and wounded lying nearby, groaning. Walking back to my truck I figured out that I had been separated by no more than thirty seconds from being where that ill-fated ARVN truck and its passengers met their fate.

And thinking to myself, how many times can I get away with this kind of luck?

85
Main Gate Camp David Land

O ur arrival was no secret to the North Vietnamese and within days they were casually dropping 122mm rockets and mortars to let us know. That was what we all believed. The Marines obviously had some experience in dealing with this, which explained the necessity for nearby trenches and foxholes, and lots of them. They were everywhere. We didn't have to run too far to seek refuge. The need for sandbags on the roofs of all buildings became very clear when high winds, coupled with heavy rain, signaled the start of the typhoon season. The seasonal shift was almost as frightening as incoming rockets and mortars.

My duties were mostly limited to security of the main entrance at Camp David Land, as NCO-in-Charge of two Marine Armed Forces policemen and two Army MPs tasked with screening military personnel and vehicular traffic in and out of the compound. Fortunately, one of the assigned soldiers was SP/4 Delton Propes, a former 3rd Platoon Bushwhacker. The Marines true to form were highly regimented and fiercely loyal to their creed. If these guys were told to stand on their heads and remain in that position until properly relieved, they would do so without question.

Which prompted me to ask my Marine Corps corporals why

their M-16 rifles retained red wooden blocks firmly placed in the magazine well, instead of the full 20-round 5.56mm load. The corporal replied, "Because we are not allowed to carry a locked and loaded M-16 without first requesting permission." Glancing at Propes, I was prompted to ask, "And why is this?" The corporal stated with a chuckle, "I guess it's so we don't shoot each other." He explained there had been an incident involving a Marine shooting at another Marine months earlier.

I turned to Propes and said, "You see anything in black pajamas or NVA khaki, kill it."

A miserable post to man twelve hours a day, but at least there was no night watch. The entire fire base was locked down at night. As a military vehicle approached our gate, a quick glance at the stenciled letters and numbers on the front bumper identifying its unit determined whether we waved it in or directed it to stop. If the vehicle was not on the register of authorized vehicles allowed free passage, it was our responsibility to examine their written orders. After the information was logged the vehicle was let through.

The list was updated daily, sometimes two or three times in the course of several hours. Within days we were able to identify an unauthorized vehicle by just glancing at the occupants. The only real challenge was to maintain a continuous flow of traffic without causing gridlock. Failure to do so increased the possibility of an ambush, a regular occurrence on any roadway in Vietnam.

The gate was generally manned by two Marines and two soldiers, I remained inside an open-air steel shack monitoring the radio and jotting down vehicle identifiers yelled out by my guys.

Duties were rotated among us, including me. The simple task of checking bumper numbers, waving through vehicles and bull sessions could be interrupted by only one of two things: The occasional landing of Marine helicopters in the open field nearby, or a moment of terror (which never occurred).

L-R: SP/4 Delton Propes, SP/4 Ed Lewin, SP/4 Doug "Bish" Bischoff.

Several days into my new job as overseer of the main gate, my Marine Corps subordinates warned me of encounters with the local population of "Rock Throwing Apes." I was to believe that these creatures could sneak into occupied perimeter bunkers, summarily beat-up the Marine occupant, snatch his rifle, and scurry off into the darkness. After almost 14 months of living in this strange land and now in possession of a hard-earned lighter shade of "green" about believing such tales, I responded, "I have seen pink elephants. I have been subjected to blasphemous insults by mystical reptiles (street-wise, English-speaking gecko lizards). And my feet have been gnawed by rats the size of cats. Now, you boys tell me this. Okay, they got gorillas here. I ain't buying they throw rocks."

Chuckles followed my disbelief. A Marine added, "Oh, yeah. We got tigers up in these parts, too. One of our guys got dragged away by one a while back." This assertion was verified by both Army and Marine sources. Still, I was highly skeptical about anything to do with rock throwing apes.

So much for keeping an open mind. I should have known better.

Two weeks passed. In addition to my normal duty, I was occasionally assigned to one of our perimeter bunkers during night watches. Bunker occupants had access to an M-60 or a .50 caliber machine gun, M-16 rifles and M-79 grenade launchers. At this stage of my time in Vietnam I made my instructions very clear to those with me inside our bunker, "Anything moves out there … kill it."

Early one evening, I was assigned to a bunker along with several newly arrived replacements (FNGs). Don't know what prompted one of them to grab an M-79 after we heard rattling from the barbed wire in front of us, but he fired his grenade aimlessly into the night.

Regardless of the why, my illumination flare revealed several small, hairy critters scampering into the night upright, on two feet. The high explosive M-79 round spits out a .40 millimeter grenade that must rotate 150 revolutions before it will detonate on a target. We heard no explosion. The errant round was either a dud or had hit something, or even possibly glanced off one of the apes.

Okay, they got gorillas here.

An hour or so later, our bunker received several thuds from what we initially thought were grenades being tossed in our direction. Another flare was launched immediately, along with some indiscriminate firing from our M-60 down range.

To everyone's amazement, maybe thirty yards off to our left, there they were standing upright, a half dozen or more apes, about four or five feet tall. Being the social creatures I had read about, they appeared to be unquestionably angry as they continued chucking rocks at us. Not bad at hitting our bunker, either. They continued this activity undaunted in spite of our display of fireworks.

We concluded that our errant M-79 grenade must have struck one these apes and in doing so we had upset the entire family clan. Minutes later, the group turned and casually shambled into the darkness. Like the monkey-eating thing told to me by the old-timer on my flight into the country: "Son, you are going to see a whole lot of things over here that you would never have believed if you hadn't seen it with your own eyes." Just another oddity.

Years later, I heard of similar experiences from former Marines who happened upon apes during reconnaissance missions. Simian ability to beat up Marines and steal their rifles remained unverified.

86
ARVNs, Bales of Straw, Diesel, 2 Hostages, Ransom, Payoff

September 6, 1970 four days before my tour ended. Four days earlier marked the first anniversary of the death of Ho Chi Minh. For weeks, rumors swirled about a possible NVA offensive in honor of the anniversary. I was relieved when September 2nd had come and gone, but I also accepted the fact that these people were unpredictable and anything was possible. Dusk was approaching. The main gate was secured and the outpost was locked down. I had just finished eating and was walking out of the mess hall when I saw people running in all directions, several coming our way screaming, "Get your gear. We're on alert!"

"Great. What the hell is this?" I asked running to my hooch. Some lifer shouted, "Rifles, bayonets, bandoleers, side arms, flak jackets, gas masks, steel pots. Form up outside in company formation. All sergeants meet me at the armory for CS grenades."

Gathering my gear, I asked if anybody knew what this was about. Nobody knew. As the four platoons started forming up in front of their hooches, I asked one of the sergeants handing out CS grenades what was going on. All he said was, "I don't know but I heard there was some kind of major disturbance in Da Nang." Disturbance, I thought. The whole damn country is a disturbance. The only kind of disturbance requiring CS Gas is a riot. I was aware that some infantry units tossed CS grenades in spider holes, we never did. We just blew them up. This being a line military police unit, riot came to mind.

Our company of some 200 men formed up to hear what the commanding officer wanted to say. He told us that two American soldiers operating a 2½ ton truck accidentally killed a South Vietnamese soldier riding on a moped, in Da Nang.

Our soldiers got out of their truck to render aid and were promptly surrounded by a company of ARVNs who disarmed them and forced them at gunpoint back into their truck. Next, the ARVN troops gathered bales of straw and completely encircled the truck, doused the bales with diesel, and threatened to set the pair on fire. The ARVN commanding officer demanded a ransom for the safe return of our soldiers. Negotiations between our Battalion Commander and the ARVN company commander were underway, adding, "We will stand by for further orders."

The announcement left us feeling we had received a sucker punch to the gut. Hostility immediately washed over everyone. There was a palpable atmosphere of disdain for our allies, the folks we defended from Communist dictatorship.

Fuming provoked questions. Among them, what are the chances all of us getting picked off like ducks in a shooting gallery by snipers as we stand like toy soldiers in riot line formation, advancing with bayonets against a mob? Had anybody given it a thought? Was I to come this far only to be killed in some senseless riot? If I assumed correctly that everyone around me was as pissed at the South Vietnamese Army as I was, were we the appropriate people to send into this mess?

My attitude had long been polar opposite to the official US position. And why wouldn't it be? It was an ARVN gunboat that fired indiscriminately at Doug Newman in his whaler, wounding him in the process. It was a company of ARVNs that surrounded Zirk and threatened his life at the French Pier. It was a young

Vietnamese woman laughing at dead American passengers and crew in a helicopter accident.

Besides, we had all heard about disputes turned deadly between American GIs and our Vietnamese allies.

Standing around waiting and keeping company with such thoughts reminded me of what I witnessed during a visit to Saigon, when I was assigned to the Honey Wagon. Destination was the Saigon docks to pick up building materials. While the truck was being loaded, I strolled a short distance away where my attention was drawn to a young Vietnamese street hustler obstructing the path of an American soldier wearing a faded 1st Infantry Division shoulder patch.

All the while, the hustler shouted in broken English, "You give me $20.00 MPC I give you watch." Over and over again. Scenes like this were shared by all who served in Vietnam. The soldier tried turning left, then to the right in an attempt to get away, shouting angrily, "Leave me alone. Get the fuck away from me!" But the young street urchin obstructed the soldier at every turn, invading his personal space and blurting repeatedly, "You number 10 GI!"

You could see it coming. In an instant, the soldier threw his right fist directly into the hustler's face causing him to slam to the cement with blood spewing from his nose and mouth, along with several broken pieces of teeth scattered nearby. There he lay, out cold and bleeding. GIs close by scattered like cockroaches, and for good reason. Nobody wanted to be detained as a witness against this guy for doing something any of us might have considered. The soldier stepped over the hustler and as our eyes locked, all he said was, "Fuck these people!" before disappearing into the crowd.

I didn't stick around either. The hustler's countrymen swarmed over him, rummaging through his pockets and removing the watch he was trying to peddle along with the one he was wearing on his wrist. The incident made it clear to me that by experience and instinct I had evolved into that 1st Infantry soldier.

Three hours into our riot standby mode and it was all over. Our hapless soldiers had been spared. The straw bales were removed and the two men were free to leave. All at the expense of the American tax payer and successful negotiations between our military brass and an ARVN company commander. The sum paid in reparations was never disclosed, but rumor said it was a hefty amount. Another conflict with a hasty resolution. Doubtful that anything associated with this event ever made its way to reporters.

87
Parting Shots

Most of the next day and entire night was spent thoroughly pickled in shots of whiskey and beer at the insistence of Bish and Lewin. My send-off back to the States. Endless discussions late into the night about the war, close calls we experienced, along with some confessions over who did what to whom and when. Early the next morning we awoke to the whistles of incoming 122mm rockets. Adrenalin catapulted us from our bunks and into the nearby trenches. Everyone that is, except me. Can't explain it. I should have been first in the trench and last out.

Instead, I remained sitting on my bunk calmly lacing my boots thinking, "if these sons of bitches want me that bad, then have at it." I remember the moment.

As the rockets rained in, each of them seconds apart, there was an instance of silence just before impact. Four of them this time, but I remained resolute in not allowing my body to move. No tremors, no nausea, no euphoria, no hunger pangs, no cowardice, certainly no bravado. A complete lack of concern. Was it possible that I had come full circle? I have always assumed the latter, thinking it was time now to reclaim the person I was before I came here.

None of the rockets even came close. All made impact several hundred yards away.

With orders in hand the following day, I reported to medical for my final physical, conducted by the same Marine captain who administered rabies vaccinations a month before. No issues noted, except for the small asymmetrical protuberance he noticed adjacent to and directly below my left eye, which we both dismissed. It was during the examination that I informed him of urinary issues acquired in the days following my consumption of Dong Nai River water. After his preliminary look, he suggested that on my return to the States I should report to the nearest Veterans Administration Hospital and request treatment for what he diagnosed as, *"Nonspecific Urethral Inflammation."*

I took him at his word. Leaving medical I met Peanuts Cortez, now in the job of company mail clerk, and made arrangements for him to drive me to Da Nang Air Force Base to catch a hop to Cam Ranh Bay.

My last night was uneventful.

Early next day I packed a bag and walked to my former duty post, the main gate. Minutes later, Peanuts arrived. I unlocked the gate (I still have a key, today), re-secured the gate and left Camp David Land trailing dust.

I had made a clean getaway, no goodbyes, no promises. The continuing saga of what remained of B Company there would continue without me.

The notion of detonating a road mine or the prospect of catching a snipers bullet on the way did dance in my head. On arrival I shook Peanuts' hand and said, "Tell the guys I said bye and don't forget to duck. You be careful on the way back. That cigarette factory back home is gonna need an experienced killer like you to run the place one day."

"I know it Bog and thanks. Thanks for everything. Go get 'em Bog!"

Excited to go home cancelled waves of sadness but awakened bouts of apathy. A new cycle had begun.

❧❧

88

Cam Rahn Bay Revisited

nonymous once again, I boarded a twin propped military transport filled with other silent, haggard-looking strangers. We arrived at Cam Rahn Bay without incident by midmorning on September 9th. Exiting the aircraft and sauntering along the tarmac, much of what I saw here during the light of day was the same as I remembered it from 14 months ago. This time, instead of being hustled to nearby bunkers, we shuffled off like automatons to the same wood-framed, screened-in Reception Center building.

I thought of the old timer from the 9th Infantry Division when we parted company, with him advising me, "Do what they tell you, kid." A lifetime ago. The remainder of the day was spent filling out paperwork, arranging commercial flights to the States the following morning, and screening all of us for contraband.

Reluctantly, I handed off my Army .45 to the corpsman who administered all those rabies vaccinations the day before I left Camp David Land. The pistol had been a trusty companion that never left my person from the time I misappropriated it from the 284th MP armory, the first day I was assigned to the Honey Wagon. I felt uneasy without it. I was fortunate on my previous visit when I dodged all the mayhem that sapper infiltration caused, a week after my departure for Bien Hoa.

I also thought about those two Air Force policemen risking their lives trying to thwart the attack only to be summarily sent to LBJ. For what? Upsetting an officer? Wonder what happened to them.

Later in the evening walking toward my temporary barracks I spotted a crowd of about thirty guys standing around smoking what I thought were cigarettes, and drinking beer. As I approached them the surrounding haze threw off the exceptionally strong odor of marijuana. Passing by, I saw a circle of ten guys seated on the ground surrounded by what appeared to be a large crudely fashioned wooden salad bowl. Long, thin hollow bamboo sticks in their mouths were four feet long and firmly attached to the base of the bowl.

As the guys huffed and puffed through the sticks, the bowl lit up like a volcano throwing out huge wafts of smoke and embers. A community pipe smoking arrangement it seemed, the likes of which I had never seen. A comical display, at that.

It wasn't so much the ritual in progress that I found disturbing, the widespread use of marijuana and heroin among our military was well known. It was their unrestrained ceremonial-like display that concerned me. Clearly, the former stern view of drug abuse had softened among the upper echelons of the Army, as evidenced by a pair of junior officers I spotted among the crowd.

All of these guys were like me, waiting for their "Freedom Bird" to the States. As I passed the crowd, I thought of guys like "Pot Head Clem" and some of the hapless GIs sent to LBJ for doing the same thing that these guys were flaunting without concern or restraint.

So much for the notion of justice for all.

❧❧

89
The Freedom Bird

At precisely 0830 the following day, I was in my assigned aisle seat on the left side of the Continental Boeing 707 just about midway down the cabin. A minute later our freedom bird sharply accelerated at a terrific speed lifted, then shot skyward like a missile. We waited in brief suspense hoping that no Soviet or Chi Com surface-to-air missile would launch to take us down. After several minutes, the voice of the plane's captain crackled over the intercom, "All right, gentleman you can rest easy now. We are no longer in Vietnam air space. Next stop, Anchorage, Alaska."

A collective sigh of relief all round, except for the guy seated next to me. He was drenched in sweat and his arms were shaking. A typical "head," he was adorned with small round wire rimmed darkly shaded sunglasses, wearing the long sleeves of his jungle shirt buttoned, not rolled up above the elbows, like most of us on the aboard.

I had seen it before at Fort Riley and Long Binh Jail. A heroin addict. Back at B Company, I happened on a man hiding behind some sandbags one night near my hooch. He had a needle in his arm. Alarmed, the sergeant begged that I not report him as I forcefully removed the syringe. A pathetic sight. The man was a good squad leader in the weeks prior to my arrival at B Company. He was demoted from sergeant to PFC for being under the influence of what was purported to be alcohol during a reconnaissance mission. My obligation as an NCO was to report the incidence, but I couldn't do it. I destroyed the syringe and tossed his baggy of powder into the nearest shit-burning barrel. I don't know whatever became of him. Two weeks later B Company disbanded.

The guy in the seat next to me was in bad shape. A PFC with the 25th Infantry Division. I leaned over and asked, "Are you holding anything?" As he glanced at my 18th Military Police Brigade patch he said, "You gotta be shitting me. You think I'm gonna give anything up to you?" "No, probably not," I responded and added, "I'll tell you what. I'm gonna go use the head. You do what you gotta do." Unlatching my seat belt, I walked to the restroom at the rear of the plane. When I came back he was curled up and sound asleep, and he remained that way for most of the 14 hour flight to Anchorage.

Arriving late in the evening we were greeted by 50 degree temperature prompting most of us to jog across the tarmac to the boarding area inside. My estranged passenger companion remained on the plane.

The airport was virtually empty save for a small contingent of culinary workers moving about a little café. Unimpressive, but nonetheless reassuring to be standing on US soil.

An hour later we were in the air again and on our way to McChord Air Force base outside Tacoma, Washington. Midway into the flight my companion asked, "What's the deal with you? Don't you MPs get off busting grunts?" "Not the ones who hump six to ten days and nights in the bush!" I exclaimed as he pushed back, "Oh man, now I've heard it all. A fuckin' MP grunt! Bullshit! No fucking way!"

This was the most common response I grew weary of hearing.

I wanted to strangle him just as Shakey wanted to slice the throat of that ignorant sergeant. Only after many more of the soldier's questions and my answers did the PFC addict accept my story. We were no longer estranged.

90

Mc Chord Air Force Base, Fort Lewis Washington

Just before landing at Mc Chord, my addict travel companion said, "I'm scared. I don't know if I'm gonna make it. What am I gonna do?" A pitiful scene and I had no answers for him except, "You better roll up your sleeves. MPs will random shake down some of us for weapons and contraband. Wearing long sleeves will only draw their attention to you. I know I would peg you for a 'head' hiding something."

"I can't. I got tracks (needle marks) on my left arm," he replied.

"Well, roll them up and stick your left hand into your pants pocket and don't even think about wearing those sunglasses." I barked back.

The Army had introduced a detoxification program that was still in the embryonic stage of development. Regardless, the admission of any drug abuse would cost him dearly. The entire weight of the Uniform Code of Military Justice would be brought to bear, routinely triggering a swift General Court Martial that invariably resulted in a conviction. He would be incarcerated to serve an indeterminate sentence and immediately spirited off to the United States Disciplinary Barracks at Fort Leavenworth. All this, to be awarded a dishonorable discharge on his release, along with a less than a warm thank you for his service to the country.

It was late morning or early afternoon when we touched down at McChord. Walking along the tarmac I told my fellow grunt to walk behind me as we approached a troupe of Air Policemen and Army MPs conducting random pat-down searches of passengers. As I came nearer I surreptitiously dropped my 201 File (personnel records) which produced the desired distraction, allowing my companion to breeze through the checkpoint without incident.

As we boarded several Army buses for the trip to nearby Fort Lewis for final processing, I heard chants in the distance. Boarding, my companion said, "That sounds like protestors. They were outside the gate here when I left for Nam eight months ago." "Protestors? They weren't here when I came through last year," I responded. "Yea, they don't like us man. They were throwing stuff at the buses and calling us names," he added. Somewhat dismayed I dismissed his story as an isolated incident.

Three buses in all, my companion and I were seated in the second bus as we headed toward the front gate. From my window seat on the right side I saw a crowd of people holding signs and screaming obscenities as we passed. An egg was tossed by a young kid standing next to a woman holding a sign with "Baby Killers" in large black letters. The egg hit the window several seats behind us. "I told you man. They don't like us." My addict reminded me. "Yea. I guess so." I muttered.

At Fort Lewis there were no protestors. My newfound friend and I entered a huge warehouse with hundreds of other soldiers. No doubt the same space with the same atmosphere I experienced fourteen months earlier. Only this time the roles were reversed. We, the returnees, handed off old worn jungle suits in exchange for ribbons, medals, and dress uniforms. All the fresh meat got issued new jungle attire. I studied the guys with me carefully, and then looked hard at the Vietnam-bound guys.

Our faces were old and haggard, theirs were fresh and melancholy. I felt sorry for them. We were shuttled to various work stations filling out paperwork, then hand carried a stack of military forms to other stations where clerical personnel stamped or signed them. During this process my traveling companion and I were split up and sent in different directions. As we parted he shook my hand, smiled and simply said, "Thanks brother. I just responded with, "Good luck." I never saw him again.

By later evening I had completed all the necessary processing. Those of us mustering out of the Army took longer than those being sent to new duty stations. The only debriefing I received was from a staff sergeant stamping my shot record. He rattled off with, "Don't talk about what you did or didn't do over there. Nobody's interested." When he asked me about my final destination, me telling him Los Angeles, he chuckled and said, "Well, after you get home, put your uniform in the closet. War heroes are not popular." I walked away asking myself, what the hell is going on here?

They gave me a bunk in a nearby barracks and handed over my plane tickets home. My flight departed early next morning from nearby Seattle-Tacoma Airport with a two hour layover in San Francisco, with a Los Angeles arrival time in early afternoon. After settling in my temporary home with a hundred other guys, we were directed to form up outside the barracks where a master sergeant marched us to the Mess Hall for a late meal. Shuffling into the building we were directed not to form a line with cup and tray in hand which was the custom, we were simply told to find a seat.

Perplexed and suspicious about the change in military protocol chatter among us evolved into a collective, "What the hell is this?" moment.

The din faded as the master sergeant called us all to attention as a captain entered the Mess Hall and barked, "As you were!" then simply added, "Welcome home, men. Tonight, the Army is serving you. A steak cooked the way you want it with all the trimmings. Enjoy it and again, welcome home!" Flabbergasted into briefly silence was quickly followed with a collective roar of laughter. If the army got anything right during the Vietnam War, this was surely one of them.

Bright and early next morning, I put on my dress green uniform sporting my service ribbons and marksmanship medals The 18th Military Police Brigade Combat Patch (double Axes) adorned on the sleeve of my upper right arm. I caught a military bus to the Seattle-Tacoma Airport. Before boarding I called Lorraine and arranged for her to meet me at LAX.

91

San Francisco Airport

A board the flight I noticed about a dozen of us, mostly Army guys seated throughout the cabin. Headed toward my seat I got a few gawks from among the cabin crowd. Fortunate, I got an aisle seat next to an older black lady who engaged me in conversation. She had just met with her son stationed at Fort Lewis. Our chat centered on the concern she held about her son being sent to Vietnam, her daily ritual in prayer for not only him but for the "boys" as she put it still over there. I remember trying to reassure her by telling her that the Vietnamese Army was assuming a bigger role in combat operations and that more guys were coming home than going over. Privately, I hoped her prayers would be answered.

Changing planes gave my mind the chance to flash backwards like snippets of an epic motion picture, with no particular chronological order. Much the way Hollywood produces a movie, starting not from point A and progressing to Z but through a series of assorted story excerpts in no sequential order. Incidents, people, places. Stopping here and there briefly on one thing, then vaulting into long deliberations on another.

Exhilarated about returning home, followed by guilt for leaving those great guys left behind. An epic adventure with no neatly tied-up ending. No resolution. Just pieces of time and place only those who were there could ever understand. Wonder. The pieces took up permanent residency in my soul.

The instant I walked into the terminal I felt completely alone even though the place was packed with people. It must be said that in those days, airport terminals were devoid of any contraband scanners or security check-in stations. People were free to roam within the confines of the airport, including the boarding/departing gates. Among the crowd I could hear faint chants of "Peace not War" out of sight, but somewhere deep in the terminal. Ignoring it, I scanned the area looking for a seat. None to be had. Leaning against a wall, I checked my travel orders trying to decipher all the acronyms. The Army was famous for applying letter jumbles and cryptic nonsense words to everything. It seemed that every written order I ever had was a challenge just to figure out what half of it meant in plain English.

On my left I saw a pair of 4-year-old eyes staring at me from underneath the bill of a San Francisco Giants baseball cap. We both smiled. His mother smiled as she grabbed the child's hand and walked away. I dismissed the encounter as normal.

Minutes later, I spotted an empty seat near the end of a long row. I eased into the seat as the man seated to my right swiftly folded up the newspaper he was reading and walked away. The woman seated on my left hastily embraced her infant daughter, rose from her seat and as our eyes met glared at me, then turned and walked away. Glancing at people across from me, I encountered a few scornful faces. Several pairs of eyes delivered a cursorily scan then spun their heads around. I was getting that same sensation I experienced walking into the mess hall after a night of laying in duck waste.

Over there it could be understood. Here absent the stench, that impression quickly evolved into a more sinister meaning. Unaware at the time, this moment turned out to be the opening shot in a long and lonely war. Never ending battles between choices. Silence, absent discussion. Acquiescence versus assertion. Ignorance instead of enlightenment. And the most challenging of all, restraint versus impulse.

So many impressionist snapshots of Vietnam in the murky corners of my consciousness where they'd been filed away, suddenly and spontaneously shot into my head.

92
Home-College

The short flight to Los Angeles filled me with excitement and anticipation. Walking from the plane toward the terminal alongside a fellow returnee, we acknowledged each other in silence. As we entered the terminal, he was immediately embraced by the open arms of what I figured was his teary-eyed wife, followed with a passionate kiss. Seconds later my eyes met Lorraine as I raced to embrace her literally off her feet. If there were any scornful faces in the crowd or antiwar chants I wouldn't have seen or heard anything. I was oblivious to anything else around me, awestruck by the sights, sounds and smells of all the things I had missed.

There I was, embraced by my mother, my sister and the firm handshake from my father who managed to reveal a ray of emotion, something I had never witnessed before. Minutes after my arrival, Rick and Patti showed up with their two-year old daughter to welcome me home, followed by celebratory drinks and salutations.

During the festive session I discovered a new talent: the ability to carry on a conversation while subconsciously grappling with flashbacks. Talking with Rick, exchanging glances with Patti and their toddler, thoughts of Rick being sent to Vietnam sickened me. I thought of guys like Jerry Perry, Delton Propes, Easy Aldrich and others who had wives waiting at home. Donnie's wife bore him a son several months before his return home. Better to send guys like me into that quagmire rather than guys like Rick with a wife and a child.

Back in college on Monday morning was a culture shock. The only guys with short hair were ex GIs among throngs of flowing long-haired people. We stood out like bulls in a herd of sheep. Anti-war posters, peace signs, along with anti-war rally notifications were posted everywhere. Anti-war sentiments were freely expressed in classrooms regardless of the subject matter. The battle over choices had begun.

I remained silent rather than join the discussions. And so it would be on more than just a few occasions for my remaining three years in the collegiate environment.

I loathed every minute of it with the exception of a very few special moments that occurred in my senior year, near graduation. During one of those silly, mandatory sociology classes I was required to take, the Vietnam War sparked debate. Nothing new there. During the discussion a pipsqueak seated in the front row in a class of over eighty students stood up and shouted, "Anybody that went over there was nothing but a *fucking* baby killer!" Silence.

Seated three rows behind him, visions of strangling the little bastard danced in my head. The sudden hush broke when the guy seated in the second row in front of me stood up. He was several years older, and obvious by appearance and demeanor an earlier Vietnam veteran. During his carefully measured response you could hear a pin drop.

I don't how or why you have come to your conclusion about me and the handful of others in this classroom you are referring to. I do know that you have been misinformed. No fault of your own. I am not a child killer but I can tell you about the children I have held and fed. I can tell you of death and destruction in a place where life is very hard and very short. I can tell you of the young men I served with, boys really, about your age that cried for their mothers in their dying breaths. And I can tell you about the terrified twenty year-old Vietnamese widow I held while she gave birth to her first child, a son, in a muddy trench during a fierce firefight. No sir, I'm not a baby killer. I am you, ten or so years ago, a young man thirsty for knowledge. It was young men like me that went there so young men like you would not have to. I forgive you and those who believe as you do, for you know not what you say. I think you will find a similar phrase in the Bible.

The class was mesmerized and prematurely dismissed by the instructor, filing out the door in silence. Six of us Vietnam Vets remained to thank him for his choice of words and for *asserting* our values instead of *acquiescing* to the status quo.

It seemed that we were to be always surrounded and outnumbered. In Vietnam and right here at home.

93

A Vietnam souvenir comes to light

Within weeks I visited the Veterans Administration Hospital in Sepulveda, California following the advice of that Marine Corp doctor. After explaining my concerns carefully, enunciating the medical term *nonspecific urethral inflammation* as the preliminary diagnosis, the VA physician rudely interjected, "Restrict your consumption of alcohol, don't drink any tea, drink milk. Get accustomed to taking more time when urinating. Anything else? I'm very busy here?" I didn't bother to tell him about the occasional swelling accompanied by minor irritation I experienced below my left eye.

My next visit to the VA was 14 years later.

That was the spring of 1984 when the protrusion began to spread, and the routine irritation that came with it increased in pain. My doctor, a reserve colonel in the Nevada National Guard, lanced it, removed a sliver of metal and said, "This foreign object looks like shrapnel to me." Six stitches later, no more swelling no more pain. I am reasonably certain that foreign object was from that errant illumination round that detonated above Cortez, Gufford and me. And so ends our Vietnam era narrative.

The years that lay ahead follow Shakespeare's Henry IV when "The edge of war, like an ill-sheathed knife, no more shall cut his master." There were any number of other sharp things to be alert to, but a jungle war with no clear aim or purpose, ineptly managed, was not among them.

But at all points in the life we built, the Vietnam experience bled through the fabric, not least the censorious political poison of the day that attempted to strip American veterans of their humanity and decency for having served. How ironic that as the new century gets underway, increasing numbers of men attempt to make hay with bogus claims of having been there with the rest of us.

Succeeding years have not been kind to my companions-in-arms. Ed Santry who worked with Easy Aldrich died of a self-inflicted gunshot wound, a scant month after he returned home. We lost Barmann in 1976 — drug overdose. Palmateer was murdered in 1997 — his brother killed him. Cortez died of heart failure in 2008, alcohol may have been a factor. Shakey stepped out in front of a car in 2007. His family believes it was suicide. Chamberlain and Bias died in 2018 of Agent Orange related prostate cancer. Tiny fought a seven year battle with cancer that invaded virtually every internal organ, also Agent Orange related. He died in 2018, too.

Jim Gufford died in 2010. He remained in the Army. During a drug bust as a CID Agent in the '70s he was shot in the same leg from which I removed a piece of shrapnel. While attending his mother-in-law's funeral he bent down, felt a sharp pain in that same leg and was sent to the hospital. Two days later he was dead. Toxic shock, we heard. Angelo Torres died in 2015 after battling cancer for over a decade.

Major Z left Vietnam under a cloud. Something to do with marketing stolen goods, but not before making a reciprocal arrangement with a fellow officer to write one another's recommendation for award of a Bronze Star medal.

❧❧

CODA

(A concluding section in a different format than
the rest of the production.)

The rest of my Life

**Marriage to Lorraine in 1972, college graduation the
following year,** took me on the road in search of a real job. My
part-time employment as a janitor for the Los Angeles School
District along with part-time employment as a sporting goods
salesman for J. C. Penney (they actually had a sporting goods
department back then) wasn't cutting it.

In those days you could enter any business or corporation,
fill out an application, then wait for a phone call or letter from the
prospective employer for an interview. In some instances, you
might get an immediate interview. This wasn't the case when I
filled out an application with Kraft Cheese Company where I was
escorted to a corporate officer seated behind a big desk in a large
and fashionable office. The man, of my father's age, reached out,
shook my hand and offered me a seat. After a short exchange
about my work experience, education and military status he said,
"It is very commendable that you completed college and I see that
you have quite an extensive work history."

I worked an assortment of menial jobs starting as a youngster
of fourteen, until I entered the Army.

"But I want to be very candid with you. I'm a little concerned about your time in Vietnam. Please take no offense, I don't think we as a company are prepared to handle some of you people. I'm sure you don't fall into that category but we have heard stories about Vietnam Veterans."

I didn't want to work there, anyway.

There were no discrimination laws against barring Vietnam Veterans from employment back then. I chose silence rather than discussion. It was easier. Thanks Hollywood.

Reno Police Department. After a series of menial truck driving jobs I found a sales position with an insurance company. Lorraine worked at a bank. The combined income allowed us to move into our first home in 1974. My son, Brian, came in 1976. My work as an insurance agent evolved into unfulfilling drudgery. I was restless.

Early in 1977 I left Los Angeles and changed course with a job as a police officer for the City of Reno, Nevada. Over ten years were spent there, five of them as a Robbery-Homicide Detective, four years as a SWAT team member, and a stint in the Intelligence Section investigating organized crime and outlaw biker gangs. My daughter, Kari arrived in 1981.

Interesting vehicle pursuits along with several shootouts marked my time in Reno. One drama took place the evening of April 15, 1981 in a vehicle repair garage. The local FBI office asked our Robbery-Homicide squad to assist them in surveillance.

Two escapees from the federal facility at Terminal Island, in Los Angeles, were to be featured in the FBI's 10 Most Wanted fugitive list for a series of violent bank robberies committed in five western states. A tip from the owner of the garage convinced the FBI that the two men would pick up a vehicle being serviced. At 8:30 pm the pair arrived. Both were armed. Confronted by FBI agents and my partner, Detective Gary Eubanks, inside the garage the pair was directed to the floor.

While one of them dithered whether or not to remove the pistol from his waistband, the other man bolted out of the garage. With Detective Lanny Marsh positioned on the rooftop and armed with shotguns, I ordered the man to freeze. He turned, glanced upward and reached into his waistband. We fired four shots, all of which hit him.

The threat ended.

Seeing an FBI agent emerge from the garage directly below, I fired one round over his head into the front windshield of the stolen vehicle they arrived in. Simple reasoning: we had not cleared the vehicle. A tactical error by the FBI agent precipitated the action. Four shots into the suspect and the windshield shot occurred within three seconds, or less.

"We won. They lost." Within 48 hours, a shooting review board convened, including a lieutenant, a patrol sergeant, a training division officer and a patrol officer. The testimony of all involved would be tape recorded and placed in an evidence locker for the criminal and/or civil suit that was invariably expected to follow.

During my testimony the patrol sergeant (years later elevated to the rank of chief of police) asked me, "What did you see in the car that caused you to blow out the windshield? Guys in black pajamas?" The suggestion hinted that I was a crazed Vietnam veteran hallucinating about Viet Cong guerillas.

He got a few chuckles.

Incensed, and as calmly as I possibly could, I answered, "No I did not. I think I may know what you're thinking. You are suggesting a possible scenario that my actions could have seriously injured or killed an innocent victim that could have been inside the vehicle. That thought did occur to me in the milliseconds I had to make that decision. I stand by the actions I took. We won. They lost."

Ultimately, I chose to allow the ignorance of the patrol sergeant's remarks to prevail instead of aggravating myself by commenting on their stupidity. It was easier.

The same type of foolish remark would came from the mouths of a patrol lieutenant (he, too, eventually rose to the rank of chief of police), and a patrol sergeant in another shooting incident four years later. The same inane VC uniform reference was made during my testimony: "I guess there weren't any black pajamas in this one." Again, I chose silence over discussion. Silence by now had become my preferred default tactic in these situations. Surrounded again, and clearly outnumbered, it was time to move on.

Los Angeles Police Department. I accepted an appointment with the Los Angeles Police Department in October, 1987. The rigors of nearly six months of basic training at the Police Academy were physically and mentally exhausting. I was 39-years of age, the oldest among a class of over seventy with a median age of twenty-five. The curriculum was dominated exclusively by all things US Marine Corps, firmly established in 1949 with appointment of Marine Corp Major General William Arthur Wharton as the 42nd Chief of Police.

In spite of it all, it was a good move for me. The next sixteen years, nearly fourteen of which were devoted to investigation of homicides, culminated with promotion to Detective II, the most junior supervisory rank and roughly equivalent to the "soft sergeant" rank of Specialist 5 I had in the Army.

It was a good fit, as I had no desire to assume any leadership role ever again. I had my fill in Vietnam. In the closing years of my career I quit counting homicide investigations I was assigned to work. My back-of-envelope tally is 300.

And what is your name? Shortly after completing the 18 -month probationary phase I was assigned to the police academy as a Tactics Instructor. Here, I trained recruits in the basics of officer survival and in-service tactical techniques to plainclothes personnel. About the second week in March, 1990 with my partner, Officer Michael Parlor, I was sent to the California Specialized Training Institute, in San Louis Obispo for a one-week course of instruction on advanced officer survival methods. During the first hour the course administrators introduced each instructor assigned to the subject matter in the curriculum, along with the expertise they possessed that qualified them to teach. All of them were retired old-timers with extensive military or law enforcement backgrounds, or both.

The live-fire nighttime tactical "Hogan's Alley" obstacle course instructor was introduced as retired Army Sergeant Major Jerald D. Massey. Hogan's Alley is police jargon for a mock setting of buildings, streets, and vehicles along with pop-up target props depicting innocent citizens, as well as armed suspects. The purpose is to subject students to stressful decision-making in a shoot-don't-shoot scenario. Hogan's Alley was synonymous with what Parlor and I routinely taught at the academy.

The introduction continued with the administrator informing us that Sergeant Major Massey had been personally awarded the Silver Star by General Douglas MacArthur for actions in the Pacific Campaign, in World War II. He added that Massey was also a veteran of the Korean War and the Vietnam War.

The man's face and the military bearing he projected, suggested a familiarity I couldn't immediately identify. I wrestled with the thought of asking him if he had any association with the 720th during the Vietnam War. I had no clear basis for asking him but the uncertainty pestered me. During the coffee break that followed I decided to ask, fully expecting my intuition to be mistaken. He said, "Yes, as a matter of fact I did, indirectly. I was quite familiar with the battalion staff there." And you were?"

"Yes sir. I was with B Company in 1969 until it was disbanded in 1970." Staring intently at me he asked, "And what is your name?" After telling him he grinned and said, "Tonight, when your group is assigned to Hogan's Alley, you will be excused from the course. You will be up in the tower with me. We have a lot to talk about. See you then." He turned and walked away leaving me thunderstruck asking myself, what the hell was that all about? Classroom instruction for the remainder of that morning and the entire afternoon was a waste. My mind was elsewhere.

Much of what I experienced in Vietnam was nothing more than fragmented tiles of a large mosaic, or isolated scenes cut from a motion picture. A chapter in an unfinished book. What did happen to those guys all shot up on that ambushed tugboat? Did those two survivors in that chopper crash actually survive? And what happened to Major Z? Had he been fragged, or was that just a rumor? What about that stolen watch along with the investigation that surely had to follow? Through all the preceding years I imagined a knock on my door from Army Criminal

Investigators wanting to interrogate me on all of those things. As the years passed, the thought gradually faded.

Here it was almost twenty years removed from that helicopter ordeal, wondering if Sergeant Major Massey had some answers, and what would I divulge, if anything? Twenty years of life experiences coupled with my intimate understanding of criminal investigations and all things associated with them would naturally guide me. The lessons learned were a benefit I did not possess when I was confronted with "And you son are looking at 99, plus 1!" when I was 22 years old.

I would rely on my instincts and weathered ability interpreting the motives people often telegraph in situations like this. I also had to keep in mind that this man was over twenty years my senior, very possibly a master himself in the art of interrogation. These were among many questions that raced around in my head.

"Personally, I wouldn't have given a damn what you or your crews would have had in mind for the bastard." Precisely at 6pm I met the Sergeant Major in the glass tower above Hogan's Alley. Seated facing the various switches and levers and with a microphone on the work desk in front of him, he motioned me to the chair next to him.

He asked about my current assignment, all the while arranging the pre-programmed pop-up targets for crime-scene scenarios selected by the range instructors. After each selected scenario, instructors conducted a brief critique on the student's performance. When the first student completed his run through the course, he spun his chair, faced me and said, "You know, I've only known one man that had a middle name that was the same as his first. You ever know anybody like that?"

I was flabbergasted but managed a tight, tight-lipped grin, shook my head slightly glancing at the floor briefly, then directly at him. He continued, "Colonel Stromfors gave you a large benefit of a large doubt." This guy was a master interrogator and as this chess game-like atmosphere between us continued through the evening, left me no doubt he had answers.

My mind scrambled for an appropriate response. He continued, "Nobody liked him you know. The man was a pain in everyone's ass. Frankly, I couldn't stand him." I was running out of patience struggling for a proper response and blurted, "He was my CO (commanding officer) back in the States. Nobody liked him there, either." Massey interjected, "You didn't either, did you?"

"No I didn't, the instant I witnessed him disrespecting NCOs with tours in Vietnam behind them, it disgusted me. These guys were my mentors."

A brief respite in the exchange followed. Then I asked, "Whatever happened to that guy?" I was convinced that one of two possible situations had occurred. Either Sergeant Major Massey was present somewhere within the confines of the Battalion Commander's Office, unbeknown to me, during my interview with the colonel, or he had access to sources intimately involved. Regardless, I hoped to confirm or deny rumors about Major Z.

Massey resumed, "That piss-poor excuse for an officer moved on to be a pain in somebody else's ass."
Slight pause.

"I do have one question. When that courier chopper went down, there was talk that some officers had their pictures taken next to the bodies of those killed. Did that happen?"

Without hesitation I answered, "It sure as hell did. It was the most disgraceful thing my crew and I ever witnessed over there."

He shook his head in disgust and said, "That's a damn shame, that's a damn shame. Look Bogison, the war has been over for a longtime. Whatever happened there stays there. I'm glad we had this opportunity to meet. Small world, ain't it?"

Our talk ended with him shaking my hand and with a chuckle saying, "Personally, I wouldn't have given a damn what you or your crews would have had in mind for the bastard. Good luck to you!"

I walked away knowing what I already knew. The question as to whether or not a fragging occurred remained unanswered. But it no longer mattered. Sergeant Major Jerald D. Massey intimated as much. Resolution had been achieved, however unsatisfactory and incomplete.

An apology and more unanswered questions. During the early '90's the annual gathering of California Homicide Investigators Association (CHIA) was hosted in Reno, Nevada and I was a participant in attendance, I was summoned by the Chief of the Reno Police Department. The former patrol sergeant who, ten years earlier, suggested I had hallucinations about men in black pajamas when I blasted the front windshield of a stolen vehicle.

As Chief of Police, he extended his hand and said, "Bogison, I am sincerely sorry that I ever made those offensive remarks to you during that review board back in 1981. I was wrong and I am truly sorry. Please accept my apology." Overwhelmed by his remarks, I simply said, "Thank you sir, and thank you for understanding." It was an awkward moment for both of us. America had started to wake up.

Throughout all those years a day never passed without

intermittent snippets of those days and nights in Vietnam, with those special men I considered my brothers. Wondering, if they made it out alive and if so, how were they were doing. Are they as troubled as I am? Have they grown as weary as I have of not being believed when trying to explain what we did as MPs in Long Binh province? Did they, too, choose silence having no remaining patience to argue the point, as I did? Do they even want to be contacted? What would I say to them? Do they have memory flashes of people, places and events like I do? Are they able to carry on a conversation and push ugly specters aside, as I have?

Questions. Haunts. Doubts. Fears.

I would be collecting blood samples at a crime scene, typing a report, interviewing a witness, screaming at a suspect or even testifying in court. There simply was no means of controlling the timing or strength of these brooding flashbacks.

With time, I became adept at swiftly pushing such thoughts aside the instant they popped up, and quickly refocus attention to the task at hand. But not always.

In 1990, teaching a class of newly minted detectives — a course in basic investigative procedures — my ability to stage-manage the old haunts all but abandoned me. Midway in my presentation of a detailed account of a case I handled in the 1983 kidnapping and gruesome murder of two little girls, I froze. The experience was identical to one I had while seated on the witness stand during the trial. Then and now, out of the blue, scenes of the French pier and the father carrying his screaming four-year old blood-soaked boy bulldozed through the reality at hand.

Abruptly excusing myself, I grappled with an overwhelming impulse to run away. I barely managed to stage a calm stroll to the door, steps away. As I closed the door behind me I took three deep breaths, forcing an immediate purge of all thoughts. Seconds later, I re-entered the classroom, completed my presentation as though the brief disruption never occurred.

The experience shattered my conviction that flashbacks were merely the substance of dime store novels or the stuff of Hollywood movies. I questioned my suitability for continuing as the seasoned, hardboiled, big city homicide detective persona I adopted years earlier. It wasn't like you could just walk into your commanding officer's office and say, "Ah boss, I have a little problem going on here. I have these visions of little people in pajamas running around screaming. Could I take a sabbatical for a couple of months to get my head screwed on properly?"

That tack would get me an immediate referral to the "Rubber Gun Squad," making biweekly visits to a therapist and spending my days with other "rubber heads" sorting and distributing police forms, moving and storing hundreds of stolen bicycles, along with one of a dozen other menial tasks while the Department decides what to do with me.

Privately, I enrolled in a self-hypnosis seminar and applied the principles I learned prior to testifying before a court of law. It worked. It helped to have good partners who instinctively knew when to step in and carry you. Me, stepping in for them on some off day or rotten moment.

All of it came to an anticlimactic end, in 2004. Several on-duty freeway accidents, some injuries received on the job led to a medical retirement.

Next stop, peace and serenity. So I thought.

Retirement-Montana. I bought twenty acres of mountain land outside Bozeman, Montana in 2000 after making a note of the area when I passed through in 1969 on the drive home from Fort Riley. The beauty and sparse population enthralled me. My dream was to live there one day. Blessed with extremely talented children, predominantly inherited from the gene pool on Lorraine's side of the family, my son Brian graciously offered to design and construct a home on the property, and we began breaking ground in 2001. Of course, I helped. The project occupied much of my time and mind and took us nearly five years to complete.

Here, in the peace and serenity of this wilderness a storm was brewing in me. Between completing household projects and regular forest maintenance undertakings, I grew restless. Having more time on my hands produced frequent bouts of self-examination spiced with images of all the people, places and challenges I faced in Vietnam.

Curiosity and concern about my fellow Bushwhackers ran a parallel track. To stem the turbulence in my soul, for several years I became a substitute history teacher assigned to local high schools. It was exactly the band-aid I needed. Until January, 2006 when my former partner and, later, supervisor Detective III Marshall White was diagnosed with terminal cancer.

He retired several years before me, picked up stakes and moved from Los Angeles with his wife to Lebanon, Missouri. His military service was on an aircraft carrier off the coast of North Vietnam. We were complete opposites in nearly every sense, but I loved the guy. Now, on his deathbed he pleaded for me to go see him before he passed.

Struggling financially at the time, I drove nonstop from my home to his bedside, a hospital in Springfield, Missouri. When I arrived, he said, "I just want to tell you that I love you."

He then directed me to pass that same message, naming each man he had toiled alongside solving murders working with various homicide units.

Minutes later, he was gone. I wept like a child.

The walls I carefully and deliberately built around me through long years were cracking. It was the beginning of their total destruction, the end of hiding behind them. Time had come to slay demons.

Four years earlier, reluctantly I had tested the waters. Surfing internet in search of information about the wounded men aboard that ambushed tugboat and the crash of the 25th Infantry helicopter crash I stumbled on the website of the 720th Military Police Battalion Reunion Association and its President, Tom Watson.

He was the squad leader among a handful of Bushwhackers responsible for successfully holding Hill 15, during the post-Tet attack on Long Binh that lasted nearly twelve hours, February 23, 1969. His background as a retired Homicide Investigator with the Gloucester County, New Jersey Prosecutor's Office produced a successful exchange of information. His extensive research into the history of the 720th was pivotal in what evolved into a storied quest for answers. It was Tom Watson who assisted me in obtaining a copy of the Army's official report of that downed chopper.

32 Year Old Mystery. At home recuperating from injuries sustained on the job, I watched a television program titled, "Vietnam Stories: The Vietnam Memorial." It was Staff Sergeant Daniel P. Ouellette's story, suffering with emotional problems, living homeless on the streets of Boston, Massachusetts for the past 32 years. Ouellette's issues began in Vietnam starting on his second tour. The lone survivor of a helicopter crash, he had no memory of the incident or what happened to him afterwards. The program also profiled members of his immediate family and their 32-year search for answers to the cause of anguish.

Half-way into the program suddenly, it hit me. Ouellette was a name listed on that accident report. I immediately telephoned the Discovery Channel, left a brief message requesting a call back followed up with an email to one of the producers of the program.

They were not cooperative.

Phone calls to the Veteran's Center in Boston, hoping to locate the former Army Green Beret counselor assigned to Ouellette, as was depicted in the program were more successful. Making contact with the counselor, I got a phone number for Ouellette's sister and mailed her a copy of the accident report along with a cover letter to the counselor, hopeful the information would benefit Ouellette's treatment.

During the telephone conversation with the sister, I sensed the information I provided answered most of the questions her family had been seeking.

Closing a chapter. After Marshall's passing, I began the task of identifying and locating surviving family members of the crew and passengers of that 25th Infantry helicopter crash. It wouldn't be easy. Interaction over the years with the next-of-kin of homicide victims reveal a darker side to the sensationalism of each story, long after it saw print in a newspaper or played out in a court of law.

The sudden impact of a deeply traumatic event on a family

generally never ends well. Once jubilant family members grow increasingly despondent, shadowed by divorce, ill health, substance abuse, suicide. Death from war would be no different. The passage of 37 years compounded the problem.

The sister of one of the pilots said the Army listed her brother's death as the result of "pilot error." In like vein, the older brother of the other pilot was told the crash was caused by "carelessness in the actions of the copilot." An uncle of a passenger was told his nephew was killed in a "helicopter mishap." All true, one way or another for all those I was able to find and speak with.

I agreed to the uncle's request to tape my recollections to share them with his extended family. The step-mother of a passenger told me "His family never recovered from the news of his passing." She said, both parents died prematurely, adding that his younger brother turned to substance abuse, living a homeless life in obscurity. What was accomplished by my effort to help bring closure after so very many years?

Confirmation of a known lesson: That passage of time does not heal.

Lack of consistency in the Army's explanation added pain to the already devastating, "We deeply regret to inform you" process. During my discussions with the family members, all registered an appreciation for receiving the information I shared with them. I was the eye witness who gave their loss a human immediacy that an impersonal telegram never could. Or the routine visit of a Casualty Assistance Calls Officer assigned locally to call on the family, could not - however earnest, kindly and well-intentioned.

Undertaking this intimate mission closed the final chapter of an unresolved issue that will forever remain with me.

A final note on the survivor of the crash who, in fact, did not truly have his life returned to him at all. By some extraordinary bureaucratic gaff, he is one of fourteen names of living personnel engraved on the Vietnam Memorial's "Wall" in Washington, DC. Following recovery from severe injuries, Staff Sergeant Daniel P. Ouellette could not cope with life. In a spiritual, wrecked physical sense his name on the Wall is true. The man became a basket case, utterly unable to cope, living on the streets of Boston for almost forty years.

Volunteering for a second tour of duty in Vietnam sealed his fate. By putting himself forward again he thought he was saving his younger brother from being sent there. The day of the crash was his first day back in-country. His injuries induced trauma, robbing him of memory. As the Discovery Channel documentary revealed, he had no idea what, when, where or how he was scooped up from the Dong Nai River.

Persuaded to seek help, his counselor suggested a visit to the Wall. When Ouellette saw his name up there along with the others aboard with him and the date of their death, he broke down completely. Attempts by media and others to find him have failed.

> "Without memory, there is no culture. Without memory, there would be no civilization, no society, no future."
>
> --*Elie Wiesel*

Epilogue:
How the Bushwhackers came to be

At 1800 hours on September 11, 1967, 2nd Battalion, 39th Infantry Regiment, 9th Infantry Division with the 720th Military Police Battalion, 89th Military Police Group, 18th Military Police Brigade launched an ambitious cordon and search mission, Operation Corral, in Bien Hoa Province, III Corps Tactical Zone, just north of Saigon.

The purpose was to locate, dissuade and destroy enemy close-in strike options directed at Long Binh Post, a sprawling logistics facility, the largest US base in Vietnam and home to about 60,000 American personnel. Viet Cong sappers attacked the base in February, destroying large quantities of munitions. And attacked again in 1969 in a Post-Tet Offensive.

Round the clock in Operation Corral 720th military police searched huts, the heavily verdant countryside and rice paddies for Viet Cong, their collaborators and enemy supplies.

In order to sustain security in the long term, Operation Corral engendered Operation Stabilize. Speculation among veterans has it that two generals informally got together to talk. Perhaps the MP Brigade one-star and his Infantry Division counterpart, a two-star. Their decision made US Army history.

On October 20th, 1967 A, B, and C Companies were jointly tasked to provide perimeter protection. In their new role, military police served as infantry in the 22-square mile Tactical Area of Responsibility (combat zone) surrounding Long Binh Post. The job included civic action program support, rapid reaction team formation, staffing village outposts, conducting reconnaissance, fielding ambush patrols, armed river patrol and commando-style stealth water-borne and ground transport.

Thus, the 720th became the first (and to date, only) MP unit in American military history to deploy in a combat zone in the traditional role of ground-pounding infantry. Operation Stabilize terminated on July 25, 1970.

In 1969 during the command of Captain (Lieutenant Colonel, retired) Harold D. "Hal" Lockhart (March 29 - July 8, 1969) the nickname "Bushwhackers" was adopted by Company B. Previously, the Company mascot was the cartoon character Snoopy, dressed in jungle fatigues with a bush hat and M-16 rifle under the saying "Hang on B Company."

Inexplicably, "Bushwhacker" achievements went largely unrecognized and have remained perversely neglected in the official history, including B Company's heroic participation in successfully repelling a determined enemy assault on Long Binh Post on February 23, 1969. The Battalion's veteran chronicler, Tom Watson, provides a coda to the forgotten epic:

And with the final deactivation of the Battalion's lettered companies in August of 1972, the special legacy of this unique and historic mission performed during a war that our national government just wanted to forget, was forgotten and relegated to the dustbins of the national archives by the Military Police Corps and their historians of the era.

This book puts the saga on record.

❧❧

Acknowledgements

Living combat veterans are the sum of those who love us and give their selfless support in peace and war. Our survival on the battlefield depended on grace, the solidarity of a supportive family back home, and on the immediate cohort of brothers-in-arms who had our back. For the grace we can offer prayers of thankfulness. For family and fellow soldiers, we owe a debt of boundless gratitude.

I have tried to remember and identify everyone who featured in my Vietnam experience. But time erases much we think is unforgettable. I beg clemency from those whose names should have, but did not, appear in this book.

All errors are mine.

Family.

Lorraine, my wife, by my side always from the day I left for Vietnam and through all the years that followed. The very crutch I needed without whom I could not have carried on.

My son Brian, who stood tall, like many of the sons and daughters of Vietnam Veterans, he took the blows thrown at him from peers and much of academia over their disdain for the Vietnam War and those who fought in it. My daughter Kari, like her brother vigorously pushed back at those voicing contempt for the Vietnam Veteran. Thank you.

720th Military Police Battalion:

Lieutenant Colonel Robert E. Stromfors, the man who gave me the benefit of a large doubt.

Command Sergeant Major William J. Wilkinson, who interceded on my behalf when there was a critical need for someone in my corner.

B Company:

First Sergeant Hardin Collins. Owed so much and never thanked enough. The most misunderstood man in all of B Company.

SP/4 John Pedemonte, fellow Bushwhacker, Vietnamese linguist from California and the voice of the tactical operations center who always ensured I received whatever I needed when it really counted.

The Bushwhackers of the 3rd Platoon:

Staff Sergeant Larry Mintec, my first Ambush & Recon Platoon Sergeant, who patiently laid the groundwork for my assuming the responsibility for leading the 2nd squad of the 3rd Platoon.

Staff Sergeant Fred Pazmino, reluctant hero who masterfully kept the platoons he led out of harm's way, and among the most humble men I have ever encountered.

Sergeant Ron Snider, from Northern California. Admired for his patient guidance as a fellow squad leader, a role model I tried to emulate. The one guy who could wring sense out of the no sense we were all subjected to.

Sergeant Hank "Tiny" Fraley, from Maryland, a fine fellow squad leader, who guided me to be the squad leader I became, and the confidant I sought when I needed it the most.

SSG Donnie Ray Thomas, country boy from Louisiana instrumental in keeping all of us alive with his natural instincts and backwoods ways. An outstanding platoon sergeant and master diplomat who successfully kept 2nd lieutenants in check.

Sergeant Angelo Torres, hardnosed Bushwhacker NCO and the second most misunderstood man in all of B Company. We share a boundless admiration for B Company, the 3rd Platoon. He harbored no malice for those who misunderstood his intentions.

SP/4 Mike "Ambi" Ambrose of San Francisco, the 1st Infantry Division MP replacement who never complained or refused to do anything I asked of him. A team player and a Master M-79 Grenadier.

SP/4 Glenn Barmann, from New York. Small in stature big on delivery in the bush and on the water.

SP/4 Richard Bias, from a small town in Ohio, the able pathfinder and minesweeper for the 3RD Platoon to whom I am grateful for pulling me out of knee-high muck on more than one occasion.

SP/4 Doug "Bish" Bischoff, the gentle giant from Michigan, Master M-60 machine gunner. The calming force in the partnership of "Lewin & Bish" on whom I could always rely regardless of the situation.

SP/4 Tommy Chamberlain, from Maryland, admired for his maverick ways, intuitive intelligence, and philosophical discussions.

SP/4 Jack "Peanuts" Cortez, the kid from New Jersey, Master M-79 Grenadier. Trusted to wreak havoc on any distant target.

SP/4 Stan Galonski, citizen soldier from Los Angeles, commended for "intellectual engineering ingenuity" turning warm cans of beer cold within minutes. Outstanding rifleman. He never questioned anything I asked of him.

SP/4 Jim "Hoss" Gufford, the North Carolina boy who always reminded me to check myself for alien tropical critters invading my body.

SP/4 Jared "Loco" Kelley, Kentucky native who stood by me, right or wrong, good times and bad in the bush and afloat. Master M-60 machine gunner, Master whaler Operator and among the first to volunteer for an assignment regardless of the danger involved.

SP/4 Carlos "Chuck" Lozano, from Southern California, to whom I am greatly indebted for accepting me as one of the "Bushwhackers" on my very first mission. The go-to-guy everybody sought for comfort. A natural leader, brilliant photographer capturing on film reconnaissance operations in the bush and PBR operations.

SP/4 Ed Lewin, the Bull from the Bronx, Master M-60 machine gunner, faithfully providing us hours of entertainment which produced some seriously interesting times. The guy I could always turn to when it counted.

SP/4 John Main, the kid from Alaska, everyone believed was an Eskimo but was a Japanese-American born in Japan, who I leaned on exclusively as the RTO for the 2nd squad. He always knew precisely where and when I needed access to the radio. Master M-79 Grenadier.

SP/4 Robert "Crazy" Marich (accurately named), from Detroit, Michigan, who never disappointed being a player front and center, especially involving anything nefarious. Underneath that eccentric façade resided an unwavering loyalty for his fellow Bushwhackers. An integral member of the 3rd Platoon.

SP/4 Ed "Shakey" Marley, streetwise guy from Philadelphia, Master whaler Operator relied on to perform any task in the bush or on the river.

SP/4 Wilber "Gomer" Martinmoss, the silent guy from West Virginia, a gifted pathfinder and highly capable soldier.

SP/4 Bill Parker, another North Carolina boy, admired for his no-nonsense demeanor along with his consistent concern for the safety and welfare of all of us.

SP/4 Jerry Lee Perry, from Paducah, Kentucky, who accepted directives without hesitation, irrespective of the dangers. Master of all weaponry in the platoon and loyal to the core.

SP/4 Robert Lynn, Michigan, Master .50 caliber machine gunner. Terrific, morale-boosting dry sense of humor precisely timed when one needed. No team - anywhere - ever had a better man.

SP/4 Delton Propes, the reliable guy from Kentucky. His squad leader, Sergeant Fraley, never had to tell him to do something twice. Neither did I. Outstanding rifleman and pathfinder.

SP/4 Jon "Rookie" Purvis, Iowa, always in the right place at the right time assisting a fellow Bushwhacker in need. Master rifleman, pathfinder and intensely loyal.

SP/4 Richard Radcliff, Ohio, admired for his Can-Do attitude in the bush and underway. I also appreciated his helping hand pulling me up on those 2 ½ ton trucks enroute to drop-off locations, then pulling me out of the mud when we got there. Master .50 caliber machine gunner.

SP/4 Greg Thompson from Phoenix, Arizona, who did much to make me into the squad leader I became.

SP/4 Glenn Ward, Southern gentleman, backwoodsman, farmer from North Carolina. The oldest among us and the man from whom I went for expert advice on adapting to life in the swamp. Master of all weaponry in the platoon. A soldier's soldier.

SP/4 Bruce Zirk, Wisconsin, ever ready with an amusing, homespun tale in lieu of an explanation for something gone wrong. Master .50 caliber machine gunner, super loyal. Outstanding on foot in the bush and on deck in the river.

PBR Boston Whaler Crews:

SP/4 Ed "Easy" Aldrich, Master RTO man, M-60 machine gunner and whaler Operator. The go-to-guy when I needed to get something done. A loyal Bushwhacker ashore and afloat.

SP/4 Joseph Keene the reliable, even-tempered guy from Kentucky. Master .50 caliber machine gunner.

SP/4 Edmond "Klinger" Kelleher, Master .50 caliber machine gunner from Michigan. The guy that stuck to me like glue when I desperately needed another hand, on more than one occasion.

SP/4-Sgt Chris Lowe, Bushwhacker from Maryland. Master .50 caliber machine gunner. Despite working on opposite watches, this Master PBR coxswain diligently applied mechanical skills that enabled our PBRs to fly at speeds in excess of 40 miles an hour.

SP/4 Harry Marineau, Master .50 caliber machine gunner. The silent, loyal guy from Missouri who never complained. An expert photographer responsible for capturing some of our PBR operations on film.

SP/4 Ronald Mason, Master .50 caliber machine gunner, Texas, never had to be told twice to do something.

Sergeant Doug Newman, the big guy from Southern California. Master whaler Operator, freely, unhesitatingly offered assistance in completing any perilous task anywhere, any time.

SP/4 Jim "Sandy" Sanders, Ohio, always knew when to complete a task before being asked to do it. Although working on opposite watches, this Master .50 caliber machine gunner ensured that our PBR weaponry was properly maintained. Essential team player.

SP/4 Denny Taylor, the guy from Illinois relied on to assist in overseeing PBR operations. Master M-79 Grenadier and .50 caliber machine gunner. Outstanding Bushwhacker in all elements. My rock to get things done on the Dong Nai River.

458 Transportation Company: Circumstances of war brought together our two disparate units. And we made it work. 458 trained by the US Navy at Mare Island knew their boat-handling business inside and out, and we learned from their example.

Lieutenant Steinberg, appreciated and much respected for his discreet support of unauthorized decisions made contrary to the standing orders he was duty-bound to abide by or report. If not for his strength of character I would have faced a court martial, likely ending with a reduction in rank, at the least.

Sergeant Ed York, mild mannered native Hawaiian, a master coxswain who acquiesced to my unauthorized requests with muted disregard for the consequences.

SP/4 Chuckie Bowen, streetwise guy from Chicago who patiently instructed me on all the complexities of piloting a PBR. Master PBR coxswain, fiercely loyal to the 458 Transportation Company.

SP/4 Gary Rasmussen, master PBR mechanic and master coxswain from Wisconsin who always had a solution to every mechanical breakdown we encountered on the water.

SP/4 Swensen, master PBR coxswain, a Minnesota native who enthusiastically offered and delivered his services for *any* task I asked of him.

Correctional Training Facility, Fort Riley, Kansas

Sergeant Alan Drever, 300th MP Company. The California boy who latched on to me in Military Police School at Fort Gordon, Georgia in April of 1968 then on to Fort Riley, Kansas until we both parted ways for different units in Vietnam. He remains a loyal friend to this very day.

Staff Sergeant Donald J. Smith I considered my mentor and squad leader at Fort Riley, Kansas. He educated me on the perils he faced as a military policeman with the 9th Infantry Division escorting convoys on the highways in the Mekong Delta.

284th Military Police Company, LBJ, Long Binh Jail, South Vietnam.

SP/4 Jim Connell 284th MP Company, who helped me keep sane and the guy who always had my back in the bowels of the asphalt jungle of Long Binh Jail.

Retired Washoe County Public Defender's Office Investigator Robert Howell. Formerly, SSG Robert Howell, 1st Cav, 2nd Battalion, 7th Cavalry, wounded on May 6, 1966 during Operation Davy Crockett. Left for dead an NVA soldier fired one shot from an AK-47 directly into his mouth while NVA soldiers systematically began shooting his fellow wounded troopers. A longtime friend and kindred spirit, he was the inspiration behind the writing of this memoir years earlier.

Los Angeles Police Department. My former homicide detective supervisors and partners who unknowingly carried me during those days when my mind was 10,000 miles away, in a time and place I could not escape. I am forever grateful they knew when to ham and when to egg:

:   Homicide Detective III Al Ferrand

        Homicide Detective III Marshall White

        Homicide Detective III Michael Oppelt

        Homicide Detective III Ismael Aldaz

        Homicide Detective III Woodrow Parks

        Homicide Detective II Thomas Townsend

        Homicide Detective I Bradford Cochran

        Homicide Detective II Orlando Martinez

Last but nowhere near least, the editors who took a manuscript and made it into a book:

Trudy Rutherford, a dear friend who years ago proofread the early drafts of this work.

Eric Dietrich-Berryman edited the entire manuscript and brought the book into production. Born in Berlin, he came to the United States as a 17-year old unaccompanied immigrant on the German quota for 1957, and promptly enlisted in the US Army. He was a PFC-SP/4 in Company C, 720th MP Battalion, Fort Hood when it was activated and became the 560th MP Company, the first military police unit sent to Vietnam and scattered throughout the country, in 1962.

Among his "non-MP" jobs in Vietnam was helicopter door gunner with the "Soc Trang Tigers" of the121st Assault Aviation Company. Following his discharge from the Army in 1964, he rode GI Bill benefits to a PhD in English literature at the University of

New Mexico (1971).

Briefly an assistant professor of English in the Massachusetts university system, he had the good sense to switch services and retired in 1993 from the US Navy as a commander. He retired again in 2003, this time from the federal civil service intelligence community where he served as a staff officer with the Geospatial Intelligence Agency, press chief and senior speechwriter to the director, retired US Air Force Lt. General James Clapper.

Design and production: coordinated by **Brayton Harris** — who has been working in printing and graphics since he was managing editor and staff-artist for his high school newspaper, 1949. In the years since, he has also been the author/co-author of some 20 books and several hundred magazine articles, held political appointments in both the Carter and Reagan Administrations, and — by a rather strange coincidence -- served (as a Navy commander) in Vietnam, 1969-1970 . . . the same period as Robert Bogison.

They said it best

In the making of this book, surviving members of B Company "Bushwhackers" were asked to provide some favorite military related proverbs (the sources, presented here in parenthesis) and add any thoughts of their own. As always, the guys came through and often in their own, idiosyncratic, independent style.

SP/4 Ed "Easy" Aldrich

"Above all, Vietnam was a war that asked everything of a few and nothing of most in America." (Myra MacPherson)

"In war, our elders may give the orders . . . but it is the young who have to fight." (T. H. White)

"Not all days in the field were unhappy ones. You had to have fun sometimes or you would go crazy." (Lanny Starr)

"We are fighting a war with no front lines, since the enemy hides among the people, in the jungles and mountains, and uses covertly border areas of neutral countries. One cannot measure [our] progress by lines on a map." (William Westmoreland)

"I have done the math."

"We shed blood, sweat and tears in the performance of duties that were indistinguishable from any US infantryman who earns thereby the award of a Combat Infantry Badge. By contrast, acknowledgement of exemplary Bushwhacker performance in the same line of work received no recognition whatsoever."

SP/4 Doug "Bish" Bischoff

"It is not possible to explain what it feels like to be on ambush in a dark dangerous place at 3 am, in total silence, just waiting for movement."

"In 1969 we were young, trusted each other, and we were dedicated to the mission. Now I feel like we were just put out there as bait for Charlie."

"The best friend I will ever have I met in Vietnam. We went through it all together, side by side. Now, years later, when I introduce him to others, I say, "This guy I trusted totally and I knew he always had my back." But I will also just add that after you get to know him better, you will be truly amazed that I am still alive."

"Special moments in life are few. One I will never forget is the time spent with buddies from my squad almost 50 years after our time together in the bush. The reunion represented the true meaning of brothers, always. God Bless each of you."

Cathy "Cat" Fraley (widow of Sergeant Hank "Tiny" Fraley)

"Tiny always said, 'Those who died in Nam were probably better off than those who have to live through the hell of Vietnam their whole life.'"

SP/4 Edmond "Klinger" Kelleher

"In war no one wins."

SP/4 Jared "Loco" Kelley

"Don't Mean Nothin' "

Dropped a class in '69.
Don't mean nothin'
Drafted away from a life so fine
Don't mean nothin'
Sent to the land of the Viet Cong
Don't mean nothin'
Learned to shoot,
Learned serious skills
Learned to cope
and how to kill
Don't mean nothin'
Then we lost some brothers
and it meant everything.

SP/4 —Carlos "Chuck" Lozano, Acting Sergeant and Squad Leader, 1969 Recon Patrol, 3rd Squad, 3rd Platoon, 1970. Acting Sergeant PBR River Boat.

"You do not survive a war… you die a long lingering life."

"I didn't meet friends in Vietnam, I discovered unknown brothers."

"You don't remember war … you feel, smell, taste and relive war daily."

"I grew up in Southern California, but I became who I am in Vietnam."

"As a Military Policeman, we all worked with a partner that we worked well with, got along with, and depended on. During my time in Vietnam, I was lucky to have two partners that I depended on to survive our time in war."

"In 1969, as part of the "Bushwhackers" doing recon patrol, I had the luck to partner with Ron Snider. Ron was the quarterback that made you feel just as important as he was. His manner with the job in hand was beyond his young age, and was respected by all. I always will be thankful to have been his partner in a time that will define everything for the rest of my life."

"In 1970 when Ron went home, I was transferred to PBRs and again gained a partner that to this day is a part of my life, Jim Sanders had big shoes to fill, and that he did. I learned about responsibility just by observing Jim's way of life. There was no job, good or bad that Jim did not jump into without giving it his best. *I could not have chosen a better man to depend my life on than Jim Sanders."*

SP/4 Edward Lewin

"I realized that, in the heat of battle, I wasn't fighting for my country. I fought for the guys next to me. We were brothers. I was prepared to die for them, and they were prepared to die for me. There is nothing stronger than that. Nothing." (Sammy Lee Davis)

"War is organized chaos!" (Stephen Grey)

"Chess is a game of strategy with an end game, war has no winners!"

"War never ends we live with it every day!"

SP/4/Sergeant Chris Lowe

"Television brought the brutality of the war into the comfort of the living room. Vietnam was lost in the living rooms of America and not on the battlefields of Vietnam." (Marshall McLuhan)

"I was a young snot-nosed kid when I got to Vietnam and didn't have a clue who was fighting who or why the hell I was there. The first thing I learned was I had to be a druggie or a beer drinker, the latter of which I chose! I was lucky and got assigned to the PBR detail and proceeded to have fun for the next year until we gave the boats to the gooks and they sent me to a fire support base 5 miles from Khe Sahn Valley. What I got out of the 14 months I was there, was the greatest camaraderie and of the brothers one person could ever want. The memories, I will never forget and the brotherhood that still continues today will far surpass anything I will ever do in my life."

SP/4 John Main
"No soldier ever really survives a war." (Audie Murphy)
"It is fatal to enter a war without the will to win it. " (Douglas MacArthur)
"Men and women who are willing and sometime unwilling to sacrifice their lives for each other are the true heroes."
"The guys I served with in Vietnam are my family whom I love and best of all my friends."

SP/4 Robert "Crazy" Marich
"Yes. War is hell but through that I met my brothers for life."

SP/4/Sgt Doug "Dougie" Newman
"In peace, sons bury their fathers. In war, fathers bury their sons." (Herodotus)
"I do not believe that the men who served in uniform in Vietnam have been given the credit they deserve. It was a difficult war against an unorthodox enemy." (William Westmoreland)
"No soldier ever really survives a war." (Audie Murphy)
"We left Vietnam: however, it did not leave us."
"Vietnam is an interesting part of American History. Many theories exist as to the why we went. I guess you can find one that suits you and conclude you have it figured out. To this I say, good

for you. I was there and I haven't gained such a perspective."

"I did learn that absurdity carried out in a time of conflict can be fatal. I also learned that people I served with, and those I met, especially our Australian friends, are the finest people God had ever ordained."

SP/4 Bill Parker

"No soldier ever really survives a war." (Audie Murphy)

"Congratulations, you have survived the war. Now live with the trauma." (Lori Jenessa Nelson)

"No matter how far from war we run, it always catches up with us." (Scott Westerfeld)

PFC/SP/4 Jerry Lee Perry

"Above all, Vietnam was a war that asked everything of a few and nothing of most of America." (Myra MacPherson)

"No soldier ever really survives a war." (Audie Murphy)

"The reflection upon my situation and that of this army produces many an uneasy hour when all around me are wrapped in sleep. Few people know the predicament we are in." (George Washington)

"Congratulations. You have survived the war. Now live with the trauma." (Lori Jenessa Nelson)

SP/4 John Pedemonte

"I trust another Viet Nam veteran immediately, over any other person I meet. I know what we have all been through, through the years. Society made us feel guilty for fulfilling our role of service to our country. It took me a long time to be proud of my service in Viet Nam."

"I was new in-country and got very sick with a cold/bronchitis and was moping around. My platoon leader, 1st Lieutenant

William Davidson, US Army Ranger, pulled me aside and told me, 'I'm sending you in on sick-call and I want you to come back a man. I'm not your Mama and I'm not your girlfriend so straighten up before you get killed or you get my other men killed.' That was the day a 20-year old surfer from California grew up overnight! I will always be grateful to him for giving me a slap in the face!"

"There was an unspoken conversation that took place when we sat across from each other in a deuce-and-a-half on our way to an ambush site. Our eyes would meet and we knew that we had each other's back. We seemed to say, I got you, and you got me" without saying a word. This Brotherhood is forever!"

SP/4 Delton Propes
"I will always remember my fist night on ambush. I thought those mosquitoes were trying to eat me alive."

"We did our duty but no one welcomed us home."

"All draft dodgers were pardoned. I wish my mind could forget what my eyes have seen."

SP/4 Jon "Rookie" Purvis
"Who is the enemy? How can you distinguish between civilians & none civilians? The same people who work on base during the day, want to shoot & kill you at night. How do you distinguish between the two? The good or the bad! They ALL look the same!" (Varnado Simpson)

"We are fighting a war with no front lines, since the enemy hides among the people, in the jungles and mountains, and uses covertly border areas of neutral countries. One cannot measure [our] progress by lines on a map." (William C. Westmoreland)

"No matter how far from War we run, it always catches up with us." (Scott Westerfeld)

"Fresh off a small farm in Central Iowa, 19 years old, 4

months training & I woke up in Vietnam. To say I was scared would be putting it mildly. Every aspect of my training was used while in The Nam. I did not know the meaning of Brotherhood until I was assigned to B Co. 720th MP BUSHWHACKERS." Members of the 3rd Recon Platoon took me under their wing & helped me fit in. Then I knew they had my back & that I had theirs. To this day I am still remembered by the nickname given to me by the squad, "ROOKIE."

"The Nam is in my life every day and will be for the rest of my life. No matter how many meds I'm on."

SP/4 Rich Radcliff

"It is fatal to enter a war without a will to win it." (Douglas MacArthur}

"Above all, Vietnam was a war that asked everything of a few and nothing of most in America." (Myra MacPherson)

"No soldier ever really survives a war." (Audie Murphy)

"Congratulations. You have survived the war now live with the trauma." (Lori Jenessa Nelson)

SP/4 Jim "Sandy" Sanders

"No soldier ever really survives a war." (Audie Murphy)

"It is fatal to enter a war without the will to win it." (Douglas MacArthur)

"Above all, Vietnam was a war that asked everything of a few and nothing of most Americans." (Myra MacPherson)

"The result of these shared experiences was a closeness unknown to all outsiders. Comrades are closer than friends, closer than brothers. Their relationship is different from that of lovers. Their trust in, and knowledge of, each other is total. They got to know each other's life stories, what they did before they came into the Army, where and why they volunteered, what they liked to eat and drink, what their capabilities were. On a night march they would hear a cough and know who it was; on a night maneuver they would see someone sneaking through the woods and know who it was from his silhouette." (Stephen E. Ambrose)

"Let us understand: North Vietnam cannot defeat or humiliate the United States. Only Americans can do that." (Richard Nixon)

"It is also unfair to every young kid (soldier) that was sent to this far away land to do anything but try to win. We were shortchanged!"

"The American public let every one of us vets down. I was in- country for ten and one half months. I was advised to change into civilian clothes to continue my flight home from the west coast so as to not call attention to myself as a returning veteran. So sad!"

Sergeant Ron Snider

"Above all, Vietnam was a war that asked everything of a few and nothing of most Americans." (Myra MacPherson)

"Not all days in the field were unhappy ones."(Lanny Starr)"

The result of these shared experiences was a closeness unknown to all outsiders. Comrades are closer than friends, closer than brothers." (Stephen E. Ambrose)

"Too much was asked of our shoulders while nothing was asked of the rich and influential in America."

SP/4 Denny Taylor

"It is fatal to enter a war without the will to win it." (Douglas MacArthur)

"There is no stronger bond than the bond with your buddies you went to war with. They are truly your brothers. Even after 50 years if one of the guys from our unit needed something I would do whatever I could for them."

"At the time in Vietnam there was a picture on our Como hooch of two buzzards on a tree limb looking down at a group crossing a desert. The saying under them was 'Patience my ass I want to kill something.'"

"The flag today means so much more to me than before I went to war. I fought under that flag and now everywhere I live I put up a flag pole and fly the flag every day."

Staff Sergeant Donnie Ray Thomas

"No soldier ever really survives a war." (Audie Murphy)

"Once Strangers, Forever Brothers." (Unknown)

"It was a traumatic experience knowing I was going to be sent to Vietnam, but after revisiting 50 years after setting my feet back on American soil, it was as much or more traumatic coming home. People just didn't understand."

SP/4 Glenn Ward

"Above all, Vietnam was a war that asked everything of a few and nothing of most in America." (Myra MacPherson)

"Who is the enemy? How can you distinguish between the civilians and the non-civilians? The same people who come and work in the bases at daytime, they just want to shoot and kill you at nighttime. So, how can you distinguish between the two? The good or the bad? All of them look the same." (Varnado Simpson)

"Let us understand: North Vietnam cannot defeat or humiliate the United States. Only Americans can do that." (Richard Nixon)

"Military men are just dumb, stupid animals to be used as pawns in foreign policy." (Henry Kissinger)

SP/4 Bruce Zirk

"It was a terrible horror movie that my mind experienced. First mission out someone reconnoitered the area by firing an M-60 machine gun. Oh, hell. I am going to die on my first ambush mission. Nobody told me about H&I (Harassment and Interdiction) coming from our own post. Thought it was the enemy bombing us!"

"Sights like a child's blown-off face, a woman screaming and waiting to bleed out after her lower torso was blown off and recovering many distorted and bloated bodies of Americans retrieved from a filthy river from a downed helicopter. They are forever etched in my mind."

"I hate our country for drafting me at a young age. Throwing 18 to 23 year old kids into a blood bath, and expect them to come home and be normal! Worthless political god damned war that could have been won without our so called, sub intellectual leader's tactics."

"And to pardon those draft dodging bastards who went to Canada when over 58,000 of our own died is a crime! And the fucking welcome we got when we returned home was also a crime!"

"I hate fireworks, crowds and in general do not like to be with people, especially chatter/small talk."

"Hated that god damn war that forever changed me! Still love my brothers in arms!!"

Author

Robert Bogison was born in a working class neighborhood in Pontiac, Michigan to an Austria immigrant, his mother, and a wine and beer salesman father (and first generation Armenian) seldom home, who had served in the U. S. Army Air Corps in the Pacific Theater in World War II. An uncle - Charlie - served with the 1st Marine Division at Cape Gloucester, Peleliu and Okinawa.

The first ten years were all-American impromptu baseball and football games choreographed on open fields, and as super action heroes and warriors battling evil, armed with toy guns and dirt-clod grenades. Winters were occupied with epic snowball fights.

A change in the father's employment took the family to Granada Hills, California. After graduating from Granada Hills High School in 1966 he focused on college, pool halls and part-time jobs.

In early January, 1968 Bogison enlisted in the US Army to become a Military Policeman. Basic training followed at Fort Ord, California and Military Police School, Fort Gordon, Georgia.

His first duty station was the Correctional Training Facility at Fort Riley, Kansas assigned to rehabilitate incorrigible soldiers, some of whom had circulated for many years in the military penal system since being drafted in the early 1960s.

In July, 1969 he shipped out to the 284th Military Police Company headquartered in the infamous Long Binh Jail compound.

Four months later - and by dint of unconventional personal

initiative - he transferred to B Company, "Bushwhackers," 720th Military Police Battalion to be a squad leader. B Company is the only combat infantry MP unit in Military Police Corps history. When B Company disbanded in July, 1970 for the final in-country 40 days he was sent to a US Marine Corps fire base near Da Nang.

He arrived home on Friday, September 11, 1970. The following Monday he was in classes at California State University, Northridge where he raced through the curriculum, graduating in 1973 with a BA in Sociology and a minor in History.

His wife, Lorraine, encouraged him to pursue a law enforcement career, and in 1977 he joined the Reno, Nevada Police Department. Ten years assigned to the Intelligence Unit investigating organized crime families and outlaw motorcycle gangs were followed by four years on the SWAT Team and five years with the Robbery/Homicide Unit.

In 1987 he was appointed to the Los Angeles Police Department as a Tactics/Officer Survival Instructor, Homicide Detective and Homicide Detective Supervisor until he was medically retired in 2004 for job-related injuries.

Nineteen years were devoted to homicide investigations. He stopped counting after 300 murders.

Since 2004, Robert and Lorraine have made their home on twenty acres of mountain land in the forest outside Bozeman, Montana in a house designed by his son Brian. His daughter Kari is a graduate of the University of Alabama, a homemaker and mother of two daughters and a son.

Son Brian makes his home in Montana. He is a law school graduate of the University of London and father of two girls.

෴

Notes
Keyed to applicable page numbers

1/ The United States Disciplinary Barracks (USDB) established in 1874 is the Department of Defense's maximum security prison for male military personnel convicted by court martial for violations of the Uniform Code of Military Justice (UCMJ). Only enlisted prisoners sentenced to more than 10 years, commissioned officers, and prisoners guilty of national security violations serve their sentences here. The Correctional Training Facility at Fort Leavenworth is a sub-set of the USDB.

2/ The Vietnam War's official start/end dates are November 1, 1955 to April 30, 1975. It was an undeclared war and the longest in US history. It is also know as the Second Indochina War. North Vietnam calls it the American War.

4/ Chief of Staff, US Army. A 4-star general, the most senior uniformed officer assigned to the Department of the Army.

8/ Knotts Berry Farm is a 57-acre theme park in Buena Park, California.

ibid/ Khe Sahn siege by three divisions of North Vietnamese troops was broken by US and ARVN ground forces (Operation Pegasus) on April 6th, 1968.

12/ Jump boots are ordinary Army-issued boots with extended

lacing for extra re-enforcement and with the heel portion of the sole cut to an angle, to lessen the chance of snagging an obstacle in the descent.

17/ The Philippines invasion by Japan forces lasted from December 8, 1941 to May 8,1942. Allied liberation occurred on January 29, 1945.

19/ The April 18, 1942 "Doolittle Raid" of 16 B-25 bombers launched from the decks of USS *Hornet* at Tokyo, Kobe, Yokosuka, and Osaka was a US propaganda victory that boosted morale on the Home front.

22/ Cam Rahn Bay has the reputation of being the finest deepwater port in Southeast Asia. It was the major military port for US military supplies during the war and also home to a significant US Air Force presence.

28/ Biên Hoa Air Base, 16 miles from Saigon (Ho Chi Minh City) used as a principal base by US Air Force and Republic of Vietnam Air Force units from 1963 to 1973.

34/ Long Binh Post was a major US Army base, logistics center and command headquarters northeast of Saigon. It was also known as Long Binh Junction after the initials of the sitting president of the day, Lyndon Baines Johnson. Long Binh Jail (LBJ) was established in 1966 as an Army stockade to hold about 400 prisoners. Demand soon outstripped supply. The Jail was woefully understaffed and suffered several riots.

38/ Deuce-and-a-half slang for a military general purpose truck of 2.5 tons, 1951 onwards.

40/ E-8. E stands for Enlisted. Enlisted ranks start with E-1, private to E-9, Sergeant Major. Non-commissioned officer ranks begin with E-4, corporal-Specialist 4.

49/ The Phoenix Program, devised by the Central Intelligence Agency in cooperation with Australian and ARVN militaries, sought to identify and destroy Viet Cong political infrastructure via infiltration, capture, interrogation, and assassination in the years 1965-1972. In this span, Phoenix operatives "neutralized" 81,730 suspected VC. In the same period, the VC killed 33,052 Vietnamese village officials and civil servants.

60/ "Full bird colonel" is Army jargon for the metal eagle that identifies a colonel's rank insignia. A lieutenant colonel's insignia is a silver oak leaf.

68/ The serviceable "round holes" of a latrine in Vietnam had no seats to lift. A customer simply sat over the hole. As GIs soon discovered to their dismay, latrines were unisex. Except that women who came to use the facility hopped on top of the planking, straddling the hole, to do their business.

71/ Black market activity in Vietnam was rampant. The massive US troop surges brought a cornucopia of materials that fueled a thriving illicit trade and fostered widespread corruption. American products dominated shop merchandise and street vendor stands in all the major Vietnamese cities. American servicemen, civilian contractor personnel, federal workers and others realized there was a great deal of money to be made in a "bonanza" atmosphere. Major Z is rumored to have succumbed to the temptation of easy black market riches.

100/ Parasites, including mosquitoes, in Vietnam's tropical heat were common, entering the body through all available cavities as well as boring upwards through the soles of feet. Harmful effects can last a lifetime. A Department of Veterans Affairs study found a possible link between liver flukes ingested through raw or undercooked fish and a rare bile duct cancer. It can take decades for symptoms to appear. By then, patients are often in tremendous pain, with just a few months to live. CBS news item, November 21, 2017.

105/ Agent Orange was a tactical herbicide used by the US military from 1962 to 1975. It got its name for the orange band around the storage barrel. Millions of gallons of Agent Orange and other herbicides were sprayed on trees and vegetation during the Vietnam War to deny the enemy thick foliage in which to hide. For the purposes of VA compensation benefits, Veterans who served anywhere in Vietnam between January 9, 1962 and May 7, 1975 are presumed to have been exposed to herbicides, as specified in the Agent Orange Act of 1991.

109/ Tan San Nhut was Saigon's principal airport and the entryway for the majority of troops in and out of Vietnam.

123/ Drug use in the later stages of the Vietnam War was pandemic, and mirrored the recreational escapism of young civilians in the United States. From heroin to amphetamines to marijuana, drugs were so commonplace among the troops in Vietnam that, in 1970, liaison to the Bureau of Narcotics and Dangerous Drugs - Egil Krogh - told President Richard Nixon, "you don't have a drug problem in Vietnam; you have a condition. Problems are things we can get right on and solve. https://www.history.com/news/

drug-use-in-vietnam.

"The American military readily supplied its troops in Vietnam with speed. "Pep pills" were usually distributed to men leaving for long-range reconnaissance missions and ambushes. The standard army instruction (20 milligrams of dextroamphetamine for 48 hours of combat readiness) was rarely followed; doses of amphetamine were issued, as one veteran put it, "like candies," with no attention given to recommended dose or frequency of administration. In 1971, a report by the House Select Committee on Crime revealed that from 1966 to 1969, the armed forces had used 225 million tablets of stimulants, mostly Dexedrine (dextroamphetamine), an amphetamine derivative that is nearly twice as strong as the Benzedrine used in the Second World War. The annual consumption of Dexedrine per person was 21.1 pills in the Navy, 17.5 in the Air Force, and 13.8 in the Army." Lukasz Kamienski, Health magazine, April 8, 2016.

124/ Thailand played an active role in the Vietnam War, sending ground troops to South Vietnam to assist US forces. In October, 1967 the Royal Thai Volunteer Regiment was assigned to Camp Bearcat at Biên Hoà to join its US, Australian, New Zealand, South Korean and Republic of South Vietnam allies. In 1968, the Volunteer Regiment was replaced by the Royal Thai Army Expeditionary Division. In total, until Thailand withdrew from South Vietnam in 1972, 1,358 Thais were wounded and 351 were killed in action.

132/ SP/4 David Allan Johnson, PFC David Lee Hemke, and PFC Robert Lamar McArthur, B Company, members of an Ambush and Recon Team, drowned in the Dong Nai River when the River Patrol Unit boat they were being transported in was swamped during a night operation at the junction of the Rach Bien and

Dong Nai in the Tactical Area Of Responsibility.

A Shameful Lack Of Recognition, Tom Watson, 720th MP Bn Reunion Association, *Vietnam Journal Operation Stabilize*, Book II Volume II, Part 4, page 543, "In Retrospect."

139/ There are 37 species of dangerous snakes in Vietnam among a total of 140 different snake species. Company commander, Delta Company, 1st Battalion (Mechanized), 50th Infantry, 173rd Airborne Brigade in Phan Thiet, Binh Thuan Province, Ray Sarlin remembers, "The Army didn't tell us how to tell 'good' snakes from 'bad' snakes, probably because it fell into the too-hard basket! Maybe they didn't tell us because it would've spoiled the Drill Instructor's best snake joke, 'The Nam has a hundred species of snakes: 99 are poisonous and can kill you with a bite; the other one ain't poisonous but will crush you to death!'"

160/ Fragging is the deliberate attempt to kill a fellow soldier - usually a commissioned officer or enlisted non-commissioned officer, with a fragmentation grenade, and making it look like an accident. The high number of fragging incidents in the late stages of the war is symptomatic of the war's immense unpopularity with the American public, coast to coast, and the effect of anti-war activists on college campuses on young, impressionable troops serving in-country. The Army documented 900 fragging incidents from 1969 to 1972.

241/ Bushwhacker-manned PBRs was part of a larger, joint Army/ Navy "Brown Water Navy" Riverine Force initiative tasked with transporting soldiers and their equipment into combat zones. Heavily armed, the boats also provided effective defensive fire in areas void of extensive roadways.

243/ Beginning about January, 1969 "Vietnamization" was a word coined by the Nixon Administration to end direct US participation in the Vietnam War through a program described by Melvin Laird, the Secretary of Defense of the day, to "expand, equip, and train South Vietnamese forces and assign to them an ever-increasing combat role, at the same time steadily reducing the number of U.S. combat troops." The emphasis was on reducing US troops serving in a ground combat role. Vietnamization, despite its successful execution, was ultimately a failure as ARVN troops were unable to prevent the Communist north from capturing Saigon, April 30, 1975.

244/ Vietnam has a tropical monsoon climate. Generally, weather is governed by two seasons -- the southwest monsoon from April to September and the northeast monsoon from October to late March or early April.

245/ For many people in tropical Asia rats are a source of protein, particularly among Vietnam's rural areas both the north and south—though rat can also be found on the menu in urban areas, including Saigon. The popularity of these rodents probably invites breeding with the aim of achieving ever-larger body mass.

247/ National Route 1A (Quốc lộ 1A) is the trans-Vietnam highway, starting near the China-Vietnam border and ending in Cà Mau province.

256/

> "You know I love the ladies
> Love to have my fun
> I'm a high life flyer and a rainbow rider
> A straight shootin' son-of-a-gun

I said a straight shootin' son-of-a-gun."
—"Joy to the World,"
Three Dog Night (1970)

262/ Mr. Toad's Wild Ride is a dark ride at Disneyland. Its title is based on the children's story book, *The Wind in the Willows* (1909), by Kenneth Grahame.

297/ Moments after expiring, body decomposition begins as bacterial enzymes break down soft tissue and spread through the blood vessels. Putrefaction, bloat, purge, and advanced decay follow rapidly. In drowning, lungs fill with water and the air sacs inside the lungs act like a sponge. This process causes the body to get denser. However, if the victim is deceased prior to submersion, victims tend to float since their lungs are still full of air. Putrification is faster in warm, fresh, or stagnant water. The hands and feet of a floating corpse are consistently the first things to break off the body. https://www.ranker.com/list/underwater-decomposition-facts/natalie-hazen?page=2

317/ Casualty list/accident report of lost helo sourced from records of the Vietnam Helicopter Pilots Association. http://www.vhpa.org.

Report title: Accident Summary for Aircraft Casualty on 17 April 1970 UH-1H tail number 67-17706, A/25 AVN 25 Infantry Division, Cu Chi Incident Number 700417351ACD. 25th 17 April 1970, Friday UH-1h, 67-17706, A Company, 25th Aviation Battalion, 25th Infantry Division, was assigned division courier aircraft.

Helicopter UH-1H 67-17706
Information on U.S. Army helicopter UH-1H tail number 67-17706. The Army purchased this helicopter 0868
Total flight hours at this point: 00001743
Date: 04/17/1970. Incident number: 700417351ACD Accident case number: 700417351 Total loss or fatality Accident
Unit: A/25 AVN 25 INF

The station for this helicopter was Cu Chi in South Vietnam UTM grid coordinates: YT004054. Number killed in accident = 10 . . Injured = 1. Passengers = 8/ costing [$] 725,945
Original source(s) and document(s) from which the incident was created or updated: Defense Intelligence Agency Helicopter Loss database. Army Aviation Safety Center database.

344/ Cambodia invasion, April 29 to July 22, 1970. By President Nixon's policy, the invasion was meant to defeat about 40,000 People's Army of Vietnam (PAVN) troops and the Viet Cong (VC) in the eastern regions of the country where Cambodian military weakness allowed a safe zone for communist forces to establish bases. With the US shift to a policy of Vietnamization (op. cit. p.243), the invasion sought to shore up the South Vietnamese government by eliminating the cross-border threat. The effort failed to eliminate many enemy troops or to find and destroy their headquarters, but the large volume of captured materials fueled claims of an Allied success.

358/ Jane Fonda, film star and Vietnam War activist made herself infamous in 1972 by broadcasting in behalf of the Communist dictatorship and posing with an enemy anti-aircraft gun during a visit to Hanoi, wearing pieces of People's Army military uniform. Thereafter, she became known as "Hanoi Jane" and remains commonly detested by the generation of Americans who served in the Vietnam War. Her politics remain determinedly Leftist. A talented actress, she is not the brightest bulb in the pack.

361/ Tugboat ambush.

> ST 2122. The *El Cid* Incident." Statement of William H. Edwards Specialist 5th, US Army
> 5th Transportation Company (Heavy Boat)
> 159th Transportation Battalion:

Being in a US Army Heavy Boat Company meant most of our vessels were LCUs (Landing Craft Utility). There were a number of other vessels assigned to the unit, however, two of them being Army tug boats. One of those tugs was the ST 2122, nicknamed the *El Cid*. On the morning of May 18, 1970 Captain Jim Krobert and Lieutenant Paul Zeller happened to be in the 159th Transportation Battalion communication room in Cat Lai and overheard a frantic radio call indicating the *El Cid* had just been hit by RPGs on a run from Cat Lai to Cogido. They could barely understand the request for help that was coming in from Chief Warrant Officer Bob Smith, the skipper on the boat. Word of the situation spread quickly through the company area, but all we could do was hope for the best for the crew and wait for those not wounded in the incident to bring the boat back home.

The Viet Cong had fired two bazooka-like rounds from the east side of the river into the starboard side of *El Cid*'s wheelhouse. It was a direct hit. (Lt. Zeller later found a piece of one of the rockets lying on the wheelhouse floor.) The impact of the rockets blew all but three of the wheelhouse windows out and sprayed shrapnel into the crew.

The skipper, CW2 Bob Smith, had been sitting on the step to the wheelhouse on the starboard side when a large piece of shrapnel hit him squarely in the chest. He was saved by an aviator-type flack vest he was wearing. The front plate of the vest was left with a large dent in it. He was also peppered with glass shards.
The Vietnamese piloting the tug was killed instantly (this was during Vietnamization, when we were gradually turning our boats over to the South Vietnamese). CW2 Cheshire and Staff Sergeant Jerry Folse were seriously wounded. Folse had received a serious jaw injury caused by the rocket shrapnel.

Mr. Cheshire, the Chief Engineer, had manned a gun on the starboard side when the rounds hit and was sprayed with shrapnel down the entire front of his body. His helmet was later found on deck with three holes in it made by shrapnel or bullets. He was hit at least once in the side by a bullet, in addition to being sprayed with glass. The bullet hit just where the pieces of the flack-jacket lace together, the most vulnerable spot. He took a towel he had around his neck and stuffed it inside the jacket to help stop the bleeding and continued to fire on the enemy.

When Captain Krobert and Lt. Zeller finally got to the boat up in Cogido, there was blood all over the deck and inside the wheelhouse. They learned that two or three of the crew who were not seriously wounded were able to return fire and call for helicopter gunship and med-evac support. River patrol escort PBR's provided immediate fire support and security while the most seriously injured crew members were removed from the tug, placed on PBRs, and moved to the river bank where a medevac 'dust-off' hovered.

A few days after the incident, I volunteered to ride shotgun on a jeep run to take mail to Mr. Cheshire at the 24th Evac Hospital in Long Binh. I remember a large, open bay of wounded people, both Vietnamese and Americans, some moaning incoherently. I made my way to Mr. Cheshire's bed and found him wrapped in bandages from head to toe, like a mummy from some Boris Karloff flick.

He couldn't speak to me and simply shook his head 'no' when I quietly asked if he'd like me to read a couple of the letters to him. I put the letters down next to his bed, patted him on the shoulder, wished him luck, left the bay, and never volunteered to make the hospital run again.

When I returned from Vietnam I still had about nine months left in my three-year enlistment. I was assigned to Fort Story, Virginia the Army's amphibious base on the east coast. Some weeks after I had settled in, I was walking down one of the company streets when I noticed a familiar face. It was Chief Warrant Officer Cheshire. He recognized me but didn't remember too much about my visit with him in Long Binh.

When I asked how he was doing he responded, "Well, other than about a pound of shrapnel still in me, I feel great!" He looked good, but you could see a couple of fresh scars. We wished each other luck and went our separate ways. That was the last time I ever saw Mr. Cheshire. I'm glad he made it.

381/ "Opposition to the war within the military can be classified into two broad categories—dissent and resistance. The dissenters were part of what became known as the GI movement, soldiers publishing 'underground' newspapers, signing antiwar petitions, attending protest rallies and engaging in various forms of public speech to demand an end to the war. The resisters were those who disobeyed orders, defied military authority, refused orders, went absent without leave, committed acts of sabotage, and in some cases attacked their own officers and sergeants." David Cortright, "Antiwar resistance within the military during the Vietnam War, October 17, 2017. http://www.vietnampeace.org/blog/antiwar-resistance-within-the-military-during-the-vietnam-war#_edn3.

410/ Relationships between US infantry personnel and their ARVN counterparts at this stage of the war might best be capsulized by the line, "Be glad to trade you some ARVN rifles. Ain't never been fired and only dropped once." Cowboy, *Full Metal Jacket.*

Made in the USA
San Bernardino,
CA